HUNT THE DEVIL

HUNT THE DEVIL

//

A DEMONOLOGY OF US WAR CULTURE

ROBERT L. IVIE AND OSCAR GINER

THE UNIVERSITY OF ALABAMA PRESS

Tuscaloosa

The University of Alabama Press
Tuscaloosa, Alabama 35487–0380
uapress.ua.edu

Inquiries about reproducing material from this work should be addressed to the
University of Alabama Press.

Typeface: Caslon and Orator

Manufactured in the United States of America
Cover photograph: A soldier from the 1st Battalion, 68th Armor Regiment,
3rd Brigade Combat Team, 4th Infantry Division participates in a dismounted
presence patrol through the Beida neighborhood of Baghdad, Iraq, on
Feb. 29, 2008; courtesy of the US Department of Defense
Cover design: Michele Myatt Quinn

∞

The paper on which this book is printed meets the minimum requirements of
American National Standard for Information Sciences—Permanence of Paper for
Printed Library Materials, ANSI Z39.48–1984.

Library of Congress Cataloging-in-Publication Data

Ivie, Robert L.
Hunt the Devil : a demonology of US war culture / Robert L. Ivie and
Oscar Giner.
pages cm
Includes bibliographical references and index.
ISBN 978-0-8173-1869-7 (hardback) — ISBN 978-0-8173-8819-5 (e book)
1. Demonology—United States. 2. Tricksters. 3. Imagery (Psychology) 4. War
and society—United States. 5. Rhetoric—Political aspects—United States.
I. Giner, Oscar, 1953– II. Title.
GR525.I85 2015
133.4'20973—dc23

2014046403

To Nancy, for sharing the journey with abiding faith and steadfast commitment
R. L. I.

For Margarita, who loved me through the years when love seemed lost
O. G.

Contents

Acknowledgments

This book was written with the support of a sabbatical license for Oscar Giner from the Herberger College of Design and the Arts and while on leave from the Barrett Honors College of Arizona State University.

A portion of chapter 1, "Evildoers," appeared initially in Robert L. Ivie and Oscar Giner, "Hunting the Devil: Democracy's Rhetorical Impulse to War," *Presidential Studies Quarterly* 37.4 (December 2007): 580–98.

A portion of chapter 2, "Witches," appeared initially in Robert L. Ivie and Oscar Giner, "Genealogy of Myth in Presidential Rhetoric," in *The Sourcebook for Political Communication Research: Methods, Measures, and Analytical Techniques*, ed. Erik P. Bucy and R. Lance Holbert (New York: Routledge, 2011), 300–320.

Introduction

Devil Myth

The subliminal figure of the devil haunts US political culture. Satan is the accursed face of evil that threatens the nation's democratic soul. He is Legion—the unclean spirit that animates pagan gods—a dark and unholy presence, a demon that lurks and relentlessly schemes, testing the nation's devotion to its special calling. This mythic devil is repeatedly discovered and exorcised from the body politic by redemptive acts of war. He is the savage that disfigures American identity and provokes an exceptional people to war in the name of civilization. His immanence overshadows the nation's democratic inclinations, deferring the promise of peace into an ever-receding future.

The mark of the devil is a mythic force weighing heavily on the national conscience and, as such, a rhetorical foundation of US war culture. We aim to clarify this wearisome relationship. The goal of our study of political myth is to identify veiled images of the devil so that a troubled national identity might be deciphered. To unveil the myth, we hunt for outward projections of the devil onto the faces of America's enemies. We circle back in time to see the construction of an enduring devil imagery that governs the present-day rite of redemptive war. This illumination results in a hierophany, which reveals America's arrested democratic soul. One of the underlying concerns of our study is whether Americans will make peace with diversity instead of condemning it as the dark foe that carries the mark of evil.

Throughout the nation's history, as W. Scott Poole observes, evil has been located in apparitions of "dark foes" who "must be destroyed" to redeem American "innocence."[1] Political culture exists in myths and rituals that infuse national stories with symbolic significance. Each ritual enactment of political myth contains both the permanence of the ancient and the ephemeral spontaneity of the present. Each cultural expression of political myth is both more and less than an exact replica of previous iterations. The image of democracy never stands starkly alone or apart from other constituents of national identity, especially as the nation's political imaginary inclines toward a Manichean struggle against evil in which empire masquerades as a "precondition" of democracy.[2] Democracy is part of the larger narrative of a self-proclaimed exceptional nation—a chosen people with the evangelical spirit of a divine mission.[3]

Myths of origin (the Taínos emerging from cave Cacibajagua in Haiti; the Navajo emerging from the fifth world to their sacred lands encompassed by four mountains) are not historical narratives. They relate history not as it happened but as the people who share a belief in the myth perceive that it happened. Myth is an aesthetic creation that reflects a people's truth and sense of themselves. The foundational myth—in Giambattista Vico's sense of the word—of American empire (comparable to the myth of the founding of Rome by Aeneas in Virgil's epic poem) is a sacred story of struggle, especially struggle with the devil. It consists of the following key themes:

1. Fleeing from tyranny and economic hardship, escaping by ship "into the wilderness from the face of the dragon," a holy people cross an ocean, invade, and settle a new land.[4] This equals in their mind the establishment of a New Jerusalem, a civilized outpost in an alien territory—a "fatal environment," in Walt Whitman's eloquent phrase.[5]
2. Committed to the pursuit of freedom, individualism, and the acquisition of worldly riches as evident proof of salvation, the people choose an organizing political system that guarantees (so the people affirm) community and equal opportunity. As an early exponent of the government of New England churches proposed it, "It seems most agreeable with the light of nature that if there be any of the regular government settled in the church of God, it must needs be a democracy."[6]
3. The worldview of the settlers is immediately challenged by hostile forces, which are associated with the natural landscape of their surrounding environment. The people come to believe that the strange world around them is evil. Their fears and shared anxieties recall and forge the mask of the devil—their ancient millennial enemy and sacred antagonist—in the crucible of their souls.
4. The devil's impassioned contours are projected onto external sources. The new land (and by later extension, the rest of the world) harbors his presence. A discourse of diabolism swiftly follows to paint a threaten-

ing picture of evil savagery. The savage becomes the face of the American devil.

5. This internal, misshapen, demonic Mr. Hyde—forged in the cradle of collective weaknesses—also creates a national ambivalence toward the political system the people claim to honor. Besieged by enemies without, the people also fear enemies within their own society: wayward souls among them, members of a fallen race who can steer their nation away from the path of salvation. The demos can instantly transform into an irrational, impassioned, and savage mob.

6. The displacement of a troubled national identity, the projection of the people's own seeming vileness onto others ("in order to wipe it out with their blood," in Arthur Miller's words) is a recurring spur to foreign wars and internal persecutions.[7] The world must be subdued to conform to the mental constructs of the settlers. Hearing the sound of angel trumpets (the drumbeat of a war dance), the people call out for a holy war—even a savage war—to defend the nation's holy democratic soul against civilization's wicked foes. Enemies who wear a recognizable mask of evil Otherness must be pursued like Ahab hunted Moby Dick: "That inscrutable thing is chiefly what I hate; and be the white whale agent, or be the white whale principal, I will wreak that hate upon him."[8]

7. Democracy provides on Earth only a pale reflection of the Kingdom of God in Heaven. Given a perpetual state of siege, democracy's ideal must be postponed until an ever-receding future comes to pass. To cleanse the nation of internal diabolonian corruption and to kill the foreign devil-enemy is to reaffirm the nation's special virtue as an exceptional people destined to overcome malevolence so that civilization may prevail.[9]

Within this complex of symbolic relations, democracy is conceived as a point of vulnerability. It is a dangerous weakness that must be contained and sheltered from the forces of evil and a chronic anxiety that constitutes a recurring motive for war.

We develop the argument of the book by mapping the demonology of America's war on terror, a war rationale that features a flattened image of evil savagery. We investigate formative moments of this naturalized mythology. In *Moby Dick*, Melville traced a genealogy of whalemen that included the mythological figures of Perseus, St. George, Hercules, Jonah, and Vishnu.[10] We examine how the dark symbolic presence of Satan assumed the face of the American Indian in the crucible of the Salem witch trials, how it developed from there in the ensuing American Indian wars of the nineteenth century, and how it evolved into a justification for total wars of extermination in the twentieth century. An enduring image of evil savagery extended beyond the American frontier through the righteous quest for empire and global hegemony of a self-proclaimed exceptional people. This mythic projection nearly buried the nation's democratic impulse under the sinister sign of a distempered polity. Emptied of political vitality, democracy was relegated to a legitimizing symbol of American exceptionalism and a rationale for militarism.

We also identify telling moments of recognition and awareness in this recurring pageant of good versus evil, such as when the Cuban missile crisis, driven by the logic of Cold War demonology, prompted an act of critical self-reflection. Certainly, Americans are prone to exaggerate their vulnerability to the forces of evil and culturally predisposed to rush to war in righteous wrath under the flag of democracy. "Tales of a battle between good and evil," Ira Chernus notes, "must depict the world as a threatening or even terrifying place, full of monsters."[11] Democracy, though, is a resilient political idiom with a potential for critical reflection, which occasionally is tapped by political actors to construct more productive relations of interdependence among adversaries. Recognizing the formative influence of the devil myth, we suggest, is an initial step toward eliciting this democratic aesthetic and its potential for transforming the "pasteboard mask" of American exceptionalism.[12]

Genealogy of Political Myth

Political myths are foundational narratives with sacred origins and secular uses. They purport to convey true accounts of past, present, and future events, that is, accounts that "are not a matter of uncovering *facts*, but of revealing *truths*" and in which myth and reality are "intimately tied together" to express the meaning of an experience as its "underlying message."[13] They support and shape the national identity, often in contrast to what is perceived as alien, evil, and subversive. Myths such as American exceptionalism operate in this way as necessary fictions.[14] In the "mythopoeic constitution of humanity," as Giambattista Vico understood, archetypal images are the source of a people's commonsense and political sensibilities; metaphors, operating as myths in miniature, express the "poetic wisdom" embedded in the commonplaces of collective identity and political will.[15]

Given that political culture is grounded in the poetic wisdom of myths and metaphors, political authority is less a matter of who governs than of how the mythic means of governance are managed. Accordingly, two related purposes for the present study are served by identifying the foundational myths embedded in political discourse. First, the detection of entrenched myth reveals the cultural source of political authority. Second, the genealogy of myth exposes the conventional wisdom of war making to the transformative potential of a democratic logic of community building. The mythic dimension of contemporary war rhetoric can be rendered transparent by being placed in a broader historical and cultural context. Understood as a mythic rite of redemptive war, a presidential rhetoric of evil imbued with the language of savagery translates into a cyclical quest for national salvation. The bond of the belligerent nation exists in its divining of founding myths. The beast, as noted by Umberto Eco, is the legendary sign of the presence of the devil.[16]

As an approach to cultural analysis, genealogy recognizes that political knowledge and authority constitute a circular dynamic, in which truth and power are so thoroughly enmeshed that they are interdependent to the point of reproducing one another.[17] Any cultural heritage of this kind, Foucault argued, is "an unstable assemblage."[18] Unlike a traditional historical method that searches for "fixed truths, laws, finalities, or origins," genealogy is alert to discontinuities among recurrences and to the dynamism of interconnections as it investigates "the primacy of origins and the reification of truths."[19] Genealogy "can illuminate contradictions, controversies, and conflicts surrounding [the] authority and use" of pivotal terms within particular discursive formations for the purpose of producing "a space of reflexivity" about "the taken-for-granted concepts or categories of existence that condition consciousness."[20] Seeing the strangeness of the past helps us to perceive incongruities in an otherwise habituated present.

Genealogy is alert to lines of development from past to present and fascinated by recurrence and repetition but is skeptical of grand narratives of progress and naturalized logics of the linear unfolding of events inevitably toward present conditions or future outcomes.[21] From Foucault's standpoint, genealogy "does not map the destiny of a people" or reveal an "uninterrupted continuity." Rather than revealing the origin or "inviolable identity" of something such as evil, genealogy instead uncovers dissension, derision, and irony, teaching us "how to laugh at the solemnities" of an origin—divine or not—by cultivating the "details and accidents that accompany every beginning." In Foucault's apt analogy, dispelling the "chimera" of a troubled origin is akin to exorcising the "shadow" of a pious man's soul.[22]

Our genealogy of the devil myth, consistent with what William Doty calls mythography, applies a critical perspective to the study of myth and ritual in the modern world.[23] It provides a "curettage device" for removing mythical debris from contemporary perspective and yields a resource for revitalizing society and enhancing moral choices in present time.[24] It reflects both a synchronic and diachronic dynamic in which the devil myth transcends history even as it is grounded in time and place.

Synopsis of Chapters

Our study of political myth advances through the following chapters, each a step in identifying and reflecting upon rhetorical appropriations of devil imagery in US war culture. In tracing the projected image of evil savagery back to originating moments in the American experience, we aim to illustrate how the devil myth was constructed in response to exigent circumstances within a cultural framework of interpretation. We offer a cautionary account of a redemptive nation's impulse to violent scapegoating. As the story unfolds, we also call attention to a democratic undercurrent of critical reflection on the demonology of war. This, too, we suggest is indigenous to the national identity and indicative of a largely uncultivated potential for resisting the easy projection of evil.

Chapter 1: Evildoers

The rhetoric of evil, so evident in President George W. Bush's public discourse, projected a national shadow onto external enemies and articulated a prime motive for declaring a global war on terrorism. The president's rhetoric of evil savagery was a manifestation rather than an aberration of US political culture, a legacy of Ronald Reagan's cinematic vision, inspired by George Lucas's epic *Star Wars*, of combating the Soviet Union's evil empire. Upon close inspection, it reveals the presence of the inherited mythos of a democratic demon contained within the republic and is illustrative of various ways in which the projection of this devil figure is rhetorically triggered.

The theme of diabolism in presidential war rhetoric reflects the nation's troubled democratic identity. It functions as an inducement to evacuate the political content of democracy, leaving a largely empty but virulent signifier in its place, which reproduces a culture of war. The president's war on terror was fought symbolically in Indian country, a largely tacit analogy in which evildoers were imagined by soldiers, policy makers, and filmmakers alike as merciless primitives who must be hunted down and dispatched on an untamed frontier in order to secure the advance of civilization.[25]

Chapter 2: Witches

The dark eminence of the European devil surfaced in the wilderness settlement of Salem, Massachusetts, to assume the form of the American Indian. When the Puritans sensed the presence of the Evil One in their midst, they fixed the blame on those tinged with Otherness. The cultural legacy of this prototypical projection later gave birth to Arthur Miller's sinister allegory of McCarthyism in his 1953 play, *The Crucible*.

The Salem witch-hunt first led to Tituba Indian, a slave woman purchased in the West Indies by Salem Village's parish minister. Ominously related to the Indian tribes that besieged New England's Puritan communities of "saints," she was driven to confess that she worshipped the devil. Her confession blended a Native American mythology of spirits with Old World narratives of devil possession. In a syncretization of mythological images, Tituba allowed her own demigods and spirits to assume the masks of the characters of the Salem Christian Passion play of good and evil. As Mary Beth Norton has suggested, behind the devil in Salem lurked the face of the American Indian—natural and mysterious, alien and threatening, a mental construct ripe for the projection of Otherness.[26] This devil-Indian avatar became a constant symbol of hostility and violence in the strange and threatening landscape of the New World.

Chapter 3: Indians

The tragic agon of the Battle of the Little Bighorn, in which the US Seventh Cavalry was defeated by a large contingent of Lakota and Northern Cheyenne warriors, crystallized the visual imagery of the devil myth for nineteenth-century America. With Sitting Bull cast as the red devil antagonist in opposition to George Armstrong Custer's Christian protagonist, Little Bighorn rendered a historical drama for the systemic struggle between Satan and saint, Indian and conquistador, in the New World. The remembrance of Little Bighorn was propagated by ritual reenactments in Buffalo Bill's *Wild West*. The symbolic, cultural forces evoked by the bellicose dynamic of the devil myth resulted in the Sioux tragedy at Wounded Knee. The Spanish-American War provided the denouement for the historical drama born at Little Bighorn. Myth and ritual of the American Indian wars produced the rhetorical justification that transformed a flawed, democratic nation into a nascent empire.

Chapter 4: Dictators

After the Spanish-American War, the United States claimed ownership of two empires: an Atlantic empire facing Europe, based on the newly acquired territories of Cuba and Puerto Rico in the Caribbean, and a Pacific empire facing Asia, which extended over the newly acquired islands of Hawaii and the Philippines. Henceforth, Asians were considered Indians, and European enemies were rendered Oriental; both were represented as evil. Likewise, the image of America's momentary eastern allies, whether

Russians or Chinese, was westernized. The European devils of two world wars—the kaiser and the führer, German reincarnations respectively of Attila the Hun and Genghis Kahn—were dictators who aimed to crush freedom, democracy, and ultimately the church. Parting from the premise that "courage was not enough" to oppose a rising tide of demonic forces, Charlie Chaplin's *The Great Dictator* performed in trickster fashion a parody of Hitler's fearsome image and objected explicitly to the institution of war.[27] But the image of the dictator's unmitigated evil prevailed, reconfirming America's moral eminence and legitimizing total war, including the obliteration of whole cities, enabled by advancing technologies of warfare. The counterpart of this outward projection of violence was the construction of domestic concentration camps to contain the perceived internal threat of Japanese Americans. Democracy's good fight against dictators amounted to a race war in which the projected enemy was a dark, not white, devil.

Chapter 5: Reds

At the dawn of the American century, the doors to war—like those of the temple of the ancient Roman deity—were never closed.[28] World War I produced the Russian Revolution and the witch-hunt of America's first postwar Red Scare. The Roosevelt administration's recognition of the Russian Communist regime in 1933 ultimately gave way to a new demonic incarnation: red devils—Oriental, atheistic, and Communist—that troubled the decade of the 1930s and set in motion the Red Scare of the Cold War. America's red enemy, intent on world domination, threatened white hegemony from Latin America to Southeast Asia.

Whether battling Castro's Cuba or Ho Chi Minh's Vietnam, America was haunted by the savagery of Indian country and compelled by visions of the last stand. The beast within revealed itself in *Apocalypse Now*—Francis Coppola's mythical compendium of US wars. The complicity of the United States in evil savagery, revealed in Marlon Brando's Colonel Kurtz, was a devastating moment of self-recognition that set in motion a countercampaign of aggressive denial and belligerent redemption. Only after Ronald Reagan's subsequent call to defeat the Soviet Union's evil empire, followed by American troops driving Saddam Hussein's invading army out of Kuwait, could George H. W. Bush boast that America had kicked the Vietnam syndrome. War had been restored as an instrument of national redemption by the time terrorism struck spectacularly on 9/11.

Chapter 6: Tricksters

Although stifled, a sporadic yet resilient voice of critical reflection could be discerned in the context of an overwhelmingly righteous militarism. The toxic mix of the Cold War made proxy war a necessary substitute for direct confrontation with the Soviet red devil. Yet, the Cuban missile crisis demonstrated the imminence of nuclear holocaust between the Soviet Union and the United States. Smarting from the Bay of Pigs fiasco, John F. Kennedy, on the cusp of nuclear holocaust, transcended the prevailing demonologist viewpoint enough to resist the advice of his bellicose generals. His perspective-taking, stereoscopic gaze enabled him to speculate on the Soviet enemy's motives, to imagine how Khrushchev might interpret the matters in dispute, and to reflect critically on US actions from the presumed standpoint of adversaries and allies.

Martin Luther King Jr., too, momentarily broke the spell of Cold War demonology by speaking out to expose the undemocratic specter and cruel irony of sending young black soldiers abroad to fight in Southeast Asia for liberties that they did not possess at home in America. Later, when George W. Bush's open-ended war on evil bogged down in Iraq, Barack Obama stepped forward to democratize the myth of American exceptionalism. He conjured an incipient image of complementary relations among interdependent people on a global scale. He spoke in terms of partnership, cooperation, tolerance, coexistence, mutual interest and respect, listening and learning from one another, seeking common ground, and discarding crude stereotypes.

These episodic voices in an otherwise long-standing tradition of redemptive warfare elicited a democratic aesthetic for acknowledging the devil myth and resisting the easy projection of evil. This comedic vision of the trickster reflected a mythic sensibility (found in the tales of Hermes and the stories of Coyote) for shape shifting and boundary crossing to slip the trap of polarities and mediate oppositions. Even in Salem, as those who victimized the most vulnerable members of the community became increasingly the victims of their own projections of evil, the figure of the trickster enabled them to arrest the ritual of demonization and to effect a last-minute escape from self-entrapment. As a figure of fluidity and ambivalence in a world of divisive and rigid orthodoxies, trickster is the mythic archetype that undermines the unquestioned authority of petrified archetypes.[29]

During twelve years of silence between 1934 and 1946 Eugene O'Neill labored, in trickster-like manner, at the writing of a cycle of eleven plays, "A Tale of Possessors Self-Dispossessed," which told the story of an American family from before the founding of the republic to the 1930s. In 1946, with the United States flush with imperial victory after World War II and set to enter the self-proclaimed American Century, O'Neill gave an interview to a group of reporters in which he spoke about the premises of his cycle: "I'm going on the theory that the United States, instead of being the most successful country in the world, is the greatest failure. . . . It's the greatest failure because it was given everything, more than any other country. . . . Its main idea is that everlasting game of trying to possess your own soul by the possession of something outside of it, thereby losing your own soul and the thing outside of it, too. . . . This was really said in the Bible much better. We are the greatest example of 'For what shall it profit a man if he shall gain the whole world, and lose his own soul?'"[30] Throughout US history, American poets, novelists, playwrights, critics, filmmakers, and political leaders have, like Eugene O'Neill, served the trickster function of questioning political myths, dissolving petrified metaphors, and retrieving projections of Otherness. Only through a courageous acknowledgment of our own evil, and a noble acceptance of the fated struggle "in the agonized womb of consciousness" with the devil within us, will we come to realize our true commitment to democracy.[31]

Knowing more of the genealogy of America's historic pursuit of the devil is the trickster way of recognizing a dark presence within the culture, which otherwise persists in willful denial. The image of the devil is woven into the mythic fabric of the national identity. It will be with us as long as there is an America, but so will the spirit of Coyote, that fleeting and friendless figure Mark Twain admired for its ability to make our "head swim" and its potential to save our soul by tricking us into a humbling state of reflection. Encountering "the sharp, vicious bark" of Twain's nocturnal Coyote, who "lives chiefly in the most desolate and forbidding deserts" of the political landscape, disturbs "our dreams" and awakens us momentarily to the ambiguities of life.[32] This is the middle way, the muddling way of a democratic people, who would aspire to Kenneth Burke's aesthetic of "tolerance and contemplation" as an ongoing corrective to sanctimonious stridency and the "torrents of ill will."[33] Trickster disturbing the outward projection of evil is a reminder that human culture is built, in Burke's words, "by huddling together, nervously loquacious, at the edge of an abyss."[34]

Conclusion: Democracy

Historian Michael Sherry has argued that war had defined the whole of American culture by the end of the twentieth century, becoming a consuming anxiety that exacerbated the tensions of civic life and public policy no less than foreign relations.[35] Indeed, war has been central to the nation's development throughout the arc of its history, according to Fred Anderson and Andrew Cayton.[36] Militarism fused with utopian vision, observes Andrew Bacevich, put a crusader state on the path to permanent war.[37] Kelly Denton-Barhaug believes that war culture, as the nation's ritual of sacrifice, permeates its way of life.[38] David Holloway warns that this cul-

turally imbued medium—manifest in Hollywood film, visual art, literature, and political discourse—renders the war on terror an attack on the
nation's democratic ethos and institutions.[39] Reflecting democratically on
the demonology of US war culture, we maintain, is critical to unsettling the
mindset of militarism in the present age of terror.

"Democracy" is a tricky word but a necessary fiction that expresses the
ethos of the country. It runs shallow and deep in America's political imagination, but it is never a matter of indifference. The cultural legacy of this
recurring wish for empowering the people is embedded in the nation's poetry, literature, and oratory, from Ralph Waldo Emerson to Toni Morrison. It is realized in political ritual, and its aesthetic is a cultural way of becoming more responsive to pluralism, diversity, and dissent—of perceiving
the possibility of peace in the apprehension of unity among difference. Developing democracy's potential for engaging difference respectfully is the
nation's best prospect for loosening the devil's mythic grip and escaping the
dictates of war culture.

I

Evildoers

The incantation of evil casts a spell of militant insecurity on the American people. War is the national sacrament of atonement. It sacrifices a scapegoat in whom the world's evil is invested.[1] No rhetorical equation is more deadly than this "myth of redemptive violence."[2] The Manichean distinction between good and evil is a "pervasive cultural code" that militarizes US political discourse.[3]

The nation's preoccupation with evil precedes and anticipates the tragedy of 9/11 and the presidency of George W. Bush. Adolf Hitler, forever fixed in the nation's memory as evil personified, is the unredeemed Darth Vader of popular culture, a dark symbol of malevolent power. Ronald Reagan is the cinematic president eager to erect a Star Wars defense against the Soviet Union's evil empire.[4] The image of evildoers evoked by Bush after the fall of Manhattan's twin towers resonates not only with rightwing Christian fundamentalism but also with the mainstream political culture. It is rooted in the secular religion of national mission and the enduring myth of American exceptionalism.

Exceptionalism is a moralistic legacy that insists Americans are opposed to evil in their foreign relations and are "on God's side against Satan" in matters of war.[5] According to this creed, the United States is the one essential nation above all others, the beacon and exemplar of standards no other country can match. As a founding myth and national wellspring, exceptionalism turns a war on terrorism into a sacred symbol for remaking the world in America's self-image.[6]

Bush's rhetoric of evildoers is a case in point. It channeled a cultural penchant to render America's enemies diabolical. When he declared an unrestricted war on terror, he spoke in the language of a Christian crusader. In a modern rendition of the Puritan covenant of renewal, he depicted a chosen people watched over by a God who was testing the national character. He advanced a righteous call to arms that absolved the United States of any responsibility by making clear that "the evil character of an external enemy was to blame."[7] This was the "theistic essence" governing Bush's rhetorical world, a world divided by good and evil and given purpose by God's will.[8] The divine will was to be fulfilled by a people of faith in their pursuit of "moral security."[9]

Guided by his faith, Bush preached in biblical cadences to a receptive nation the message of holy battle to bestow freedom on a corrupt world. Any and all means were justified in the fight against Islamic terrorism. Despite the distinction he made between terrorism and the religion of Islam, after he had already referred to the war on terror as a "crusade," the president and his supporters persisted in the use of "coded Christian language" to invest the war with "*messianic* meaning."[10] The "greatest force for good in history" was fighting for "the glory of God."[11] This global war on terror was America's "Third Awakening."[12]

Bush's war rhetoric allowed little to no room for critical thinking. Every consideration, domestic and foreign, became a matter of national security viewed through the moralizing lens of an evil threat. National security was equated with health security, retirement security, economic security, and more. A doctrine of preemptive war was advanced to rid the world of evil before it could strike the United States. The image of Satan incarnate was the rhetorical trump card for a preventative war against Saddam Hussein's Iraq. Bringing down the demonic Hussein was "a test of national moral resolve in the face of evil."[13] The palpable malevolence of terrorism legitimized a regime of executive authority and undercut the separation of powers, even as it eroded civil liberties, deflected criticism of economic elitism, and eschewed diplomacy as a viable instrument of foreign relations.

The Demon of Distempered Democracy

This obsession with evil, revealed in a rhetorical trope deeply embedded in US political culture, is "inherently corrosive of democratic politics."[14] The trope of evil prods the nation to dehumanize its enemies and displace its own "deformities" onto a vilified Other.[15] It sets in motion a "victimage" ritual through which America redeems itself on an altar of vicarious sacrifice.[16] The more the image of the enemy is made sinister, the greater the nation feels in danger of damnation. The articulation of evil suffuses every perception, reason, and calculation for choosing war over peace. It colonizes the collective judgment. Naming the demonic enemy constitutes the peculiar state of war that turns the nation against its democratic self.[17]

Indeed, America's chronic impulse to war is provoked by democracy's shadow, which casts a dark veil of anxiety over the public disposition. This deep distrust of the people confounds the identity and bewilders the political will of a self-proclaimed exceptional nation.[18] It produces nothing short of a cultural tension that is resolved in presidential rhetoric as a commanding motive for war.

There are several continuous phases in democracy's impulse to war. We—the people—fear the enemy within: an impassioned ogre of mob violence, a deformed Mr. Hyde who reflects the common fear and shared anxiety about democracy. This internal demon—forged in the crucible of collective weaknesses, misshapen by national ambivalence toward the political system Americans claim to honor—is readily projected onto external sources that are conjured as evil and defined as the public enemy. A discourse of diabolism swiftly follows to paint a threatening picture of the enemy's evil savagery and to goad the nation to defend its holy democratic soul against civilization's wicked foes. The projection of a troubled identity, the displacement of the nation's own seeming vileness onto others—"in order to wipe it out with their blood"—is a recurring goad to fight.[19]

This demonic impulse to war assumes many guises in US presidential rhetoric. The devil, as an essential antagonist in the nation's cosmology, has had a long and notable history in national dramas playing the part of the enemy. To kill the foreign devil-enemy is to reaffirm the nation's special virtue as a chosen people destined to overcome malevolence so that civilization may prevail. This heroic mask is the stuff of political myth. In the secular rituals of presidential rhetoric, the mask pretends worldly realism in order to summon the god of war, which is a necessary posture to assume in a world of presumed enlightenment. Even as the nation dances to the drums of war, it justifies aggression in the prosaic presidential idiom of the real, the rational, and the practical. Herein lay the riddle of war's apparent complexity but basic simplicity—the extraordinary cultural appeal of the call to arms.

Detecting the presence of this powerful mythos in presidential rhetoric raises the question of its meaning for democratic culture and its implication for governance in an age of continuous warfare. Can democracy, emptied of its incentive to humanize aliens by the diabolical incantations of presidential rhetoric, function as an inclusive politics of contestation? Or must it succumb, as did the first French republic, to a culture of war?[20] To answer this question, it is important to acknowledge that George W. Bush's presidential rhetoric is not an aberration of American political culture but rather a manifestation of unresolved issues of national identity played out in a mythic ritual of redemptive violence.

As a principal constituent of political culture and a basic element of national identity, democracy is defined by the language in which it is embedded. The terms with which democracy commonly clusters, as well as the history of their separate and combined usage, establish a working notion of its sense, sentiment, and significance at a given point in time. Democracy is an attitude articulated within the polity and configured by rhetoric, especially by conventions of discourse that treat relations of similitude as relations of equivalence or virtual sameness. A constellation of figures rendered by conventional usage into language that is taken more or less literally (what we might call literalized metaphors) comprises the nation's metaphorical concept of democracy. Giambattista Vico understood that such metaphors operate as condensed myths or, as Stephen Daniel puts it, "myths-in-miniature."[21]

Throughout US history, this metaphorical or mythic conception of democracy has been fraught with tension by the troubled image of a desired but dangerous spirit of self-rule. In the American political lexicon, democracy is affirmed but also qualified by figures of containment, which work to constrain its full expression and dreaded impact on the fragile reign of reason and prudence. American democratic rhetoric often composes a reverse kind of medieval bestiary in which base or animal attributes are attached to the symbolic representation of citizens. As Benjamin Barber observes, the rhetoric of democracy in America is akin to "zookeeping." Human "creatures," situated by "liberal democratic imagery" within a menagerie of sovereign lions, bleating sheep, and ornery wolves, are reduced in Alexander Hamilton's language to one great beast. In this "political zoology," Barber noted, "liberal democracy's sturdiest cages are reserved for the People," who are admired for their proud individuality but considered dangerous as a madding crowd.[22]

Madison, at most a "reluctant democrat," was among the prevailing founders who framed constitutional barriers to popular rule as a hedge against the unruly mob.[23] Madison's republic was his "remedy" for containing the "mortal disease" of "popular councils," his "proper cure" for democracy's "common impulse of passion," his "guard against the confusion of a multitude," his hedge against the "malady" of "sinister" prejudices and "wicked" schemes. In his republic of representative governance, the "wisdom," the "enlightened views," and the "virtuous sentiments" of a superior few—the natural aristocracy—substituted for the degradations of "factious tempers," "local prejudices," and "sinister designs," all of which were "sown in the nature of man" and thus inherent to popular rule.[24] The "confusion and intemperance of a multitude," he believed, "never fails to wrest the scepter from reason."[25] The uncontained, undisciplined demos was seen as a violent mob under the evil influence of primal passions, allowing the savagery of chaos to prevail over reason, order, and justice. This was the distempered, demonic beast of democracy that so troubled federalist elites—their dark, mythic image of human depravity. Through the healing principle of representation they exorcised the people from government in order to found the nation.[26]

This mythos of the democratic demon contained within the republic has haunted the nation throughout its history, even as Americans have struggled in fits and starts to create a more democratic republic. Whigs complained in the nineteenth century, for example, that Jacksonian demagoguery had caused the republic to "degenerate" into a democracy—that is, to become a "mobocracy" ruled by evil passions and the vulgar ignorance of the poor masses.[27] The new democratic style of middling political communication was considered by political elites to be a dangerous development of "catering to the *demos*," which they believed was undermining moral probity and rectitude in public affairs.[28] Twentieth-century critics, such as Walter Lippmann, doubted that education could reform a degraded public.[29]

Previous to the fall of Communism, scholars had warned that a rising rhetorical presidency constituted a serious and growing threat to republican governance—that a worsening condition of presidential demagoguery, or direct appeal to the masses, bypassed responsible deliberation in Congress.[30] In the midst of this worry over properly containing and disciplining domestic democracy, the nation's political leadership endorsed a theory of democratic peace that prescribed a thin veil of democratization as the way to global peace.[31] This assumption legitimized an aggressive post–Cold War foreign policy and a subsequent doctrine of preemptive warfare for fighting the tyranny of terrorism.[32] George H. W. Bush's Gulf War quickly launched a brave new world order of "moving toward democracy through the door of freedom" and "toward free markets through the door to prosperity," exuding a distinctly crusading spirit that Amos Perlmutter considered "mission oriented" and aimed at world domination.[33] Bill Clinton, nervously following in Bush's presidential footsteps, proclaimed that America, as the one essential nation, must secure "democracy's triumph around the world."[34] Overtones of national insecurity and vulnerability resonated throughout Clinton's rhetoric of democratic world order. Even the extension of democracy—assuming "the ennobling burdens of democracy" to foster a "global village"—in these uncertain and tenuous times was a risky affair, it seemed, when the world's "oldest democracy" continued its "most daring experiment in forging different races, religions and cultures into a single people."[35] Democracy was hazardous at home and abroad.

By the logic of the prevailing metaphorical construct, securing the demon of democratic passion inside a rational container was equivalent to

quelling the forces of savagery that threatened civilization. The inner conflict paralleled the outer struggle, and suppressing the forces of savagery was
the mythic motive for America's historic mission of spreading democracy's
empire. From the beginning, as Robert Kagan argues, America was perceived by much of the world as a dangerous nation because of its "aggressive
and seemingly insatiable desire for territory and dominant influence." This
abiding desire for control, along with a craving for ideological and commercial hegemony, posed the ongoing danger of "swallow[ing] up those cultures
with which it came into contact." Yet, a lack of self-awareness about these
expansive tendencies, "even as the United States has risen to a position of
global hegemony," has left Americans perplexed when they discover that
others hate and fear their powerful reach.[36] Empire was America's unacknowledged vocation, its mythic calling expressed as the sacred mission of
an exceptional people to advance civilization by overcoming the evil forces
of savagery and securing a lasting democratic peace.

After 9/11, terrorism became the threatening face of savagery in democracy's troubled empire.[37] Indeed, terrorism became not just democracy's
mortal antagonist but also its evil counterpart, at once an enduring cause
for unlimited warfare and a ready pretext for unruly democracy's restraint.
The demon of distempered democracy was symbolically subsumed under
the war on terror. The face of the terrorist enemy was a semblance of the
face of the inner savage. The terrorist was the dark brother, if not offspring,
of the democratic demon. Democracy served ambiguously as war's purpose and provocation, sought after in the ideal but arrested in the present
while its distempered, totalitarian shadow remained dangerously at large.
Such a "disowned shadow" in troubled hero myths, as Janice Rushing and
Thomas Frentz note, is readily projected onto an Other toward whom "we
then relate . . . in an unconscious, undifferentiated way, usually with auto-
matic and dogmatic hatred or fear."[38]

Democracy remained, in Sheldon Wolin's astute term, a "fugitive"—a
paradoxical marker of national identity at a time of increasing alienation
between the people and their rulers. Its invocation in American political
rhetoric and media was "a tribute, not to its vibrancy, but to its utility in
supporting a myth that legitimates the very formations of power which
have enfeebled it" by means of antidemocratic strategies such as appeals
to efficiency, stability, emergency, and so on. In this way, America's superpower "claim to democracy" was "a form of hypocrisy," a shallow symbol
without a substantive, participatory practice. Democracy's basic principle
of collective self-rule was "fictitious" in the contemporary world that reduced "majorities" to "artifacts manufactured by money, organization, and

the media."[39] Whether America's claim to a democratic identity was paradoxical, hypocritical, or fanciful, it was freighted with tension, distrust, and apprehension.

The force of this chronic democratic unease—this hellhound of national self-doubt and even self-loathing in the most extreme cases—must be understood as a primal impulse to war that projects an odious self-image onto the persona of an evil, fearsome enemy. This projection of democracy's shadow is difficult to observe and acknowledge because, viewed directly, it appears too grotesque and raw to emanate from the core of the national temperament. America sees itself as an enlightened and pacifically inclined agent of liberty and human advancement in a dark landscape of diabolical spirits, not as an imperial beast of prey let loose upon the world, because "*we* are on the side of Light, *they* on the side of Darkness."[40] The mythic shading of the repressed enemy within—a deformed representation of the people, a distempered image produced by an ingrained fear of democracy—is therefore expressed obliquely in presidential war rhetoric.

George W. Bush's Rhetorical Demonology

George W. Bush's rhetorical demonology—his war on evil—probed the archetypal recesses of terror. After awakening from the nightmare of 9/11, the president spoke to the nation in mythical overtones of an enemy that spewed hellfire and inhabited dungeons. "We must defeat the evildoers where they hide," he declared.[41] An image of sheer evil configured this presidential vision of a global war on terror, so much so that tracking the single term "evildoers" through the first weeks and months of Bush's war rhetoric leads directly to the perception of a gnawing internal tension, which expresses itself in the quasiliteralized metaphors and pseudorealistic narratives of an exorcism of foreign devils.[42] This was "a different type of struggle to defeat an enemy that's sometimes hard to see, and sometimes hard to find," Bush proclaimed: "Now is the time to root out evil so that our children and grandchildren can live with freedom as the beacon all around the world."[43] The president positioned himself as St. George slaying the mythical dragon. Behind the armor of St. George were more familiar masks: the Jesuits exorcising devils in Loudun or the Salem ministers pursuing compacts with the devil in Salem.

Here is where the president's rhetorical demonology is especially revealing. As a deadly earnest exercise in political myth, it spins a beguiling story for the willing consumption of a nervously receptive public, a story that positions the nation resolutely but precariously as a heroic avenger on a salvific errand. "We should reflect on the national character we inherited from our forefathers," Bush urged, "and on the obligation we now have to stand for morality and virtue in the face of evil and terror." This "is a war to save the world."[44]

The raw image of the evildoer that America would subdue was suggestive of collective misgivings too mortifying to manage without delegating them to a sinister surrogate: "This is good versus evil. These are evildoers," Bush insisted urgently and repetitively.[45] In this regard, the president's story of evil was like the surcharged symbolism of a disturbing dream sequence. The ambivalence of the dream, which the president's rhetoric of evil aimed to resolve wholly on the side of American virtue, was over the question of whether the devastation of 9/11 somehow was deserved. How could anyone hate the United States enough to perpetrate such a terrible attack against an innocent people, unless America's innocence was to be called into question and no longer could be presumed? Was it conceivable that at least some of the blame could be attributed to the nation's own misdeeds? Were there serious flaws in the American character?

The president awkwardly posed this haunting question of American culpability and nervously replied as follows: "You know, I'm asked all the time—I'll ask myself a question. (Laughter.) How do I respond to—it's an old trick—(laughter)—how do I respond when I see that in some Islamic countries there is vitriolic hatred for America? I'll tell you how I respond: I'm amazed. I'm amazed that there is such misunderstanding of what our country is about, that people would hate us. I am, I am—like most Americans, I just can't believe it. Because I know how good we are, and we've got to do a better job of making our case." Bush's expression of incredulity, his suggestion that any conceivable criticism of the United States was reducible to a simple misunderstanding that could be corrected by better communication through public diplomacy, and his affirmation of the nation's innate goodness left the bulk of the question to be answered by attributing evil motives to evil deeds. "We're fighting evil," he resolved, "and we cannot let it stand."[46]

The face of these evildoers—these terrorists in whom evil had "found a willing servant"—was a featureless, flat surface. This blank façade presented an exterior devoid of any discernable interior. "These are evildoers," Bush observed. "They have no justification for their actions. . . . The only motivation is evil." Motivation was impossible to fathom beneath the actual act of evil. The stark exterior provided no depth of perspective, no explanation for the devastation and suffering it wrought. This was "a kind of a faceless enemy," the president allowed, "an enemy who sends young men to die on suicide missions and they, themselves, try to hide in caves." Evil was something to hunt down and purge, not to understand—something to deny, not transcend. In the president's words: "I see things this way: The people who did this act on America, and who may be planning further acts, are evil people. They don't represent an ideology, they don't represent a legitimate political group of people. *They're flat evil.* That's all they can think about, is evil. And as a nation of good folks, we're going to hunt them down, and we're going to find them, and we will bring them to justice."[47] These emboldened but anxious words were emblematic of a profound absence in a shallow presence—an empty explanation that contained nothing other than itself. There were no meaningful features articulated either to characterize these agents of evil or to elucidate their cruel acts.

Evil's flat exterior was the rhetorical foundation of the president's image of terror. The defacement of America's terrorist enemies set the stage for a classic psychological projection, defined as *"an unintentional transfer of a part of the psyche which belongs to the subject onto an outer object."*[48] Alluding to a Christian metaphor, Marie-Louis von Franz reminds us that projections traffic in the "well-known business of the beam in our eye which we do not see."[49] Projections are "emotionally-toned," Carl Jung observes, and characteristically "the cause of the emotion appears to lie, beyond all possibility of doubt, in the *other person*."[50]

The rhetorical manufacture of a blank slate allowed for the externalization of a vague, disturbing, shadowy persona. "Terrorists try to operate in the shadows. They try to hide," Bush allowed, but America would "rout out terrorism" no matter how long it might take. "No corner of the world will be dark enough to hide in." Cast in a sinister undertone, the president's portrait of terror depicted America struggling in the dark to conquer its nemesis. This was "a time of testing," a "time of adversity" that would reveal "the true character of the American people." It would be a difficult struggle, but the president assured Americans, "We can overcome evil. We're good." Americans were fighting to prove that evildoers could not "break our spirit" or "diminish our soul."[51] America would not succumb in the darkness to its evil counterpart and alter ego.

In Jung's estimation, "projections change the world into a replica of our unknown face."[52] Behind the mask of terrorist evil, the face of the distempered demon of democracy can be observed. An observer tracking the language of terror through the president's public statements soon encounters visible markers of the enemy's crazed brutality. On the side of "chaotic violence" were the "barbaric acts" of "bands of murderers, supported by outlaw regimes" and driven by "mad intent"; these "shadowy, entrenched enemies" were the "authors of mass murder." Their "mad ambitions" and "fanaticism" constituted an "axis of evil" that threatened "the civilized world" with "mass destruction." The "dim vision" of these "backwards," "barbaric," "cold-blooded killers" and "parasites" that "don't have hearts" was to "brutalize" their victims with "torture" and "beheadings" contrary to "all civilized norms." The "fanatical," "murderous ideology" and sheer "savagery" of these terrorists marked them not only as "brutal an enemy as we've ever faced" but especially as "violently opposed to democracy" and against "the idea of progress itself." America's war was a quest to "leave the desert of despotism for the fertile gardens of liberty."[53]

This composite sketch of the terrorist threat is a profile of evil incarnate. Terrorists are fanatical religious fundamentalists and wicked ideologues. They are power-hungry thugs without heart or conscience. They harbor a grim vision of theocratic intolerance. They commit unspeakable acts against innocent civilians, including rape, torture, and murder. Their agenda is death by violence. They are shadowy, cowardly characters that hide in caves, plant roadside bombs, and behead defenseless captives. They hate freedom, crush dissent, and operate on the assumption that Americans are too decadent to defend their own freedom. They show contempt for civilized rules of warfare and are intent upon the ruin of civilization. The whole world is their battlefield. Their barbarism cannot be appeased.

Viewed as a symbolic projection of America's dark shadow, the president's representation of evil reflected a rogue nation of power-hungry religious fanatics attempting to remake the Middle East in its own image by perpetrating immoral acts of violence on a massive scale and with criminal disregard for the rules of civilized warfare—a war machine leveling whole cities, condoning torture, and hiding behind superior technologies of death; decadent imperialists with an insatiable appetite for power who detest freedom and dissent; insecure ideologues determined to impose their rule and their way of life on the world.

This mirror image of American wickedness is too stark for most Americans to recognize or abide. Bush's post-9/11 war rhetoric and his ritualized invocation of the scapegoat displaced any acknowledgment of error or malfeasance by a nation that considers itself "the most Christian of nations."[54] Even anxieties over democracy are difficult for Americans to acknowledge. Such apprehensions can be expressed only indirectly by attributing them to an old ideological adversary frequently revisited in presidential rhetoric. "The murderous ideology of the Islamic radicals" was "like the ideology of communism," the president allowed, in that it "is elitist. . . . teaches that innocent individuals can be sacrificed to serve a political vision. . . . pursues totalitarian aims . . . [with] endless ambitions of imperial domination. . . . is dismissive of free peoples. . . . [and] contains inherent contradictions that doom it to failure."[55] This projection of fear and distrust onto a totalitarian antagonist (in abnegation of democracy) was purportedly a display of what democratic America precisely was not (elitist, authoritarian, imperialistic, aggressive, belligerent, murderous, and doomed to defeat). Yet the dark image of this totalitarian, Islamic, Communist-like enemy corresponded, perhaps too closely for comfort, to the nation's compliance with presidential rule and a regimen of continuous global warfare.

In this regard, George W. Bush was the mythological son, spiritual successor, and political disciple of Ronald Reagan. Both men were cowboy figures, self-proclaimed ranchers from the American West, with "a fondness for . . . open spaces and don't-fence-me-in rhetoric" that advanced "evangelical themes and suggested that America has a divine assignment in the world to spread what Reagan called 'the sacred fire of human liberty.'" They shared a spiritual and ideological lean to the right that mixed Christian moralism with nationalism and laissez-faire economics, and they reduced the complexities of world affairs to simplistic black and white images. Both resisted the constraints of treaties and international organizations on a unilateral exercise of American power, and their administrations accordingly were marked by "obsessive secrecy, a premium on loyalty, a taste for working through foreign proxies, [and] an impatience with Congressional oversight." Reagan's "evil empire" was matched by Bush's "axis of evil" as an assertion of moral certitude and righteous purpose.[56]

In the darkness of the underground battlefield of the global war on terror, it was critical not to confuse and conflate good and noble America with the terror of evildoers, not to intermingle an antagonist's savagery with the hero's civilized morality. Critical to the desired outcome was the imposition of a "Manichaean dualism" on the mythic identity struggle.[57] The contrast between good and evil had to be marked as clearly as possible under the difficult circumstance of fighting terror on its own dim terrain. The sustained image of terrorism's mad barbarism signified the "moral and ideological divide" between the hunted and the hunter.[58] The visage of yet another, even older antagonist, was borrowed in order to recognize, seek, and destroy the intended prey.

Americans think they are too modern and rational to believe in the medieval devil, but the fire and destruction of 9/11 made the nation susceptible to the suggestion that the devil and his legion (Osama bin Laden and his al-Qaeda army) had perpetrated the event. In the nation's language and history, in its arts and spirituality, beneath the cornerstone of America's political and economic systems, the devil lies shallowly buried, ready to surface at any moment that he is summoned or conjured. The devil was present in the virgin forests that first greeted the American colonizers. The mystery of the Salem witch-hunt outbreak of 1692 still fascinates the national imagination.

At the Little Bighorn, one soldier remembered that the attacking American Indians howled "like incarnate fiends"; after the battle, the Bismarck *Tribune* described the death of one cavalry officer as being "tortured and finally murdered at the pleasure of the red devils."[59] In his dramatic masterpiece *The Crucible*, Arthur Miller reminded Americans that the McCarthy era of the 1950s was a reenactment of ancient battles with the perpetual Christian antagonist. As bluesman Robert Johnson sings in "Me and the Devil Blues," the devil is instantly recognized:

> Early this morning
> > when you knocked upon my door
> And I said, "Hello, Satan
> > I believe it's time to go."

His presence immediately triggers aggression and hostility, an irrepressible impulse that results in violent action:

> Me and the Devil
> > was walkin' side by side
> And I'm going to beat my woman
> > Until I get satisfied.[60]

Most recently, it was necessary to portray democratic America's external antagonist as brutally satanic (a role perfectly cast in the dictatorial figure of Saddam Hussein, who was reviled, deposed, and plucked unceremoniously out of a spider hole). America's own special virtue appeared on this dark rhetorical canvas as a mere silhouette sketched in grey relief to the enemy's black barbarity, as in the satanic image of the ominous "smoke demon" seen lurking about the stricken twin towers on that fateful morning of 9/11.[61]

Under such trying circumstances, Bush suggested, America and the world needed strong, decisive executive leadership—the services of a lead exorcist or what amounted to presidential rule. He expressed this theme of presidential power by representing himself as the decider. "I'm the decider," he said, "and I decide what is best." The president had told reporter Bob Woodward a few years earlier that "I'm the commander. . . . That's the interesting thing about being the president . . . I don't feel like I owe anybody an explanation." This democratically challenged notion of presidential governance insinuated a kind of moral authority in which citizens were expected to be obedient to the rule of the village minister or father-leader. This was, as George Lakoff observed, "the values of the strict father family applied to politics" in which the idea of freedom was not the progressive ideal of expanding civil rights, appreciating diversity, enriching education, and the like. It was instead, according to the libertarian Cato Institute, a presidential "power surge."[62]

Such a blunt assertion of executive authority did not offend the public's liberal-democratic sensibilities because it was premised on a set of culturally inscribed notions, including the presumption that Christian virtue and freedom exist in and are defined by an ongoing struggle against the devil and his totalitarianism. This premise was triggered by alluding to a cosmogonic struggle between God's chosen people and Lucifer in the guise of repeated references to the war on terrorism as a fight against "totalitarian ideology"—that "dark vision of tyranny and terror" and successor to "Fascists, to Nazis, to Communists, and other totalitarians of the 20th century." This was "the decisive ideological struggle of the 21st century."[63] Neither a simple defense of endangered freedom nor a recovery of lost democracy, this was instead primarily a story of progress toward a promised world of liberty and democracy, a halting tale of a bright world that would be formed sometime in the future out of the dark violence of the present day, a promise of the Kingdom of Heaven after the tribulations prophesied in the book of Revelation. Only the faint outline of democracy was visible in a perpetual scene of seemingly endless struggle against a relentless metaphysical foe. This minimalist image reduced democracy to a thin political veneer, an endangered prospect, an idyllic ambition, an occasion and cause for heroic deeds—one of those longed-for "possibilities of a world beyond the war on terror."[64]

The terrorists' "ambitions of cruelty and murder" amounted to nothing less than an "ideology of power and domination." Led into the wilderness not by the Spirit of God but by the enemy's desire to "dominate the weak and intimidate the world," the nation was being tempted by the devil. Its character and sense of destiny were tested by Satan in the desert. The president expressed this theme of character-revealed-by-adversity when he allowed that "the evil ones thought they could affect the spirit of America" and suggested "they must have not known who they were attacking." This was a challenge, Bush proffered, that Americans would not fail to meet. In his resolute words, "We're united behind the fact that we must rise to this occasion. And rise we will."[65]

In this imperative voice, the president exhorted the nation to show its strength and affirm its morality. Demonstrating strength meant remaining steadfast, patient, calm, courageous, determined, resolved, and decisive—not being soft, not tiring of the task at hand. America "will not be intimidated by evildoers," he insisted. "We must be strong and we must be decisive," he said. "We must stop the evil ones, so our children and grandchildren can know peace and security and freedom." Bush insisted, "we will not tire and we will not fail"; "we will plant the flag of freedom forever, by winning the war against terrorism, by rallying our economy, and by keeping strong and adhering to the values we hold so dear."[66]

The imperative of affirming America's morality entailed exhortations to Christian ideals of justice, tolerance, compassion, generosity, honesty, love, faith, and commitment to family values. "In order to overcome evil, the great goodness of America must come forth and shine forth. And one way to do so is to help the poor souls of Afghanistan." America's children, at the president's prompting, donated dollar bills to send food and medicine to Afghanistan's children in need, while the military displayed America's character by "dropping food, medicine, and supplies to relieve the suffering among the victims of the Taliban regime" and the "al Qaeda parasites," thereby demonstrating that "Americans are the most generous people on earth" and that they were "engaged in a noble cause."[67]

Evildoers, the president contended, "will not take this country down" because "we are one strong nation" of great character. This was a test of the nation's character that would determine its destiny and define how America would respond in the face of threats to the "core principles of liberty, justice, and equality": "The manner in which we face these and other challenges in this war will continue to influence our country for generations to come. In fulfilling our mission with both compassion and courage, we show our children what putting American values into action means. Similarly, parents should teach their children by word and deed to understand and live out the moral values that we hold, such as honesty, accepting responsibility for our actions, and loving our neighbors as ourselves."[68] The haunting alternative was to submit to evil, to become evil, to be exposed as evil.

America's heroic persona of liberator and protector was vested in the office and the person of the president as commander in chief. "We're not conquerors," Bush proclaimed. "We're liberators. We liberated people from the clutches of one of the most barbaric regimes in the history of mankind. I cannot tell you how proud I was to see the joy on the faces of women and little girls in Afghanistan with the realization that this mighty nation has freed them to realize their dreams." The appeal was evocative of the American Indian wars in its manly image of "hunting down the al Qaeda" and rescuing captive females from Saddam Hussein's rape rooms, paternal in its theme of fighting terror "for the sake of our children and grandchildren," and personal in its presidential testament that "I will not let stand" a regime that mistreats its people. Afghanistan and Iraq were "now on the road to democracy" thanks to presidential resolve. "I'm driven by my desire to protect the American people," the president declared. "I chose to defend the country," he insisted, and "when a President says something, he better mean it. In order to make the world more peaceful, the President must speak clearly and mean what he says." What he meant was "we defeat terror and darkness with the light of democracy and freedom."[69] The light was that of the Gospel, and the task was messianic. The nation was no longer opposing human adversaries but rather specters—terror and darkness—that could and would be defeated by the light of God. For the president, democracy was the beacon in the shadows: "And the light shineth in darkness; and the darkness comprehended it not."[70] Elaine Pagels has pointed out that the Christian Gospel of St. John casts "the struggle between good and evil" as that "between light and darkness."[71] Just as in the redemptive story of Jesus Christ, the war on terror would accomplish "what God accomplished cosmologically in creation: the separation of light from darkness—that is, of the 'sons of light' from the offspring of darkness and the devil."[72]

Writing in the current era about the seventeenth-century exorcisms of possessed nuns in Loudun, Aldous Huxley comments that all of the exorcist priests who took part in the ritual ceremonies were affected by the devils they conjured and battled: "No man can concentrate his attraction upon evil, or even upon the idea of evil, and remain unaffected. To be more *against* the devil than *for* God is exceedingly dangerous. Every crusader is apt to go mad. He is haunted by the wickedness which he attributes to his enemies; it becomes in some sort a part of him." The knight dueling the dragon in order to rescue damsels in distress; the exorcist casting out devils from possessed victims; the witch-hunter chasing the witch to protect afflicted children; the sheriff tracking down the Western outlaw—none remains untouched by the evil they fear or survives unscathed the power of the darkness they persecute. "Possession," Huxley argues, "is more often secular than supernatural. Men are possessed by their thoughts of a hated person, a hated class, race or nation."[73]

From this perspective, the president's rhetoric can be considered typical of "self-made demoniacs." As defined by Huxley, the term refers to world leaders "who are possessed by, and who manifest, the evil they have chosen to see in others. They do not believe in devils; but they have tried their hardest to be possessed—have tried and been triumphantly successful." Pagels observes, too, that the "vision of cosmic war," which "has pervaded the imagination of millions of people for two thousand years," remains compelling to the present day. "Many religious people who no longer believe in Satan," she writes, "along with countless others who do not identify with any religious tradition, nevertheless are influenced by this cultural legacy whenever they perceive social and political conflict in terms of the forces of good contending against the forces of evil in the world."[74]

The evil recognized by us in others is always validated by their deeds (actual or fabricated) and presumed intentions. But it is also a reflection of our shadow within—a mirror image of our darkness, the reign of Hell opposed to the Kingdom of Heaven in our souls. The foreign terrorist is a syncretic image created from characterizations of his criminal behavior in the external world as well as from a sense of the unacknowledged evil in ourselves. The terrorist is an external threat that is amplified by our own demons; our very own devil projected onto our political enemies. As with Frankenstein's monster—created from bits and pieces of dead bodies—the terrorist's actions provide the building blocks for our idealization, but the life we breathe into him is our own.

Democracy's Faint Glimmer

Democracy's light was indeed dim in the president's rhetorical war on terror, except in comparison to tyranny's total darkness—"a totalitarian ideology that hates freedom, rejects tolerance, and despises all dissent." The president's modest measure of democracy for the here and now was limited to educating young girls, preventing their moms from being whipped in the public square, freeing families to worship their God, registering voters, and holding elections. By this standard, Bush could boast that "Iraqis are making inspiring progress toward building a lasting democracy." This was the narrow shaft of democratic light the president said would someday overcome the darkness "of a totalitarian empire that denies all political and religious freedom."[75]

Hints of a more robust democratic culture and practice, when they occasionally surfaced in presidential war rhetoric, were directed to the future rather than the present, thus deferring indefinitely a fuller realization of democracy while avoiding direct acknowledgment of a deep and abiding anxiety over actually empowering the demos. Although Iraq was "making inspiring progress toward building a lasting democracy" and Afghanistan was "on the road to democracy," the president reminded Americans that "we are now in the early hours of this struggle between tyranny and freedom." While the president occasionally gestured (and even then jokingly) to debate as the "essence of democracy" and made passing reference to "a pluralistic, self-governing society," he continued to insist that the "difficult road ahead" required "the determined efforts of a unified country" that "must put aside our differences and work together to meet the test that history has given us" in our common quest for "a shining age of human liberty."[76]

The reason for continuously deferring the fulfillment of democracy's larger promise was that tyranny, like the devil tempting Jesus, is irrepressible and only "departs for a season."[77] The present fight was a "current expression of an ancient struggle—between those who put their faith in dictators, and those who put their faith in the people"; America faced an enemy that was "never tired, never sated, never content with yesterday's brutality."[78] Tyranny always returns, restored to its full savagery, at the first sign of civilization's weakness. It never stays dead or remains permanently defeated. It continues "violently opposed to democracy," forever challenging America to "back down" and constantly requiring the nation to "fight back" in order to disprove tyranny's unshakable belief that "democracies are weak."[79]

When freedom was defined in opposition to totalitarianism—as a continuous fight with the dark ideological forces of tyranny spanning centuries, not just years and decades—it lost its focus as a positive exercise of constitutionally privileged and protected civil rights and its immediate relationship to democratic practice. Thus, fighting for freedom substituted for putting freedom and democracy into practice and hindered thinking about what a robust practice of liberal democracy might actually mean. It insinuated strong presidential leadership as the appropriate mode of governance—indeed, the stronger the better given the immediacy of totalitarianism's unending threat.

Similarly, the rationale for presidential governance was premised on the suggestion that a free and democratic people were too weak-willed to stay the long and difficult fight. This culturally engrained anxiety over freedom's frailty was provoked by the taunts of the totalitarian enemy. Thus, the president quoted Osama bin Laden as saying that "our nation is weak and decadent, and lacking in patience and resolve" and that "America does not have the stomach to stay the fight." We must "uphold our duty" and "summon the will to meet this great challenge," Bush responded. "With vigilance, determination, [and] courage, we will defeat the enemies of freedom." The president positioned the country as if it were the man of weak faith in the book of Mark who asks Christ to cast out a "dumb spirit" from his tormented son: "Lord, I believe; help thou mine unbelief."[80]

Freedom's people were called to prove their virility and challenged to overcome their self-doubt by following the firm and decisive leadership of a heroic commander in chief. "I'm not going to allow" terrorists to blackmail the free world and spread their ideologies of hate, the president assured his people. Courageous leadership and the firm hand of presidential rule—unrestrained by legislative or judicial oversight, unencumbered by constitutional protections of civil liberties, and regardless of international conventions—were required to ensure a weak-willed democratic people would "stay in the fight." An unacknowledged Orwellian state was necessary to protect democracy from its enemies. Other culturally inscribed premises supporting expansive presidential power and reflected in Bush's war rhetoric included notions such as elections are the measure of democracy; patriots respond to the president's call to fight; dissent gives aid and comfort to the enemy and is disrespectful of soldiers' sacrifices; the public is easily duped by cunning enemy propaganda; when left to their own devices, the public will not see the threat until too late; new kinds of threats require abandoning old ways of thinking and old legal barriers to effective intelligence gathering; and "we need to do everything in our power to stop the next attack."[81]

The diabolical incantations of presidential war rhetoric functioned overall as an inducement to evacuate the political content of democracy, leaving a largely empty signifier in its place. Although officially promoted, a narrowly circumscribed, truncated, and distorted simulacrum of democracy suspended ad infinitum was the diminished extent of its symbolic import. Shriveled, shrunken, and emptied of meaning, democracy was relegated to the degraded role of a political cipher—a ready and reliable but badly disfigured vehicle for sublimating a heavy burden of anxious self-loathing and transferring that unwanted load to an external object of terror. Diluted democracy in the heroic guise of world liberator and protector and under the firm control of presidential order substituted for robust democratic deliberation and a full contestation of opinions. A failure to contain democracy implied a risk of chaos, an outbreak of violence, a loss of civilization, a reign of terror. Killing terrorists substituted for acknowledging and confronting the suppressed dark side of America's political identity. The primal appeal of presidential war rhetoric, its patriarchal inducement to rescue a feminized and infantilized victim from the evil savagery of faceless tyranny, was to prove the nation's virtue and virility. This was the essence of a rhetorical diabolism that purged democratic anxiety by channeling it into an impulse to war.

We do not conclude from the above that George W. Bush was the devil. We suggest only that he was no more or less than a Burkean devil insofar as he manifested the nation's penchant for demonizing its adversaries by stereotyping their circumstances and motives. His presidential rhetoric contributed to a toxic oversimplification of the complexities of the human divide, thereby perpetuating the mythic cycle of redemptive violence. This "victimage ritual" of redemption by violence, in Kenneth Burke's terms, is a political drama that symbolically fuses secular and religious discourses. Burke captures the paradox of transforming flawed and complicated secular affairs into artificially perfected God and devil terms through an imagined conversation in Heaven in which an agile and overly hasty Satan proclaims freedom to be the hallmark of the human condition while the Lord repeatedly admonishes him to remember that human purposes and political relations are always more complicated than that.[82]

If Americans have inherited the Christian worldview from their ancestors, they have also inherited a naïve susceptibility to believe in medieval villains, a language derived from an agonic cosmology that casts the devil as an eternal, ontological adversary, and a superstitious conviction in the power of scapegoating as a ritual means of cleansing one's sins. The length of influence of old fears and the perpetuity of mental constructs are highlighted by the fact that the nation that chased devils in Salem in its infancy grows up to declare war on terror and darkness. President Bush was not an exception or even an extreme example of warmongering. What he was, as president, was the leading voice articulating the projection of a national shadow onto terrorist enemies—a shadow forged by Americans and created in the image of their fears and anxieties about democracy.

As long as these projections go unrecognized, they distort the nation's vision, delude it into making mistakes, and create an imaginary landscape that serves as a hideout for America's enemies: "The effect of projection is to isolate the subject from his environment, since instead of a real relation to it there is now only an illusory one."[83] This fanciful terrain provides camouflage for the actual threat and is even a source of mistakes in battle. At the turn of the century, arguing for a more complex understanding of the social phenomenon of Russian anarchist terrorists, George Bernard Shaw warned, "If a man cannot look evil in the face without illusion, he will not know what it really is, or combat it effectively."[84]

The true danger to the nation that is posed by unexamined projections is twofold: first, unexamined projections leave us weak and vulnerable. Having cast our vital energy on others, we are left small and terrified before imagined external dragons (like in those dreams in which we are chased by our own monsters). Second, by branding others as evil—cruel and inhumane though they may be—we position ourselves as good, leaving our "evil spirit," in the words of Robert Johnson, free to "catch a Greyhound bus and ride."[85] Because we are good, we believe ourselves justified in Abu Ghraib, in Guantanamo, in violating the rights of American citizens and disregarding the Constitution. Also—somewhat inconsistently but nevertheless devilishly captivating—we are left free to deny that these events occur, that they are wrong (How could good people perpetrate wrongful acts?), and that we are complicit in them. Thus the practical need, as well as the moral responsibility, to remove the "beam" from the nation's collective eyes. Perhaps, if we gain the means and the moxie first to recognize and eventually to reclaim the nation's projected shadow, we might then dare to move forward toward a less dehumanizing and more democratic future with a diminishing incentive for war.

Meanwhile, under the tattered banner of democracy, America blindly persists in its patriotic battle with terrorist evildoers, a fight that occurs in mythic time on the symbolic terrain of Indian country. In this Wild West "terror dream," as Susan Faludi aptly calls it, Americans set out once again to tame the frontier. "The 'unimaginable' assault on our home soil was, in fact, anything but unimaginable. The anxieties it awakened reside deep in our cultural memory. And the myth we deployed to keep those anxieties buried is one we've been constructing for more than three hundred years." Comprehending the mythic impulse and dramatization of evil savagery that resurfaced after 9/11, Faludi insists, requires a full awareness for the nation to understand itself.[86]

2

Witches

The witchcraft delusion of 1692 has attracted universal attention since the date of its occurrence, and will, in all coming ages, render the name of Salem notable throughout the world.

Charles Upham, *Salem Witchcraft*

Arthur Miller went to Salem in search of a metaphor. The times—Cold War America during the early 1950s—were out of joint. Unsettling developments were threatening a United States flush with the arrogance of its own power after World War II: there was "the recent red victory in China, the Russian demonstration of the atomic bomb, and the expansion of Soviet territory into Eastern Europe." The Washington hearings of the House Un-American Activities Committee (HUAC) and the cultural revolution of McCarthyism were terrorizing the nation into becoming a "philosophical monolith," and if—Miller believed—"the current degeneration of discourse continued . . . we could no longer be a democracy, a system that requires a certain basic trust in order to exist."[1]

Marion Starkey's classic book on the Salem witch-hunt, *The Devil in Massachusetts*, had fallen into Miller's hands "as though it had been ordained."[2] In 1952 he gave a copy of Starkey's book to Elia Kazan, the director of *All My Sons* and *Death of a Salesman*. "It's all here . . . every scene," he said, for he was contemplating writing a new play. Miller had sensed disturbing parallels between himself and Salem and between Salem—across the breach of time—and contemporary Washington. Before leaving on a research trip to what was then "a town dribbling away, half forsaken" he stopped, at Kazan's request, for a visit at Kazan's Connecticut home. In a fateful conversation in the woods that recalls Goodman Brown's conversation with the devil in Nathaniel Hawthorne's story, Kazan told Miller that he had decided to cooperate with HUAC—to confess his past and tenuous connections to the Communist Party and to publicly reveal the names of former associates. Miller loved Kazan like a brother, but he could not get past the sum conclusion: "Had I been of his generation, he would have had to sacrifice me as well." As he said goodbye, he mentioned that he was on his way to Salem. Understanding the implication of Miller's journey, Kazan's wife, Molly, exclaimed: "You're not going to equate witches with this!"[3]

Miller wrote that while driving up to Salem "the gray rain on my windshield was falling on my soul." He entered the Salem courthouse and asked to see the town records of 1692. He sat next to a window that overlooked the waters of Salem harbor and began to read the recorded words of the witch trials. After several hours of "mouthing" the language of seventeenth-century Puritan farmers, he concluded that it sounded like a "burred and rather Scottish speech," and he came to love its feel—"like hard burnished wood."[4]

Black Witch of Salem

Tituba was a woman, a slave, an immigrant, and a foreigner to Puritan society—a perfect symbol of Otherness for seventeenth-century Massachusetts and for our own time. Had she not been sold by Barbados merchants to Samuel Parris (parish minister of Salem Village in 1692) in the West Indies, she also would have been considered illegal. The legality of her status was sanctioned by her servitude as a slave. In all probability she was an Arawak Indian from the region of the mouth of the Orinoco River in South America.[5] In the Salem documents she is repeatedly called "titibe an Indian Woman," or more simply, "Tituba Indian."[6] By their resort to the descriptive "Indian," Salem folk insisted that she was separate, apart from them, ominously related to the North American Indian tribes that besieged their own community of "saints."

The Other, once defined, becomes a receptacle for fresh projections of Otherness. In time, Tituba's features have been colored by our own projections. Starkey describes her as "half Carib and half Negro." In *The Crucible*, Miller describes her as a "Negro slave," and so she was portrayed in Nicholas Hytner's 1996 film of the play. Caribbean novelist Maryse Condé titled her novel on the Salem slave *I, Tituba, Black Witch of Salem*. Tituba was married to John Indian, the second one of Parris' West Indian slaves. John appears frequently in the original Salem documents but only sporadically in later accounts of the trials. In his nineteenth-century classic history of the witch-hunt, Charles W. Upham writes: "These two persons may have originated the 'Salem witchcraft.'"[7] Together, John and Tituba exerted a psychic and spiritual manipulation of the Salem inhabitants that resulted in persecution, death, and the implosion of their community.

On March 1, 1692, Sarah Good, Sarah Osborne, and Tituba were examined at Salem Village (now Danvers, Massachusetts) for suspicion of witchcraft by Jonathan Corwin and John Hathorne (a forefather of Nathaniel

Hawthorne), assistants to the general court of the Massachusetts Bay Colony. The women were accused of devil worship and of sending their spectral shapes to torment a group of afflicted children. Over the next few days, Good, Osborne and Tituba were interrogated by the magistrates and confronted by a chorus of howling, disturbed adolescents and their relatives, in front of a large gathering of spectators and covenanted church members. Sarah Good denied tormenting the children and blamed Osborne for their ills. Sarah Osborne denied having made a contract with the devil and, revealing an easy association between Indians and devils in the minds of Puritans, claimed that instead of being a witch she was probably bewitched herself: "shee was frighted one time in her sleep and either saw or dreamed that shee saw a thing like an indian all black which did pinch her in her neck and pulled her by the back part of her head to the dore of the house."[8] Tituba, examined next, had been beaten and abused by her slave master, Reverend Parris, in order to make her confess and accuse others of witchcraft. At first she, too, refused to admit hurting the children and denied familiarity with evil spirits, but eventually she began to speak the myth that would energize the Salem witch-hunt.

Tituba said that several weeks before, when the children had first fallen ill, "one like a man Just as I was goeing to sleep Came to me. . . . he sayd he would kill the Children & she would never be well, and he Sayd if I would nott Serve him he would do soe to mee." This man, who came from Boston, "Tell me he god." He wore "black Cloaths Some times, Some times Searge Coat of other Couler, a Tall man w'th white hayr, I think." The man asked Tituba to write her name in his book:

Q. did you write?
A. yes once I made a marke in the Booke & made itt with red Bloud
Q. did he gett itt out of your Body?
A. he Said he must gett itt out the Next time he Come againe, he give me a pin tyed in a stick to doe itt w'th, butt he noe Lett me bloud w'th itt as yett butt Intended another time when he Come againe.

The Tall Man in Black often appeared in the company of the shapes of Sarah Good and Sarah Osborne, and those of two other women from Boston who also dressed in dark colors and sober fabrics: one wore a "black Silk hood," the other a "Searge Coat." On one occasion, the Tall Man and the four women had appeared to Tituba at her master's house: "the man stand behind mee & take hold of mee to make mee stand still in the hall." These spectral shapes had forced Tituba to pinch and hurt the children of the household—Betty Parris and Abigail Williams. The man, who was "very strong," had also made Tituba ride "upon a stick or poale & Good & Osburne behind me we Ride takeing hold of one another." They had traveled to Thomas Putnam's house—so the story went—to kill his young daughter with a knife. On the same pole, Tituba and the Tall Man in Black had ridden through the air but had come back to Salem Village without reaching Boston.[9]

Tituba's was the first documented confession by a Salem witch. The sexual metaphors in her language—later picked up and repeated by Salem accusers in their depositions—readily identify the Tall Man from Boston as a Medieval incubus. In subsequent examinations, the image of the Tall Man in Black would recur as an obsessive concern in the questions of prosecutors, in the hallucinations of the afflicted children, and in the relations of confessed witches (the signing of one's name in blood to a contract with the devil is a story as old as the legend of Dr. Faustus). Religious officials and Salem citizens feared the presence in their midst of a conspiracy of witches led by a Grand Wizard. George Burroughs, former minister of Salem, was tried and hung on August 19, 1692, based on evidence that held him to be the "minister with a black coat," or the "little black beard man . . . in blackish apparil" who was the "Cheife of all the persons accused for witchcraft or the Ring Leader of them."[10] Burroughs was accused by Ann Putnam Jr. of "greviously tortoring me by beating pinching and almost choaking me severall times a day." Mercy Lewis complained that Burroughs had "tortored me most dreadfully" and "caried me up to an exceeding high mountain and shewed me all the kingdoms of the earth." Elizabeth Hubbard testified that Burroughs had visited her at night, "tortoring me very much by biting and pinching squesing my body and runing pins into me."[11] Tituba's man with "black Cloaths," whose spectral shape tormented victims into signing the devil's book, had become the "dreadfull wizzard" who sounded the "Trumpett" for the "generall meeting of the Witches in the feild near Mr. Parrisse's house," and who presided over their "sacramental meeting" where they ate "Red Bread" and drank "Red Wine like Blood" in a devilish inversion of the Last Supper ritual.[12]

What the Salem folk did not perceive—what Arthur Miller sensed, but did not discover—was that a momentous shift had occurred in Tituba's discourse during her interrogation. Pressed by the magistrates, the disturbed children, and the menacing congregation, Tituba had withdrawn into her own dream world. The forces that the Puritans believed to be at work in Salem (God and the devil; angels and familiar spirits; witches and saints) existed in different forms in her own native mythology—a mythology that was organic to the natural environment of the Americas and that did not partake of the moral Manichaeism of Christianity.

Indians and Demons

The Arawak tribes of the South American continent first immigrated to the Caribbean Islands between 500 BC and AD 600. In the centuries between AD 1200 and 1500, the Taíno culture—formed by successive waves of Arawak migrations that combined with early preagricultural settlers on the islands—flourished in western Cuba, Española (today Haiti and the Dominican Republic), and eastern Puerto Rico. The Taíno language was a branch of the proto-Arawakan languages. In AD 1500, it was closely related to the Island/Carib language of the Lesser Antilles, and to the Arawak/Lokono language of the South American continent.[13] In the Caribbean Islands, the Taínos encountered Christopher Columbus and his caravels in 1492. Facing the need to communicate with native tribes, Columbus entrusted Fray Ramón Pané—a Catalonian hermit who came to the New World during the second voyage—with the task of living among the Indians of Española in order to "know and understand the beliefs and idolatries of the Indians, and how they venerate their gods."[14] Pané recorded his findings in a document entitled *Relación acerca de las antiguedades de los indios*, which is today an invaluable source for the study of the language, myths, and ceremonies of the Caribbean Taínos. Pané's brief manuscript, dating from 1498, was the first book written in the New World.

Elaine G. Breslaw has noted that the name of a young slave, *Tattuba*, appears on two slave inventories of plantations from Barbados in 1676. She suggests that this was the same slave bought by Parris in the mid-1670s and points out that the name "Tituba or Tattuba denoted an Arawak Indian tribe in South America—the Tetebetana." Coincidentally, we find in Pané's *Relación* the myth of a woman called *Itiba Cahubaba* who dies giving birth to four sons. One of them was the sacred trickster figure of Taíno mythology, Deminán Caracaracolero, who brings about the cosmogonic origin of the sea by smashing the treasured pumpkin of an old chieftain. As Itiba Cahubaba gave birth to the Taíno trickster figure and his brothers, so Tituba became the mother of the trickster rhetoric and mythology that cast the "great delusion of Satan" upon New England.[15]

We learn from the *Relación* that the Taínos believed in an Other World of spirits—or as Salem folk would call them, "shapes"—that communicated freely with human beings. At night, the spirits of the dead (*opías*) would eat of the fruit of the guava tree, celebrate dances, and come to the world to make love to the living:

CHAPTER XIII
Of the shapes they say the dead have
They say that during the day they are secluded, and at night they walk about, and eat of a certain fruit called *guayaba*, which tastes like [quince fruit] . . . and that they celebrate, and go next to the living. . . . And so they are tricked sometimes . . . and lie with some woman from Coaybay, and when they think they have her in their arms, they have nothing, because she vanishes instantly.

The House of the Dead was ruled by a dark lord:

CHAPTER XII
What they think about the wanderings of the dead, and how they are, and what they do
They believe there is a place where the dead go, called Coaybay, and it is found on one side of the island, called Soraya. They say that the first one who was in Coaybay was one called Maquetaurie Guayaba, who was lord of the said Coaybay, house and habitation of the dead.

They also believed that the living spirit of human beings could appear to others in different shapes: "When the person is alive, they call the spirit *goeíza*, and after dead, they call it *opía*; they say: *goeíza* appears many times in the shape of man as well as woman, and they say that there are men who have wanted to fight it, and when they struggled with it, it would disappear. . . . And this is believed by all of them in general, both young and old; and that it appears to them in the shape of father, mother, brothers or relatives, and in other shapes."[16]

The parallels between the Salem narratives—first framed by Tituba's confession, and infused with the Christian belief of illicit sexuality as evil—and Pané's accounts in the *Relación* are striking in their similarity of detail. Ghostly apparitions by the spirits of dead relatives were recorded by Ann Putnam Sr. in Salem: "immediately their did appere to me: six children in winding sheets which called me aunt: which did most greviously affright me: and they tould me that they ware my sisters Bakers children of Boston and that goody Nurs and Mistris Cary of Charlstown and an old deaft woman att Boston had murthered them."[17] Salem girls were "tortored" by specters; men were suffocated by familiar spirits in their houses at night: "ther came at his window the liknes of a catt and by and by com up to his bed took fast hold of his throt and Lay hard upon him a Consideribl while and was lik to throtl him at Length he minded w't susana martin thretened him with the day be fore."[18] Such visitations might as well have been encounters with the *goeíza*, or nocturnal trysts with *opías*, who seduced the living by laying "hard" upon them and by "pinching and squesing" their bodies. Tituba's Tall Man in Black from Boston, who appeared along with other spectral shapes, has his counterpart in the semblance of Maquetaurie Guayaba, Ruler of Coaybay. Her flight with the Tall Man upon a "stick or poale" is an apt metaphor for nocturnal love making. Like an *opía*, the Tall Man in Black would instantly disappear after his adventures: "they hall me and make me pinch Betty . . . and then quickly went away altogether."[19]

Other incidences of Tituba's Arawak-based story abound in Salem. The shapes of some of the familiar spirits she identified in her confession can be found among Taíno *cemíes* (carved stone, wood, or cotton sculptures of deities and animal figures). The "hairy Imp" that she described as "a thing all over hairy, all the face hayry & a long nose & I don't know how to tell how the face looks w'th two Leggs, itt goeth upright & is about two or three foot high & goeth upright like a man"[20] can be recognized in the wooden sculpture of *Opiyelguobirán*, the doglike *cemí* of the cacique Sabananiobabo, which always escaped to the rain forests at night.[21] The "little yellow bird" that caused so much havoc in Salem, which sucked Goody "Good betwene the fore finger & Long finger upon the right hand," may have had its progeny in the bird *inriri*, which carved out the female sex from four wooden creatures when the Taínos lost their women.[22]

Even aspects of the Taíno myth not relayed by Tituba, at least not in the extant documentation, can be found in later narratives by witches and witch-hunters. One Andover witch confessed to John Hale that she and two others would fly and land at Salem Village to attend the Witch Meeting, where they would consume the ceremonial red bread and blood; so would the *opías* consume the guava fruit (similar in appearance to the quince fruit, with yellowish-green skin outside, red as the pomegranate inside) and celebrate their dances in Coaybay. Similar to the Taíno men who tried to combat the *goeíza*, Benjamin Hutchinson and Eleazar Putnam, prompted by Abigail Williams and Mary Walcott, engaged in a spectral combat with myriad shapes at Ingersoll's ordinary: "the roome was full of them then the said hucheson & Ely putnam stabed with their raperres at a ventor then said mary & abigell you have killed a greet black woman of Stonintown, and an Indian that comes with her for the flore is all covered with blod. then the said mary and abigaill looked out of dores & said they saw a greet company of them one a hill."[23]

Otherwise powerless before the Salem magistrates, the slave Tituba allowed—by mythological translation and adaptation—her own demigods and spirits to assume the masks of the cast of characters of the Salem Christian Passion play of good and evil. Forty years after his original research for

The Crucible, Arthur Miller commented on Tituba and the Salem Puritans: "They gave her inadvertently the power to destroy them by investing her with this mysterious power from hell. They then proceeded to destroy each other, once that was let loose among them."[24] By accepting the power they conceded her, Tituba created the mythos that informed and compelled the witch-hunt. Through a graphic syncretization of mythological images she invigorated the threats that the Puritans perceived, and exacerbated their fears. She became a queen of spirits and a priestess of the dead. Thus was the fury of the witch-hunt unleashed upon Salem.

If Tituba gave birth to the demons that tormented Salem, then her husband, John Indian, became the instigator who whipped them into shape. John and Tituba had baked the witch-cake (a mixture of rye meal and urine from the afflicted children) that raised the devil in Salem.[25] Ever since that time, according to Samuel Parris in his rebuke of Mary Sibley (March 25, 1692), "apparitions have been plenty." The devil's "rage is vehement and terrible; and, when he shall be silenced, the Lord only knows."[26] Soon after Tituba's testimony, John Indian joined the ranks of the bewitched. In a complaint lodged against John Proctor (April 1692) he appears in the role of accuser: "Then John [Indian] cryed out to the Dog under the Table to come away for Goodm: Proctor was upon his back, then he cryed out of Goody Cloyse, O you old Witch, & fell immediately into a violent fit that 3.men & the Marshall could not without exceeding difficulty hold him."[27]

From Nathaniel Cary's account of the examination of his wife, Mary, it is clear that by May 1692 John Indian had crafted his convulsions into a masterful performance: "The Indian before mentioned, was also brought in to be one of her Accusers: being come in, he now (when before the Justices) fell down and tumbled about like a Hog, but said nothing. The Justices asked the Girls, who afflicted the Indian? they answered she (meaning my wife) and now lay upon him; the Justices ordered her to touch him, in order to his cure . . . but the Indian took hold on her hand, and pulled her down on the Floor, in a barbarous manner; then his hand was taken off, and her hand put on his, and the cure was quickly wrought."[28] There is a precedent for John Indian's "fits" in Pané's *Relación*. His gambols and mountebankery were part of the ceremonial practices of Taíno *behiques*— medicine men who were known to speak to the gods and to the dead. Both the "touch test" applied in the case of Mary Cary and John Indian's pulling of Mrs. Cary to the floor existed among the healing rituals of the *behiques*: "the *behique* stands up, and goes toward the sick person who is seated alone in the middle of the house . . . and then stands before him, and grabs him by the legs, touching him by the thighs and down the feet; then he pulls strongly, as if he wanted to tear something away. From there he goes to the entrance of the house and closes the door, and speaks to it saying: 'Go to the mountains, or to the ocean, or where you will.'"[29] John Indian also preserved himself by the simple tactic of affirming the narratives that the Puritans were disposed to hear. For his sins, he was spared the witch-hunt, and thus brought destruction on his Salem masters.

The syncretic crystallization of images that fused the contours of the European devil with the substance of American Indian divinities had a long history in the new continent previous to 1692. In Pané's *Relación, cemíes* are described as "demons" and as "idol or devil."[30] Bartolomé de las Casas (1474–1566), the Great Defender of the Indians, writes that through the Taíno statues "it is believed that the devil speaks to the priests, called behicos [*sic*]."[31] In 1562 Diego de Landa (1524–1579), provincial head of the Order of Franciscans in Yucatán, ordered an auto de fé to combat the idolatries of the Maya. Over five thousand idols, altars, sacred stones, and pottery objects were destroyed; twenty-seven books of hieroglyphs were discovered, and "because they contained nothing but the falsehoods and superstitions of the demon, we burned them all, which they felt and grieved deeply."[32]

Puzzled by the mysteries of an unknown environment, anxious at the loss of familiar spiritual and social contexts, European colonizers tried to apprehend the geography and nations of the Americas through their own inherited images. When those New World landscapes proved threatening and harmful, they projected onto them, for safety and recognition, their own mental constructs. Massachusetts Puritans, "flying from the depravations of Europe," had come to an American "Indian wilderness" in order to live and celebrate the "Wonders of the Christian Religion."[33] Experiences such as that of Mary Rowlandson, victim of an Indian raid upon the settlement of Lancaster in 1676, moved them to comfort and reassurance in the discovery of an old enemy—the one that haunted their fears and theology and was the principal antagonist of their Christian faith: "It is a solemn sight to see so many Christians lying in their blood, some here and some there, like a company of sheep torn by wolves, all of them stripped naked by a company of hell-hounds, roaring, singing, ranting and insulting, as if they would have torn our very hearts out."[34]

Behind the mask of the devil in Salem there was always the face of the American Indian—natural and mysterious, alien and threatening, a sign of Otherness and a constant symbol of violence, danger, and distance from the natural landscape of the Americas. In the nineteenth century, Charles Upham was convinced that Tituba and John Indian contributed to the Salem witch-hunt by borrowing "from the wild and strange superstitions prevalent among their native tribes, materials which, added to the commonly received notions on such subjects, heightened the infatuation of the times, and inflamed still more the imaginations of the credulous." Upham concluded that many of the stories and images that flourished in Salem were to be found in other native cultures from the Americas: "Persons conversant with the Indians of Mexico, and on both sides of the Isthmus, discern many similarities in their systems of demonology with ideas and practices developed here."[35] Upham also reminds us of Cotton Mather's moral certainty in the seventeenth century: "the *Black Man*" (shades of Maquetaurie Guayaba) is what "the Witches call the Devil; and they generally say he resembles an *Indian*."[36] In our own time, Mary Beth Norton has explored the connections between King Philip's War, King William's War (Second Indian War), and the Salem witchcraft crisis: "The association among Indians, black men, and the devil would have been unremarkable to anyone in the Salem Village meetinghouse. English settlers everywhere on the continent had long regarded North America's indigenous residents as devil worshippers and had viewed their shamans as witches."[37] Conceding the compelling nature of Breslaw's evidence with regard to Tituba's origins, what Tituba and John Indian contributed to this association was a specific iconography that was based on Christian beliefs and on the mythology and ritual practices of Antillean Arawaks.

Puritan Resistance

If the New England Puritans are to be remembered for the Salem witch-hunt, they must also be remembered for their efforts to bring the witch-hunt to a halt. If the violence and zealotry that characterized the witch-hunters serve as a warning against the excesses of ideological fundamentalism, we must remember that it was also Puritans, who finding strength in their faith, bravely resisted tyranny, delusion, and the dominion of folly. Patricia Roberts-Miller has noted the presence of a monologic discourse in Puritan rhetoric: "Puritans imagined only two possible identities in an audience: the reprobate and the elect." Puritanism, she argues, "*required* a degree of dissent that it could not manage." Oppositions in Puritan rhetoric were not antitheses, but rather "dualities whose apparent conflict results from man's fallen nature. In a state of grace, the apparent paradoxes dissolve, but in this world we must hear the voices from both sides." It contained within itself an unmanageable impulse to dialogism. On one hand, "Puritans were dissenters in search of religious freedom who treated their own dissenters with no mercy and forbad religious freedom to everyone else." On the other, true piety required a "difficult balancing of dual positions" in a fallen world. Those cast in the roles of reprobates were to take comfort in the belief that affliction was a path to salvation: "The righteous individual . . . will some-day be forced to stand firm against a group of persecuting sinners who ver-bally abuse the saint."[38]

The threats in Salem were real and felt by all. The devil was a cultur-ally inherited image with deep moral and religious associations;[39] the New World landscape was a perpetual source of vague, unnamable anxieties; armed conflicts with Indian tribes and their French allies were regular oc-currences in the colonists' lives: "There was scarcely a village where the marks of savage violence and cruelty could not be pointed out, or an individual whose family history did not contain some illustration of the stealth, the malice or the vengeance of the savage foe."[40] Salem children and adult vic-tims were palpably sick in 1692.[41] The region's livestock and farm animals were distempered as if with a plague. Even Arthur Miller, who put no cre-dence on witchcraft and who was at best ambiguous about the credibility of the symptoms of the bewitched, acknowledged the presence of natural disturbances in Salem: in *The Crucible* he narrated an outbreak of mass hys-teria caused by the wounded sexuality of a teenage Abigail Williams and the adulterous guilt of John Proctor.

The devil/Indian avatar that Tituba and John Indian unleashed was an aggregate sum of living terrors, a crystallized antagonist that signified dis-parate threats, a literalized metaphor that obsessed both accused and witch-hunters alike. Little wonder that the Reverend Deodat Lawson, in a sermon on March 24, 1692, exhorted his former Salem Village parishioners in the following terms: "*ARM, ARM, ARM!* handle your arms, see that you are fixed and in a readiness, as faithful soldiers under the Captain of our sal-vation, that, by the shield of faith, ye and we all may resist the fiery darts of the wicked; and may be faithful unto death in our spiritual warfare; so shall we assuredly receive the crown of life."[42] Following Carl Jung, Marie-Louis von Franz observes that "the shadow is exposed to collective infec-tions to a much greater extent than is the conscious personality."[43] Tituba received the abuse, the derision, the accusation of witchcraft and demonic practices—all projections of the shadow archetype of the self—and turned them back on to her Salem accusers, leading them to believe that the devil lived among them. She played the villainous part of the Nahuatl divinity Tezcatlipoca (god of darkness and shadows) in the Mesoamerican legend of Quetzalcoatl (Tezcatlipoca defeated the king/priest of the Toltecs by asking Quetzalcoatl to "envision" himself in a two-sided, magical mirror).[44] Von Franz calls this psychological phenomenon of projections "re-flexio," which means that the "image which has been 'radiated' outward onto another ob-ject is 'bent back' and returns to oneself."[45] Projections of the shadow side of the collective self, when reflected back upon the subject, are never at first discovered to lie within ourselves but always elsewhere—usually among our neighbors. When the works of the devil were discovered in Salem, the blame was fixed upon those who were tinged with Otherness.

How to combat the literalization of metaphors, or to retrieve projections of the archetypal shadow? Salem Puritans struggled mightily against the witch-hunt from different perspectives. First were the resolute denials of the victims. There was Martha Corey, proclaiming before her accusers that she was a "Gosple-woman." Her husband, Giles Corey, was pressed to death for refusing to answer the charges of witchcraft. In the face of howling accusations, Rebecca Nurse declared: "I am as innocent as the child unborn." Elizabeth Proctor warned one of her accusers: "There is another judgment, dear child." At Gallows Hill, moments before his death, George Burroughs repeated the Lord's Prayer without fault and spoke so fervently that the gathered crowd almost turned against the witch-hunters, save for a timely oration delivered by Cotton Mather. Mary Esty, petitioning the court not for her own life but so that "no more Innocentt blood may be shed," asked the court "to examine theis Afflicted Persons strictly and . . . to try some of these confesing wichis I being confident there is severall of them has belyed themselves."[46]

Not only the condemned resisted or tried to pierce the clouds of fear that oppressed Salem. In the cases against John and Elizabeth Proctor, thirty-one neighbors signed a petition declaring "upon o'r Consciences we Judge them Innocent of the crime objected."[47] A deposition submitted in favor of Mary Bradbury of Salisbury (ancestor of science fiction writer Ray Bradbury) contained the signatures of ninety-three of her neighbors. When petitions did not move the court, Puritans took stronger and more direct action. Margaret Jacobs recanted her confession: "What I said, was altogether false against my grandfather, and Mr. Burroughs, which I did to save my life and to have my liberty; but the Lord, charging it to my conscience, made me in so much horror, that I could not contain myself before I had denied my confession, which I did though I saw nothing but death before me."[48] Thomas Bradbury and supporters orchestrated the escape of his wife from jail and kept her in hiding. Nathaniel Cary smuggled his wife out of jail and helped her escape to New York. Philip and Mary English, encouraged by the Reverend Joshua Moody and aided by Massachusetts governor Sir William Phips, also escaped to New York.

On July 23, John Proctor sent a petition to several Boston ministers alleging that the confessions of witches were being obtained through torture ("Popish Cruelties").[49] After reviewing Proctor's letter, Increase Mather and other Boston ministers declared unanimously against one of the key assumptions of the trials. They concluded that the devil *could* appear in the shape of an innocent person, although they qualified their statement by admitting that such instances were "rare and extraordinary."[50] At a conference of ministers in Cambridge, the elder Mather later warned in sterner tones against spectral evidence and denounced the "touch" test.[51] An opinion by Dutch and French ministers from New York sent to Governor Phips by Joseph Dudley also denied that spectral evidence was sufficient grounds upon which to condemn witches. Richard Pike, magistrate of Salisbury, and Thomas Brattle, merchant from Boston, wrote letters denouncing the premises of the trials: "I cannot but admire that the justices, whom I think to be well-meaning men, should so far give ear to the devil, as merely upon his authority to issue out their warrants, and apprehend people."[52] Starkey reports that numerous preachers came to the defense of individual parishioners: "The credulity and pitiless zeal of Nicholas Noyes and Samuel Parris, far from being characteristic of the ministers of Massachusetts, seem to have been the conspicuous exception."[53]

Still the witch-hunt raged, and the witch-hunters continued down their cruel path. The Kingdom of Satan had descended in great wrath, legions of the devil's servants were torturing the minds and bodies of the faithful, a score of condemned persons had been executed on Gallows Hill, and the jails were filled with confessed witches and wizards. "There is such a passionate drive within the shadowy part of oneself that reason may not prevail against it. A bitter experience coming from the outside may occasionally help; a brick, so to speak, has to drop on one's head to put a stop to shadow drives and impulses."[54] Such a "brick," such an irreconcilable chasm between delusion and reality, such a personal calling to account for the consequences of unexamined projections of evil, was to fall squarely on the head of the Reverend John Hale. In October 1692, Mary Herrick of Wenham complained of being tormented by Mrs. Sarah Hale—the reverend's wife. Being "fully satisfied of his Wife's sincere Christianity," the reverend could no longer believe that the devil could "Afflict in a good Man's shape." He shifted his attitude "when it came so near to himself."[55]

There were others who were spared and protected from accusations. In his famous "letter," Thomas Brattle complained "that some particular persons, and particularly Mrs. Thatcher of Boston," had been accused by the afflicted persons yet remained at large, even while others had been apprehended "upon the same account." Mrs. Thatcher was the mother-in-law of Jonathan Corwin, one of the judges and chief witch-hunters of the trials. Mary Cary, Mr. and Mrs. Philip English, and others had escaped from prison, but no effort had been made to reclaim them, even though "in other capital cases this has been practiced."[56] When the Revered Samuel Willard (who made efforts to oppose the witch-hunt), one of the most distinguished ministers in Boston, was accused, the judges rejected the charges outright.[57] And when Lady Mary Phips, the governor's wife, was cried out against by the bewitched, the accusation was ignored.

When the relatives of the rich, the eminent, and the powerful became the object of accusations, the witch-hunt came promptly to an end. By comparison, prosecuting a few sacrificial soldiers for the sins of the Abu Ghraib prisoner abuse in Iraq was not the bitter, mind-clearing experience of a brick falling on the head of the powerful. Indicting the secretary of defense or the president himself for violating international law, however, might have been a brick of sufficient force to halt the projection of evil. And so Salem in the seventeenth century—and not the United States in the twenty-first— learned the lesson contained in the myth of Iphigenia: when the witch-hunter is made to pay a personal price, when the warmonger is extracted a cost for his war, his actions become sober and wise.

Relieved by Prayer

The witch-hunt, instigated by Tituba's vision of the Tall Man in Black, came to an end with a second, compelling vision by one of the bewitched girls. On September 22, 1692, Mary Herrick (she who had complained of the spectral shape of Mrs. Hale) saw the shape of Mary Esty (Rebecca Nurse's sister) on the last day of the witch hangings. The spirit of Esty spoke to her: "I am going upon the ladder to be hanged for a witch . . . but I am innocent and before a twelfth-month be past you shall believe it."[58] In late October the Court of Oyez and Terminer, which had been appointed by Governor Phips to hear witchcraft cases, was dismissed. Through the course of the following year, witches arrested and condemned on the grounds of spectral evidence were pardoned and reprieved. Once error was perceived, once the conviction of delusion was gained, Salem Puritans reacted with humble apologies, public confessions, and rituals of reconciliation to the horror of the Salem crisis. In 1696 the General Court of Massachusetts Bay proclaimed a "Day of Prayer, with Fasting throughout this Province," so that "whatever mistakes on either hand have been fallen into . . . refer-ring to the Late Tragedy . . . [God] would humble us therefore and pardon all the Errors of his Servants and People."[59] On the day of the fast, January 14, 1697, Judge Samuel Sewall, lamenting the "reiterated strokes of God upon himself and family" because of his "Guilt contracted" during the Salem Trials, stood in the South Meeting-House of Boston while the Reverend Samuel Willard read his apology: "[Samuel Sewall] Desires to take the Blame & Shame of it, Asking pardon of Men, And especially desiring prayers that God who has an Unlimited Authority, would pardon that Sin, and all other his Sins."[60] Jury members of the Salem trials, fearing that they had brought upon the "People of the Lord" the "Guilt of Innocent Blood," released a public document that stated: "We justly fear that we were sadly deluded and mistaken, for which we are much disquieted and distressed in our minds; and do therefore humbly beg forgiveness, first of God for Christ's sake for this our Error."[61] Troubled by the crisis, John Hale wrote his book, *A Modest Enquiry Into the Nature of Witchcraft* (1702), to "at least give some light to them which come after, to shun those Rocks by which we were bruised, and narrowly escaped Shipwreck upon."[62]

Perhaps the most significant apology was that of Ann Putnam Jr. A bewitched child during her young years and one of the ringleaders of the accusing circle of girls in Salem, Ann had been raising her younger brothers and sisters since the death of her parents in 1699. On August 25, 1706, the Reverend Joseph Green read a "relation of her conversion experience and a confession"[63] of her past deeds to the congregation at the Salem Village meeting house: "That I, then being in my childhood, should, by such a providence of God, be made an instrument for the accusing of several persons of a grievous crime, whereby their lives were taken away from them, whom now I have just grounds and good reason to believe they were innocent persons . . . for which cause I desire to lie in the dust, and earnestly beg forgiveness of God, and from all those unto whom I have given just cause of sorrow and offence, whose relatives were taken away or accused."[64] Not even the kinsmen of the condemned Towne sisters—Rebecca Nurse, Mary Esty, and Sarah Cloyce—who sat in attendance, objected to Ann's entry into full communion in the Church.[65]

Modern psychoanalysis holds that "the withdrawal of a projection . . . is almost always a moral shock." Jung compares the process to that of a fisherman sailing on the sea of the unconscious: "He hauls fish (the contents of the unconscious) into his boat, but he cannot fill the boat (i.e., integrate unconscious contents) with more fish than the size of the boat allows; if he takes in too many the boat sinks." The process of individuation requires that vital forces contained in the retrieved image (shadow/devil) be integrated into the conscious personality. In terms of the Salem Puritans this would have meant coming to the realization that the devil they feared was within themselves; that whatever else he may be he was also a formal manifestation of the shadow archetype; that he was the alternate face of the Puritan coin; that he was their dark brother, or an artful representation of their own shadow. This far the Salem folk could not go; Puritan theology could not brook such a compromise. Lacking acquaintance with modern theories of the self's phenomenology, Puritan identity in 1692 would have been characterized by Jung as archaic, "one in which [man] saw all psychic processes in an 'outside'—his good and evil thoughts as spirits, his affects as gods (Ares, Cupid) and so on."[66]

Ann Putnam Jr. was characteristic of others in assigning blame for her actions to the external devil she battled as a child and renounced as an adult: "What I did was ignorantly, being deluded of Satan."[67] The General Court proclaimed that the witch-hunt had been "raised among us by Satan and his Instruments, thro the awful Judgment of God."[68] The jurors of the Salem trials also blamed their mistakes on a devil beyond themselves: "We confess that we ourselves were not capable to understand, nor able to withstand the mysterious delusions of the Powers of Darkness, and Prince of the Air."[69] Samuel Parris, in his grudging apology to his mutinous parishioners in 1694, was convinced that "God . . . has suffered the evil angels to delude us on both hands."[70] The very devil they had fought had tricked them, outsmarted them, but the devil—and their belief in him as an external phenomenon—remained very much alive.

Following Freud, Jung writes about the process of transference in psychotherapy: "Many projections . . . resist integration, and although they may be detached from their original objects, they thereupon transfer themselves to the doctor."[71] Projections that are withdrawn but that cannot be integrated into the conscious self will be "transferred" to other "concrete persons and situations." Detached unconscious contents will be projected again, thus repeatedly creating new threats and fears. At a later time in history (what Arthur Miller revealed in *The Crucible*), when witches and Indians were no longer perceived as threatening, the devil was found (once again) to exist among Reds and Communists. Like Massachusetts Puritans, we have yet to see the devil as a projection of our own darkness. We prefer to fancy him a living, breathing, external enemy.

During one of Miller's last days in Salem, he observed several framed etchings of the witch trials on the walls of the Salem Historical Society. He immediately recalled his own childhood memories of devout old men praying in a New York synagogue: "It became my memory of the dancing men in the synagogue on 114th street as I had glimpsed them between my shielding fingers . . . both scenes frighteningly attached to the long reins of God. I knew instantly what the connection was: the moral intensity of the Jews and the clan's defensiveness against pollution from outside the ranks. Yes, I understood Salem in that flash, it was suddenly my own inheritance."[72] Driving back to New York he discovered that he had already committed to writing his new play.

There are lessons to be found in this troubled precursor of contemporary political culture's struggle to suppress and purge the satanic forces of terrorism—lessons about listening to dissenting voices and about the limited possibilities of retrieving a projected shadow given such strong tendencies to deflect blame onto Others inside and outside the community. The people of Salem did not accept communal responsibility for an acknowledged error. Instead, the protests, professions of innocence, and admonitions of the condemned, the petitions of loved ones, neighbors, and moral figures within the community, and especially the calamity of the rich and powerful who eventually became ensnared in the growing web of accusations had the collective effect of prompting those involved to play the role of victim of an evil deceit. The category of evil—the presence of the Evil One—remained untouched by the acknowledged and lamented tragedy of the witch-hunt, just as it continues to rend American politics today in the form of self-sustaining and self-righteous rites of redemptive violence in the wake of disenchantment over the Iraq and Afghanistan Wars.[73] Like Communists and fellow travelers of yesteryear, terrorists and their homegrown counterparts have become the witches on whom the powerful deflect blame for the troubles of the present era. Powerless and vulnerable people of color are ethnically profiled, accused of providing Islamist terrorists with material support, and investigated by a Congressional committee on homeland security in search of homegrown terrorists.

The presence of a myth in society—its dormant latency in collective consciousness—may compel a "subjective reality" to be raised to the level of a "holy resonance" given a precise, semiotic manipulation of the contents of the myth.[74] The story of Salem would become a prescient magical object that fused two corners in time—always the present, and ever the recurring past. Having erupted into the geography of the New World on the face of the American Indian, the devil would return repeatedly, waging mythic wars that were only past events repeated in cyclical time. The stage was set for a future battle against the forces of darkness in the nineteenth-century American frontier, specifically at a place called Greasy Grass by the devil, near the Bighorn Mountains, during the time of the Moon of Making Fat.

3
Indians

Ere long whole tribes must take the spirit trail
As once they travelled to the bison hunt.
Then let it be with many wounds—in front—
And many scalps, to show their ghostly kin
How well they fought the fight they could not win,
To perish facing what they could not kill.
John G. Neihardt, *Song of the Indian Wars*

That "old serpent," the Indian devil Puritans had faced in the French-Indian wars and confronted at Salem, was cast out across the Mississippi River during the Jacksonian removal of the 1830s. There, from the US point of view, hydra-like and cognate with the seven-headed "red dragon" of John's book of Revelation, the devil had reared his head once more against the light of civilization. His legions had terrorized European settlers: miners in search of gold, ranchers, and farmers—all those inclined to spread the Kingdom of God through territorial expansion. Like angels come down from Heaven with great keys and chains, blue-coated armies of US soldiers—tempered in the crucible of a bloody civil war—with long knives and Hotchkiss guns materialized in the Plains territories, bound Satan in the bottomless pit of frontier reservations, and shut him up, removing his life source and his movement.

Wolf of the Washita

The expedition was haunted from the moment it left Fort Lincoln. The wives, children, and older relatives of the Arikara sang mournful songs to accompany the deployment of their warriors. The scouts beat their drums and sang death songs for miles down the road. When the regimental band played "The Girl I Left Behind Me" the officers' wives, who had stood bravely at their doors waving goodbye, ran into their houses to hide their grief. Elizabeth Custer saw the ghostly mirage of a long column of army cavalry and equipment reflected against the early morning mist. When Brevet Major General George Armstrong Custer departed with the Seventh Cavalry, a "premonition of disaster" and an "uncontrollable anxiety" weighed Mrs. Custer down.[1]

On Saturday, June 24, 1876, the expedition passed an abandoned Indian camp where a Sun Dance had been performed. Prehistoric petroglyphs on the banks of the Rosebud River were interpreted by Arikara scouts as a warning not to follow the Sioux into the Little Bighorn Valley. In the camp of the Seventh Cavalry, when all had retired in preparation for a forced march that night, a solitary voice was heard singing "Nearer, My God, to Thee." On that same June 24, Sitting Bull crossed the Greasy Grass and offered a prayer on a high ridge: "Father, save the tribe. I beg you. Pity me." At a Sun Dance early in June, he had offered one hundred cutout bits of his arms in sacrifice to the Great Spirit. In a vision, he saw soldiers and horses approaching an Indian village. They came upside down, feet and hoofs to the sky, hats falling to the ground. He considered it a great sign and told his followers that Indians would win a great battle, but they were not to take spoils.[2]

On June 25 at Reno Creek, the Crow scouts removed their army-issue clothes and changed into traditional battle wear: "Tell [Custer]," they said, "that in a very short time we are all going to be killed." On a nearby hill, interpreter Fred Gerard saw a party of warriors heading toward the Indian camp. He waved his hat toward Custer and yelled: "There go your Indians, running like devils!" By sundown, naked bodies of the Seventh Cavalry lay sprawled on the same Montana bluffs where Sitting Bull had prayed. On June 26, troops from General Alfred Terry's command saw more than sixty Indians galloping on a ridge wearing blue uniforms and flying an Army guidon. From a distance the next morning, the bodies on Custer Hill were mistaken by Terry's column for "skinned buffalo carcasses" and their dead horses for "buffalo skins." It was midsummer.[3]

Myths are formed by human experiences coined in aesthetic patterns that coalesce in a universal cauldron of mythic lore. "To the Greek mind," writes William Arrowsmith, "all exceptional human action really aims at . . . the immortality of memory, of memory become myth." This inclination—and its inevitable consequences—produces palpable substance and numinosity: "Classical Greeks understood heroism—in the firm belief . . . that the hero in some real sense survived his own death and achieved the permanence of myth as an exemplary and abiding presence." Legends exist within the confines of the time and space of our ordinary reality. Dressed and constructed with elements from what Jung named the "personal unconscious," they are referential of history and its specific details. Myths properly reside in Jung's universal realm of the "collective unconscious." They are mined by the dreams of shamans and the imaginary work of creative artists.[4]

The story of the Battle of the Little Bighorn presents the case of the development of a heroic legend that ultimately reveals a veiled myth. George Armstrong Custer had achieved "an illustrious reputation as a cavalry leader" and the rank of brevet major general under the command of Phil Sheridan in the Civil War. After the Fetterman Fight in 1866, echoing the universal sentiments of an aggrieved nation, William Tecumseh Sherman telegraphed Ulysses S. Grant: "We must act with vindictive earnestness against the Sioux, even to their extermination, men, women, and children." In 1868, Sheridan gave express orders to attack an encampment of Plains Indians in present-day Oklahoma and "to destroy their villages and ponies, to kill or hang all warriors, and bring back all women and children." The Battle of Washita River created a bright reputation for Custer (now a lieutenant colonel) and the Seventh Cavalry as Indian fighters. After the battle, Sheridan spoke to a Comanche chief who was surrendering: "The only good Indians I ever saw were dead." In 1874 Custer was ordered to undertake a scientific/military expedition of the Black Hills, a small mountain range sacred to the Lakota and Cheyenne tribes that was located within the confines of the Great Sioux Reservation. Custer's expedition brought back reports of a "wonderland" region in which gold could be found "in plenty from the grass-roots down." The subsequent intrusion of the Northern Pacific Railroad into Indian hunting grounds and an invasion of gold seekers into the Black Hills angered the Lakota and Cheyenne.[5]

Within days after June 25, 1876, newspapers proclaimed the defeat of the Seventh Cavalry and Custer's death as events of epic proportions. The *New York Herald* wrote that Custer and his men had died "as grandly as Homer's demigods." Custer's dead brothers and relatives fallen in the battle were compared to the Roman Curiatii and the Hebrew Maccabees. The *Herald* also began a campaign for the construction of a permanent monument to Custer, memorializing him as a Spartan Leonidas at Thermopylae. In spite of Custer's history as a Civil War cavalry officer for the Union, the *Richmond Whig* saw him as a hero that belonged to all Anglo-Saxons: "We behold in him the true spirit of that living cavalry which cannot die, but shall live forever to illustrate the pride, the glory, and the grandeur of our imperishable race." Not all reactions were laudatory. President Ulysses S. Grant, who disliked Custer, pronounced a judgment shared by a majority of army officers: "I regard Custer's massacre as a sacrifice of troops, brought on by Custer himself, that was wholly unnecessary." According to Colonel Samuel Sturgis, regimental commander of the Seventh Cavalry and father of Lieutenant "Jack" Sturgis (killed in action at Little Bighorn), Custer was "guilty of disobedience and of sacrificing good men's lives to win notoriety for himself." Countering press clamors in favor of the extermination of Indians, abolitionist Wendell Phillips posed the following question in the *Boston Transcript*: "What kind of war is it, where if we kill the enemy it is death; if he kills us it is a massacre?"[6]

The early mythification of the Little Bighorn can be perceived in Henry

Wadsworth Longfellow's "The Revenge of Rain-in-the-Face." The poem pictures a "Savage, unmerciful" Sitting Bull waiting in ambush with three thousand warriors for Custer. The hero rushes headlong into battle, "sword in hand." Longfellow envisions the warrior Rain-in-the-Face fleeing from Little Bighorn at night:

> Uplifted high in the air
> As a ghastly trophy, bore
> The brave heart, that beat no more,
>   Of the White Chief with yellow hair.

The number of Custer's dead is rounded up to a Spartan three hundred. Custer's "yellow hair" (repeated three times) brings to mind the refrains with which Homer identifies gods and heroes in *The Iliad* ("white-armed" Hera, for example, or "red-haired Menelaus"). Longfellow blames the US government's sad history of Indian treaties for the Bighorn slaughter:

> And say that our broken faith
> Wrought all this ruin and scathe,
>   In the Year of a Hundred Years.

The first Custer biography was published scarcely six months after his death. Frederick Whittaker's influential *A Complete Life of General George A. Custer* pronounced the American cavalryman as "worthy to stand beside Hannibal's 'thunderbolt' Mago; Saladin, the leader of those 'hurricanes of horse' that swept the Crusaders from Palestine; Cromwell, Seydlitz or Zieten; a perfect general of horse." Whittaker wrote that at the end of the battle, after emptying his pistol, Custer had fought like a tiger with his saber, and had struck down three enemies before he was shot by Rain-in-the-Face. Three hagiographical books by Elizabeth Custer—*Boots and Saddles* (1885), *Tenting on the Plains* (1887), and *Following the Guidon* (1890)—contributed to the perpetuation of her husband's heroic image among the public in the years that followed.[7]

Joseph Campbell has argued that mythology was historically the mother of the arts. When myths become manifest, they acquire corporeal form without forsaking sacred origins: "Myth is the secret opening through which the inexhaustible energies of the cosmos pour into human cultural manifestation." Art frees us from the tyranny of "reference" and serves to reveal an immanent experience. The multiplicity of paintings about the Little Bighorn during the last two centuries is proof of the activation of a myth in consciousness. A partial list of Western painters who have produced versions of the Last Stand would include John A. Elder (1884), E. S. Paxson (1899), W. R. Leigh (1939), and J. K. Ralston (1959). Acclaimed Western painters Frederick Remington and Charles Russell also produced several works on the Custer theme. In 1881, John Mulvany completed a twenty-by-eleven-foot oil painting, entitled "Custer's Last Rally," that was enthusiastically received in viewing galleries in Kansas City, Boston, New York, Louisville, and Chicago. At a viewing in New York, Walt Whitman sat "for over an hour before the picture" and saw an outpouring of the dark side of the American experience: "Altogether a Western, autochthonic phase of America, the frontiers, culminating typical, deadly, heroic to the uttermost; nothing in the books like it, nothing in Homer, nothing in Shakespeare; more grim and sublime than either, all native, all our own and all a fact."[8]

In or about 1885, a St. Louis artist and Civil War veteran by the name of Cassily Adams completed an oil painting for the St. Louis Art Club entitled "Custer's Last Fight." In an attempt to re-create Mulvany's success, Adams's painting was exhibited in Cincinnati, Detroit, Indianapolis, and Chicago. It was eventually sold to John G. Furber, a St. Louis saloonkeeper who kept the painting on permanent display in his establishment. After Furber's death, the Anheuser-Busch company acquired ownership of the painting. "Custer's Last Fight" was improved and lithographed by Otto Becker. Beginning in 1896—in the midst of the Cuban War of Independence that preceded the Spanish-American War—the company distributed over 150,000 copies of the Adams-Becker work to saloons and restaurants as an advertisement. The Adams-Becker version of the Battle of the Little Bighorn was viewed "by a greater number of the lower-browed members of society—and by fewer art critics—than any other picture in American history."[9]

In Ernest Hemingway's *For Whom the Bell Tolls*, Robert Jordan recalls "that figure in the buckskin shirt, the yellow curls blowing, that stood on that hill holding a service revolver as the Sioux closed in around him in the old Anheuser-Busch lithograph." Custer stands gallantly brandishing a saber aloft. The saber, according to Whittaker, was the "queen of cavalry weapons," and Custer was "the bravest and best swordsman of all." But there were no sabers at Little Bighorn. They had been left behind boxed on the Powder River, since Indian battle tactics made sabers an encumbrance. Because of the heat on June 25, Custer had worn a blue, not a buckskin, shirt. His fabled long "yellow hair" had been cut short before the battle. The Lakota and Cheyenne warriors did not know, until long afterward, that Custer had been present on Custer Hill.[10]

A telling corrective to the Western iconography of Custer's death can be found in pictographs drawn by Indian warriors who participated in Little Bighorn. From the native point of view, the Battle of the Greasy Grass elicited illustrated accounts by (among others) Amos Bad Heart Bull, Kills Two, No Two Horns, One Bull, and Standing Bear (Lakota); White Bird, Lame Deer, and Wooden Leg (Northern Cheyenne); and White Swan (Crow). In 1898, Frederick Remington asked Kicking Bear, a survivor of Little Bighorn and later apostle of the Ghost Dance, to draw his own recollection of the battle. A roundel of fallen soldiers and Indian warriors surround four prominent Indian heroes, standing center: Sitting Bull, Rain in the Face, Crazy Horse, and the artist, Kicking Bear. Custer lies dead, off-center of the picture, recognizable by his buckskin clothes and long yellow hair. Kicking Bear adds to his pictogram one remarkable component that is rare in Custer iconography: outline drawings of spirits leaving the corpses of the dead.[11]

The Dark and Bloody Ground

The Last Stand is a mythos of the American imaginary that keeps us constantly at war irrespective of whether our warlike stance is justified by historical circumstances. It repeats perpetually the story of a holy society that is besieged by devils and unholy forces. It features a necessary, perennial sacrifice in an everlasting conflict. It sets up a public, painful, bloody ritual of victimization that sounds the trumpets and beats the drums that conjure the deliberate slipping of the dogs of war against projected enemies. Its remembrance kindles bellicose aggression.

The genealogy of the Last Stand can be traced back to the besieged Troy of Homer's *Iliad*, once described by Jorge Luis Borges as a "rumor of men who defend a temple that the gods will not save." It also references the classic tale by Herodotus of the three hundred Spartans who died at Thermopylae defending Greece from the Persian invasion of Xerxes. Sacrifice creates memory, memory begets legend, and legend, in turn, constructing metaphors through what W. B. Yeats called the "vehicle of symbol and incident," signifies myth. Slotkin considers the construct of the Last Stand to have been an essential component of the American "Myth of the Frontier." He defines it as a "scenario in which heroic representatives of American civilization sacrifice themselves to delay the advance of a savage enemy."[12]

The Last Stand makes its first American archetypal manifestation in the events of the Salem witch trials. Later it appears in the legend of the Alamo, in which a superior Mexican army of "godless invaders and barbarians" defeated a small garrison of Texan and American soldiers at San Antonio de Béxar. On the eve of the fall of the Alamo, Colonel Travis wrote: "My bones shall reproach my country for my neglect." Just as in Salem, Santa Anna's early dawn attack on the mission garrison was described by one newspaper as a rush "forward with the fury of devils, and, in less than an hour, every man in the garrison was murdered." One immigrant to Austin commented in the aftermath: "Texas . . . will call it a second Thermopylae, but it will be an everlasting monument of national disgrace." The symbolic association with the Greek tale sanitized the complexity of contemporary contexts: "The slaughter of the Alamo garrison was transformed into a . . . necessary sacrifice for the establishment of a dominant Anglo-Celtic civilization." For the Last Stand is also a righteous condition, a symbolic fabrication that provides a justification for empire.[13]

The genealogy of the Last Stand reaches an epiphany in US war culture during the American Indian wars of the nineteenth century. Custer's defeat at Little Bighorn by a gathered population of hostile Indians crystallized the heroic visual imagery of the mythos for turn-of-the-century North America. The story was used as an aegis—Zeus's shield, borne by his daughter Athena, goddess of civilization and democracy—that compelled, cried out for, the extermination of Indians, or at the very least, their absolute containment. Given their total victory in battle, and the mutilations inflicted on the dead bodies of the Seventh Cavalry, how could the Sioux and Cheyenne not be evil? How could savages defeat a modern army and rub out a renowned military tactician? The dramatic imagination set up Sitting Bull as antagonist to Custer's protagonist in a mythic agon. Sitting Bull—so ran some of the contemporary legends surrounding him—had received a Western education by missionary Jesuits; the "Red Napoleon" had studied military tactics as a cadet at West Point. The association with black-robed Jesuits and Bonaparte confirmed the devilish contours of the Hunkpapa spiritual leader. The Sioux, as one of Custer's Irish troopers put it, were "rid nagurs."[14] The devil—his wiles and savagery—had defeated Custer, not Crazy Horse or Sitting Bull.

We consider, following Vico, that new nations are formed on the basis of new foundational myths. These trigger ritual, mimetic, collective action. The Last Stand is a "mytheme"—what William Doty defines as a "small unit of a complex myth"—of the devil myth, brought forth by a people at their time of origin. It is reflective of a point of crisis, the product of a mythological explosion against an overwhelming array of threatening evil forces. The Last Stand is seldom an accurate portrayal of what happened, but it is always a truthful representation of how the aggrieved choose to view the sacrifice they lament. The demonization of the antagonist—a stern belief in his evil savagery—cannot be sustained unless his victims are blameless of agency in their own destruction. All complexities are washed away in fabrication. During a tour of Canada, William F. Cody reflected soberly upon the events at Little Bighorn: "The defeat of Custer was not a massacre. The

Indians were being pursued by skilled fighters with orders to kill. For centuries they had been hounded from the Atlantic to the Pacific and back again. They had their wives and little ones to protect and they were fighting for their existence." The initial attack upon the Indian village by Custer and the Seventh Cavalry is ultimately erased by constructions of the Last Stand narrative. Only the Lakota and Cheyenne affirm this part of the story in their pictographs.[15]

The mythos informs our military victories and reinterprets our military defeats. There may be errors of strategy (like at the Alamo) or of execution (like at Little Bighorn), but never flaws in the basic premises of the war stance. The eventual surrender of Crazy Horse and exile of Sitting Bull to Canada one year after Little Bighorn perpetuated a faith in Anglo-American exceptionalism and helped to secure the privilege of a self-serving nation. The Last Stand is a spiritual disposition, with which North Americans approach the external world. It has become part of American mythology and is an integral component of American war culture. The belief that there is gold to be found in the frontier, that energy and exertion are all that is required, and that salvation depends on our efforts are the fuel that set in motion the Last Stand. Thus policies of containment and extermination of evil enemies are served and justified.

Magnificent Spectacle!

Ritual is a kinetic pattern of image and sound constructed in order to express myth. Oral cultures enact living, foundational myths through ritual performances. Performance allows the power of the thunder beings of the west (as Black Elk would have it) to reach the tribe and become manifest in our world of time and space. It compels the cleansing process (according to Aristotle) of catharsis upon an audience. Ritual—which contains immanent presence—accentuates the impact and consequence of performative actions and engraves them in memory. For Black Elk, performers (*heyokas*) are naturally selected individuals whose visions give them power, which they share with the tribe through comic actions: "When a vision comes from the thunder beings of the west, it comes with terror like a thunder storm; but when the storm of vision has passed, the world is greener and happier; for wherever the truth of vision comes upon the world, it is like a rain. The world, you see, is happier after the terror of the storm." Truth comes into the world with two faces: one is "sad" (tragedy) and the other one "laughs" (comedy), but it is "the same face laughing or weeping." This recalls the premises of classic Greek drama: theater (from the Greek *theatron*) was the "seeing place" where the ancient gods appeared and spoke. The actor was a vehicle for communication with the gods—a performer who carried out the actions of the mythos that Aristotle claimed was at the heart of tragedy.[16]

The strength and force of the operation of a myth in a given culture depends crucially on the artistic quality of the vehicle. The weight and substance of the Last Stand cannot be carried by a mirage. Literate cultures (book and newspaper cultures) follow the strict and abstract visuality of script. The full power of vision, the breaking through of the gods into our temporal world, can occur only in reenactment (performance). With regard to ancient tragedies, Aristotle held that "the elements by which they imitate are two (i.e., verbal expression and song composition)," and "the manner in which they imitate is one (visual adornment)." In the case of Little Bighorn, the expansion of "manner" generated the number of prints, woodcuts, paintings, and lithographs that tried to interpret the combat at Custer Hill. It would take the special talent of a unique performer to crystallize a ritual based on the Custer story.[17]

Enter Buffalo Bill: government scout and tourist guide; Pony Express rider and buffalo hunter for the Kansas Pacific Railroad; Indian fighter and later friend to the Indian; protagonist of dime novels and plays; master showman and most successful of American theatrical personalities during the last half of the nineteenth century. William F. Cody and George Armstrong Custer were different iterations of the same hero archetype—mirror images replicating themselves into the future—of the western frontier. Both Cody and Custer were called "Long Hair" by the Sioux. Custer adopted Buffalo Bill's "scout" image in dress and manner and won considerable notoriety during the Black Hills expedition of 1874. After Custer's death, Cody cultivated the link with Custer's story throughout his career. In following years, a series of Buffalo Bill novels featured Cody as Custer's scout: some located Cody at the Little Bighorn; one of them—*Buffalo Bill's Gallant Stand* (1903)—had Cody fighting Indians alongside Custer, both with sabers in hand, at Last Stand Hill.[18]

From 1885 to 1905, according to Richard Slotkin, Buffalo Bill's *Wild West* was "the most important commercial vehicle for the fabrication and transmission of the Myth of the Frontier." In 1886, José Martí lived in New York and wrote chronicles of North American customs and politics as a foreign correspondent for several Spanish American newspapers and literary magazines. One of his articles for the Argentinean publication *La Nación* described Buffalo Bill's *Wild West* as an "enterprise" at the gates of New York, which consisted of an "army" of Indians, cowboys, Mexicans, horses, buffaloes and "amazons." In the *Wild West*, "the triumph of the strong and the domination of Nature are reproduced in a great and iniquitous drama." Martí recorded his eye-witness account of Cody's performance: *"Buffalo Bill*, the chief, is the celebrated scout of the campaigns against the tribes, who speaks to Indians in their own languages, who has stripped from dead Indian warriors their feather headdress with the same knife and the same gesture with which now he repeats the feigned battle of his deed every afternoon." In January 1887, Cody presented "Custer's Last Rally" as an addition to a series of historical pageants entitled *The Drama of Civilization*. Elizabeth Custer attended the premiere at Madison Square Garden in New York. The part of Custer was played by Buffalo Bill himself, and the show included some of the Indian warriors "who had exchanged fire with Custer's men that day."[19]

A myth is a mysterious symbol; it can be liberated from the trappings of a specific context. In May 1898, when the First Arizona Volunteers Cavalry (or the Arizona Cowboy Regiment, future "Rough Riders") boarded the train at Prescott for military training in San Antonio, the railroad cars were decorated with slogans. One of them read: "Remember the *Maine!*" That year, Cody staged a new version of "Custer's Last Rally": "With its central image of a slain Custer atop Last Stand Hill, the Little Bighorn turned out to be a battle that provided an ideal icon for the United States during its confident expansionism in the twentieth century." In 1899, the military spectacle of the Battle of San Juan Hill replaced Little Bighorn as a ritual of remembrance. Cody played the part of Theodore Roosevelt, Indians played the part of Spanish soldiers, and the *Wild West* contracted a squad of "Roosevelt's Rough Riders" to appear in the "Grand Review." An official program for the *Wild West*'s 1899 season also lists squads of "Cubans," "Hawaiians," and "Filipinos." Roosevelt substituted for Custer; the imperial victory at San Juan Hill replaced the defeat at Little Bighorn. In imaginative performance, Buffalo Bill completed Act Two of the Last Stand drama initiated by the Seventh Cavalry. In the mythic terms of the *Wild West* one had compelled the other—as if the blood spilled at Custer Hill was washed away, avenged and glorified by victory in Cuba and the Philippines. Ritual was both symbolic and evocative of the cultural forces unleashed by the bellicose dynamic of the Last Stand: "This substitution of an imperial triumph carried off in 'Wild West' style, for a ritual reenactment of the catastrophe that symbolized the end of the old frontier, completes the Wild West's evolution from a memorialization of the past to a celebration of the imperial future." In 1901, the Cuban campaign of Santiago was replaced in the *Wild West* by "The Battle of Tien-Tsin"—a presentation of the rescue of European and foreign legations besieged in Peking by the Boxer Rebellion.

Indian performers "assumed the role of the Boxers"; soldiers and cowboys played the parts of the foreign armies that stormed the city.[20]

For the 1885 season, Sitting Bull agreed to join Buffalo Bill's *Wild West*. By 1886, Sitting Bull had returned to Standing Rock Reservation in the Dakotas and was no longer performing. According to Agent James McLaughlin, Sitting Bull "had not profited by what he has seen, but tells the most outlandish falsehoods to the Indians."[21]

When José Martí exited the *Wild West*'s "magnificent spectacle," walking past the Indian Village on the grounds of Cody's "enormous circus," he encountered not Sitting Bull but his ghostly semblance: "Next to the strongest and most distant of pine trees, his upright figure made giant by the shadow over the horizon, bristling with feathers, the sad medicine man looks over the disappearing white people, bony hands crossed on his chest, shield at his feet, dry eyes, earthen face." Martí's closing descriptive tableau was prescient. In a few short years, a grand ritual dance—forged from a myth found in vision—would spread like prairie fire among Native American tribes, uniting all in spiritual rebellion. Preached by a native shaman, the Ghost Dance would announce the end of the white race, an onrushing thunder of buffalo herds, and the return of the Indian Way.[22]

The Killing of Crazy Horse

In his epic poem "The Song of the Indian Wars," John Neihardt captured the sentiment of a young and arrogant American empire at the sight of one of Satan's archangels. Scarcely a year after Little Bighorn, Crazy Horse surrendered his starving band of hostile followers at Red Cloud Agency (in modern-day western Nebraska) on May 6, 1877. In September of that year, brought to Camp Robinson under false pretenses of a parley, he was mortally wounded in a jailhouse scuffle by the stab of a bayonet knife. At the sight of the dying war chief—according to Neihardt—an onlooker exclaimed: "*Kill that devil quick!*"[23]

The killing of Crazy Horse was merely the instant reflection of a ritual sacrifice that had recurred throughout the centuries in the Americas since the first years of the colonization by Spain. In 1542, Fray Bartolomé de Las Casas documented the first genocide of indigenous nations in his *Brief Account of the Destruction of the Indies*: "The reason why Christians have killed and destroyed so many and such an infinite number of souls only because they have gold as their ultimate end, and becoming bloated with riches in very few days, and climb to very high states out of proportion to their persons, it is good to know, is because of their insatiable greed and ambition, which has been greater than it could have been in the world, because these lands are so blissful and rich, and the people so humble, so patient and so easy to subjugate." "If demons had gold," Las Casas added, "[the Spanish] would attack them to steal it from them."[24]

When the conquistadores entered new territory, their custom was to stage a "cruel and notorious massacre so that those gentle sheep would tremble at them." The lords and leading men of the tribes were burnt at the stake in "living flames." The rest of the Indians were killed with lances, sword-thrusts, and fierce dogs, and their villages were set on fire. Those who survived were enslaved. The Caribbean chieftain Hatuey escaped from Española to Cuba in order to remove himself and his people from the "slavery, torments and perdition" of the Spanish encomiendas. Like a heretic condemned to an auto de fé, Hatuey was burned at the stake by the Spaniards of the Diego Velázquez expedition to Cuba. Moments before his death, a friar offered him Christian baptism, salvation from Hell, and the promise of Heaven after death. Hatuey refused the offer, saying that he preferred to go to Hell than to meet with such cruel people as Christians in Heaven.[25]

Hugh Thomas has suggested that it is impossible to recapture today the "physical attraction . . . gold exercised in men's minds in those days." In 1532 in Peru, the Inca ruler Atahualpa was captured during the Battle of Cajamarca, in which several thousand natives were slaughtered by fewer than two hundred Spaniards. Atahualpa promised Francisco Pizarro four million castellanos—and "paid fifteen"—in exchange for his freedom. In a room at the temple of the sun, he reached above his head and drew a line on the wall with white chalk. He would fill the room up to that height with "gold—jars, pots, plates and other objects" and twice the size of the room with silver. After his subjects delivered the ransom, the Spanish accused Atahualpa of raising an army of warriors against them. He was condemned to die at the stake unless he converted to Christianity, in which case he would be strangled. He accepted baptism, "whether to save his children, save himself from a fiery end, or to guarantee himself access to the Inca afterlife is unknown," and was killed with the garrote for his presumed betrayal. His corpse was set on fire after death.[26]

Both of these stories from Las Casas—so often retold by later chroniclers—have become cornerstones of the mythology of the Spanish conquest of the Americas. Amid the cruelty and barbarism of the deeds, they single out the pressing need of the conquerors to inflict a ruling ideology upon their victims. It was not only imperative that Indians accept the theft of their gold, the destruction of their societies, and the subjugation and extermination of their relatives. It was also important that they consented to the rite of baptism. The conquest was prompted by an ideology that compelled and legitimized the acquisition of gold. The human sacrifice of Indians was a supreme act of ritual expiation. Just as the crucifixion of Christ had opened the doors to salvation in the next world, the burning of caciques and the extermination of Indians proved to be the alchemy that unearthed the gold of the Americas. Thus the Spanish in imperial arrogance brought to the Indies "Christ the Merciful, with his shackles and stakes," his cosmic duality of good and evil, his wars, his demons, and his Hell.[27]

The Great Sioux Reservation

The Custer Wars of the 1870s were provoked by the discovery of gold in the Black Hills; the breaking up of the Great Sioux Reservation in 1876 was fueled by rage at Custer's defeat. In August, Congress proposed to suspend all food and rations guaranteed by treaty to the Sioux who had remained in the agencies during the wars until they consented to a new agreement with the government. Like classic Romans forcing early Christians to offer sacrifice to Roman gods, the Manypenny Commission appointed by President Grant gave the Sioux three choices: die in battle, starve to death, or agree "to cede the Black Hills, to give up their other rights outside the permanent reservation, and to grant rights of way through the remainder of their land." The Sioux would be "dispossessed" of seven million acres of reservation land (including most of their arable land) and restricted in their use of another forty million acres of unceded Indian Territory. Only 10 percent of the Indian population signed the Manypenny Agreement. Congress ratified it in 1877.[28]

Between 1876 and 1882, the great buffalo herds vanished from the northern Plains. Along with the buffalo, traditional Lakota diet, clothing, lodgings, and tribal customs also began to disappear. When Sitting Bull and his 287 followers (from a peak of 5,000 in 1878) returned from Canada in 1881, the Lakota medicine man gave his Winchester rifle to his young son, Crow Foot, to deliver to the army officer in charge at the formal surrender ceremony in Fort Buford (in North Dakota): "I wish it to be remembered that I was the last of my tribe to surrender my rifle. This boy has given it to you, and he now wants to know how he is going to make a living." Sitting Bull was referring to the ration and annuity system that would now govern the lives of his people. He was promised that he could join his friends and relatives at Standing Rock Agency. Instead, he was sent down the Missouri River to Fort Randall (in South Dakota, near the Nebraska border) to remain there for the next nineteen months as a prisoner of war.[29]

In 1887, the General Allotment (Dawes) Act stipulated that after seeking and attaining agreement from individual Indian tribes, each Indian head of household would be assigned 160 acres of land in trust (less for single adults, orphans, and minors). All "surplus prairie" remaining in Indian reservations after land allotment would be purchased by the government and sold to homesteaders at low prices. After twenty-five years, Indians would be granted ownership of their individual plots and would be free to sell or continue to use the land as new American citizens. "The basic idea," writes Vine Deloria Jr., "was to make the Indian conform to the social and economic structure of rural America by vesting him with private property."[30]

By the agreement of 1877, the Sioux owned the most "surplus" land of all Indian tribes. In 1888, the government proposed—even *before* land allotment was consented to or approved by the Lakota—to break up the Sioux reservation into six smaller separate reserves, and in return for some minor reparations, confiscate nine million acres of territory according to the provisions of the Dawes Act. Like Spanish friars offering baptism or death at the stake, the Crook Commission explained the political context of the proposal to tribal members: "It is certain that you will never get any better terms than are offered in this bill. . . . When you can't get what you like best you had better take what is the best for you." Neither Sitting Bull nor Red Cloud and other older chiefs signed the agreement, but three-fourths of the required eligible adults "rushed forward to sign the death warrant of the 'Great' reservation."[31]

In the years before 1890, a cascade of miseries fell upon the Lakota: Congress reduced the Indian Appropriations Act and rations were cut; cattle herds were ruined by disease; crops failed in 1889 and 1890; clothing and annuity goods did not reach the agencies in time for winter; deadly epidemics of measles, influenza, and whooping cough ravaged the reserves; and in spite of protests by members of the Crook Commission, treaty promises were not honored.

Then on January 1, 1889, an eclipse of the sun occurred over Mason Valley, Nevada. A full-blood Paiute by the name of Wovoka was struck down with a high fever and was taken up to Heaven. There Wovoka saw everyone who had died—old friends and relatives were found happy, young, playing games, and busy with usual occupations. God told him to go back and tell Indians to love one another, work, not lie or steal, give up old war practices, and live in peace with the whites. If they followed God's message, they would be reunited with their dead. Wovoka was given a dance to take back to his people. By performing this dance at frequent intervals, they would hurry up the event. When he recovered from illness, Wovoka began to preach the doctrine. He came to be known as "Our Father" to Indians and as the Ghost Dance "messiah" to whites.[32]

The Sioux first heard of the messiah by word of mouth from the Shoshoni and the Arapaho in 1889. Much like the followers of an Islamic jihadist movement at the dawn of the twenty-first century, who would use modern technology and digital media to organize recruits, the Indian graduates of government schools—proficient in reading and writing the English language—spread the news of the messiah among tribes with different languages now scattered throughout different reservations. A council of Sioux chiefs held at Pine Ridge appointed a delegation of tribal members to visit the west and find out about the messiah. In the spring of 1890, the delegates returned with tidings of the new gospel. The Ghost Dance was formally inaugurated by the Sioux, with the recent delegates acting as apostles of the dance ceremonial.[33]

In his definitive study of the Native American Ghost Dance, James Mooney summarizes the doctrine of the Ghost Dance: "The great underlying principle . . . is that the time will come when the whole Indian race, living and dead, will be reunited upon a regenerated earth, to live a life of aboriginal happiness. . . . The white race, being alien and secondary and hardly real, has no part in this scheme of aboriginal regeneration, and will be left behind with the other things of earth that have served their temporary purpose." Mooney finds antecedents to Wovoka's Ghost Dance in the visionary doctrines of the Delaware Prophet of 1762 (an inspiration for Pontiac); in the teachings of Tenskwatawa (the Shawano prophet and brother of Tecumseh); and in the rites of Smohalla of the Columbia River Indians and Nochedelklinne of the Apaches. Wovoka's own father, Tavibo, "did not preach, but was a 'dreamer' with supernatural powers." Parting from an animistic conception of the universe and a profound devotion to the earth, these previous Indian messiahs had preached good behavior, the renunciation of bad habits (drunkenness, quarreling, gambling, etc.), and a decision to discard the practices and commercial products of whites.[34]

By 1890, traditional Indian dances either were being modified or had disappeared before the Western cultural onslaught that had besieged Native American tribes. The Ghost Dance doctrine revived the need for traditional ceremonial practice. Four characteristic elements based on earlier religious manifestations can be perceived in the movement of the 1890s:

1. A circular movement of the dance around a central point or axle (as in Nochedelklinne's dance).
2. A physical and emotional displacement, which results in a hypnotic

trance that transports participants to an imaginary world, followed
by accounts of experiences in the "spirit land" during trance (as in the
Smohalla "Dreamer" religion).
3. An ecstatic vision of the destruction of the present and the return of
aboriginal time (as in the revelations of the Delaware Prophet).
4. A Judeo-Christian parallel (or influence, or foundation), to be found in
New Testament prophecies of the coming of the Messiah and the resurrection of the dead (as in the doctrine of Tenskwatawa, the Shawano
prophet).

A composite account of Ghost Dance mythology among the Sioux would
hold that the messiah—the "father," as he was called in Ghost Dance songs—
was the son of the Great Spirit. The Indian millennium was at hand, and
the "return of the ghosts" was a sign of deliverance. In the spring of 1891,
Ghost Dancers would be reunited with the returning dead. A tornado
would precede an onrush of new land that would cover the old earth. Ghost
Dancers would be lifted up in the air, flying with the sacred feathers, which
they wore while dancing. Whites would perish in the avalanche. The ghosts
would drive before them herds of buffaloes, ponies, and wild game.[35]

Medicine leaders would gather in the center of the dance circle. An opening prayer was offered, asking for communication with dead relatives. The
dancers then held hands and stepped counterclockwise while chanting ceremonial songs. As the dance progressed, some participants became dizzy,
broke from the dancing ring, and fell into a trancelike state. Dancers returning from the ghosts were brought to the center to relate their experiences in the spirit world. Participants often returned with the memory of
sacred objects, songs and melodies, and tales of conversations with relatives. Significantly, "no weapon of any kind was allowed to be carried in the
Ghost dance by any tribe."[36]

Early in October, Sitting Bull invited Kicking Bear—one of the Sioux
emissaries to Wovoka and leading priests of the Ghost Dance—to come to
Standing Rock and lead a dance in Grand River Valley. McLaughlin's Indian police removed Kicking Bear from the reservation the following week.
From then on, given his stature as spiritual leader in the community, Sitting Bull became chief overseer of the religion at Standing Rock (although
he did not direct the dances or participate in the ritual). On October 18,
McLaughlin wrote a letter to the commissioner of Indian Affairs in which
he referred to Sitting Bull as "high priest and leading apostle of this lat-
est Indian absurdity." He condemned the Hunkpapa medicine man in the
strongest terms: "abject coward, disaffected intriguer, polygamist, libertine,
habitual liar, active obstructionist, and chief mischief-maker." McLaugh-

lin urged the adoption of the Spanish strategy in the time of Las Casas: do away with the leaders and the Indians could be controlled easily.[37]

By November, all agents were in agreement that ghost dancing was out of control in the Sioux reservations. The new agent at Pine Ridge, Daniel F. Royer, telegraphed Washington: "Indians are dancing in the snow and are wild and crazy." He requested the presence of at least one thousand soldiers at the agency. Major General Nelson Miles, commander of the Division of the Missouri, mobilized the army. Ominously, on November 26, the Seventh Cavalry—including veterans of the Battle of the Little Bighorn—arrived at Pine Ridge reservation. Approximately three thousand troops were eventually dispatched to the land of the Sioux. Agents were requested by the Indian Bureau in Washington to turn in lists of troublemakers to be arrested by the War Department. The most prominent name on the lists was that of Sitting Bull. The stage was set for sacrifice.[38]

Death of Sitting Bull

The death of Sitting Bull is a two-sided mirror—an event that looks backward and forward in genealogical time. Looking back, it finds correspondences in the deaths of Crazy Horse and in the burning executions of Hatuey and Atahualpa. Looking forward, the death of Sitting Bull would be repeated in both the killing of Ché Guevara in 1967 and in the termination, at the dawn of the twenty-first century, of an Islamic spiritual leader who had inspired—just like Sitting Bull—heinous crimes against the United States.[39]

In the early morning hours of December 15, 1890, an armed contingent of Indian policemen gathered at the cabin of Lieutenant Bull Head, three miles west of Sitting Bull's camp in Grand River Valley. They had received orders from McLaughlin to arrest Sitting Bull, who was planning a visit to Pine Ridge "as God was about to appear." They did not board stealth Black Hawk helicopters, or carry Special Forces ordinance—this was the nineteenth century, and the territory was well known to them. Besides, they had been entrusted with the detention of a relative and admired leader, rather than with the eradication of a foreign terrorist.[40]

At dawn, Bull Head's police command—a biblical forty plus four strong—galloped into Sitting Bull's camp. They entered Sitting Bull's lodgings, roused the old medicine man from his sleep, and told him that he was being arrested. Sitting Bull offered no resistance. His older wife, one of his young daughters, and his son Crow Foot were in his quarters that night. His wife began to wail. Sitting Bull took his time to dress ceremonially. Crow Foot—his young son who had surrendered Sitting Bull's rifle years before—

berated his father: "You always called yourself a brave chief. Now you are allowing yourself to be taken by the *ceska maza* [metal breasts]." Hearing the words of Crow Foot, Sitting Bull refused to go with the soldiers.

He was taken out of his cabin by Lieutenant Bull Head and Sargent Shave Head, with Sargent Red Tomahawk following behind. A crowd of 150 Ghost Dancers and neighbors, awakened by the dogs, horses, and the lament of Sitting Bull's wife, had gathered around the cabin—some of them armed with rifles, knives, and clubs. "You shall not take our chief!" shouted the crowd. Then Catch-the-Bear—a loyal follower of Sitting Bull—shot Bull Head, who in turn shot Sitting Bull. Shots and a furious struggle ensued between the crowd and the police, lasting for about an hour. The wounded Indian police were carried into Sitting Bull's cabin, where Crow Foot was hiding. Three policemen clubbed him, and shot him dead.

When Navy SEALs successfully completed their mission to kill Osama bin Laden, they radioed Admiral William McRaven, commander of the Joint Special Operations Command: "For God and country, I pass Geronimo. Geronimo E.K.I.A [Enemy Killed in Action]." It was said that at the moment of Sitting Bull's death, his spirit possessed the horse given to him by Buffalo Bill—the same one Bull had ridden in the *Wild West*—and the horse danced.[41]

Thus came the demise of the most renowned Native American leader of his generation. Historians agree that Sitting Bull participated in the Ghost Dance reluctantly, from a doubtful perspective, but once engaged he lent the new doctrine the full measure of his towering prestige and spiritual legitimacy. The massacre at Wounded Knee would occur two weeks later, but as Robert Utley concludes, "it was the end of Sitting Bull that symbolized the end of the Indian wars." In the eyes of James McLaughlin, the "good" resulting from the conflict over Sitting Bull's death could "scarcely be overestimated, as it has effectively eradicated all seeds of dissatisfaction sown by the Messiah Craze over the Indians of this Agency." When the ghosts promised by Wovoka did not materialize in the spring of 1891, the outward expressions of the dance faded away from the northern Plains tribes.[42]

The Dead

The Ghost Dance religion was "the inspiration of a dream. Its ritual is the dance, the ecstasy, and the trance. Its priests are hypnotics and cataleptics." With characteristic Christian aversion to the rites of primitives, "the music, screams and shouting of the awful dance" were described by Euro-Americans as a sham propagated by pseudo-priests such as Kicking Bear, a "false prophet and cheat." The religion was a "dangerous doctrine" for a "superstitious and semi-civilized people," who "abandoned their houses" and gave up "industrial pursuits." The secretary of the interior objected to the "bad advice and evil councils" of Sitting Bull and other medicine men who were diverting Indians from the "ways of civilization." Reinforced by sensational newspaper accounts, it was feared that the ritual ecstasy of the dance—and not the deplorable treatment of Indians—would lead to open rebellion.[43]

And yet no serious trouble had resulted from Ghost Dancers until the mobilization of troops into the reservations in November. Open hostilities did not erupt until after the arrest of Sitting Bull; war did not break out between the Sioux and the US Army until after the massacre of women and children at Wounded Knee on December 29, 1890. Ghost Dancers had warned that they would resist if the government tried "to put a stop to the messiah question," but they believed that the destruction of whites would take place (just as the destruction of Rome had been prophesied in the book of Revelation) "entirely by supernatural means."[44]

Why were the whites afraid of an Indian dance? Because of the profound psychological threat conjured by ecstatic physical and spiritual movement in an orderly dominant culture; because of the horror of a Protestant society when confronted by a flowering belief in a ritual aesthetic; and, finally, because of the misreading of Indian cultural metaphors by a literal, hegemonic mentality. The ceremony was meant to provide a ritual means to hasten the desired catastrophe by channeling hostility into an aesthetic dynamic, thus sublimating rightful anxieties about the present. The dance was an appeal to forsake violence through dance and prayer. Who were the truly superstitious: the dancers and medicine men and women who belonged to a culture conversant with the fluid nature of vision, knowledgeable of the signifying quality of metaphor, or the Euro-Americans who, entrapped in their own mythological complex, literalized Wovoka's vision and concluded that an Indian outbreak was imminent?

What proved fatal to the Sioux was the resurrection spell, which had an undeniable parallel in Christian teachings. The vision of an apocalypse that only Indians would survive was entirely believable for whites immersed in Bible prophecies and the book of Revelation. The Ghost Dance turned their prophecy of the end of days against them. Whites were the damned ones, the followers of Antichrist, the force of evil that would perish. Before this trickster-like reversal of roles, they reacted with full military and judicial power in the months that followed.

The Ghost Dance was a spiritual rebellion, a yearning for liberation from civilized order and the strictures of time, from technological and political hegemony through Dionysian ecstasy. Its chaos had clear objectives and a grim purpose: the cyclical renewal of the sacred earth not as a return to the past but as an affirmation of the future. The Dreamer Prophet Smohalla preached that private ownership of land—the parceling of lots for homesteads—was against the laws of nature. The earth was a divinity that belonged to no one, just as sun, wind, moon, and stars existed for the benefit of all: "God . . . commanded that the lands and fisheries should be common to all who lived upon them; that they were never to be marked off or divided." Based on an economic and ecological indictment of whites, Smohalla's gospel proceeded from the viewpoint of what Friedrich Engels called a "primitive Communistic society."[45]

In the mid-1920s, Carl Jung voyaged to North America and visited the Pueblo Indians of New Mexico. He observed: "The Americans present us with a strange picture: a European with the style of a black and the soul of an Indian. He shares the destiny of all usurpers of foreign soil. Certain Australian aborigines claim that it is impossible to take possession of foreign territory, because in the foreign territory live foreign ancestral spirits, and these ancestral spirits will incarnate in new-born children. There is a great psychological truth in this. The foreign country assimilates the conqueror." The impulse to conquer and take possession of foreign land is doomed to failure. We sense the presence of Jung's ancestral spirits within us. These "spirits"—being earth—oppose the profanation of the land, and therefore we identify them as foreign antagonists and project them onto external enemies. Beyond our psychological boundaries, painted with our moral judgment, the earth and its children become the devil and his legion. The Ghost Dance is the ritual of the dead that brings the devil and his rebel angels back to life. For Ghost Dancers—and for Carl Jung—the end result is beyond doubt: the earth will win, the dead will come back. Like the Communist prophecy of the end of the state, like the cyclical catastrophe ordained by the Maya calendar, the Ghost Dance affirms, unimaginably: "The unconscious of the conquerors sinks to the level of the autochthonous inhabitants."[46]

In the demonology of US war culture, the pageant of the Last Stand provokes the sacrifice of a hero and his army, and compels the ritual extermination of the devil and the containment of his followers. In our day, the image of fighting evil terrorism in Indian country represents itself as a benign convention of war talk. It invites no critical reflection on its mythic origins and entailments. It works under the guise of a dead metaphor used by the US military to signify "hostile, unpacified territories in active war zones," as Stephen Silliman notes, and to draw implicitly on the "narrative of U.S. colonialism, triumphalism and Othering that operated in discourses about Native Americans in the past." The heritage metaphor of Indian country was recast in the Vietnam War, where the Vietnamese enemy was the Indian gook, an inferior race of savages that could be massacred along with their water buffalo. The same racist language and its embedded perspective informed the Gulf War of 1991 and the war on terror in Afghanistan and Iraq after 9/11.[47]

The analogy of the nineteenth-century frontier maps onto the twenty-first-century defense of civilization an image of "dark skinned savages with little technological development, no adherence to Christianity, warring tribes and factions . . . and [a] knack for guerrilla fighting." Historical detail and accuracy is not required for the analogy's assumed legitimacy and moral force. Its "deeper symbolic connection" is "rooted in colonialism and aggression" and "feeds on a belief in the continued rightness, historical legitimacy, and expected military successes of the United States." The Battle of the Little Bighorn was "the 9-11 of its day," a temporary setback and dramatic reminder of the nation's imperative struggle for salvation. The events of September 11 issued forth a new manifest destiny. In the words of former Foreign Service officer John Brown, quoting the Puritan preacher and witch-hunter Cotton Mather, "Our Indian wars are not over yet."[48]

4

Dictators

Adolf Hitler is the personification of evil, the devil incarnate. No other political figure is more reviled. His name conjures an image of utter wickedness—demagogue, megalomaniac, racist bigot, and "chief instigator of the most profound collapse of civilization in modern times."[1] He is the face of Nazi atrocity, of genocide and holocaust, the satanic dictator who has become a modern archetype, the perfect example of villainy to which all subsequent enemies are compared. He is the symbol of crazed authoritarianism, vitriolic propaganda, and deadly racism, the demon who hijacked democracy, bewitched the German people, and turned them into a mindless killing machine in the service of territorial expansion for more living space. He cast an evil spell to enslave the world and spawn the sacrilege of a millennial Third Reich.

The legacy of Hitler's defeat is America's redemption. The good war is an American story of vanquishing a fiendish foe, a narrative of victory over evil in which the irony of projection goes mostly unremarked. American imperialism, as Amy Kaplan notes, persists by way of denial, displacement, and projection in opposition to "evil empires": "imperial politics denied at home are visibly projected onto demonic others abroad, as something only they do and we do not." Engaged in the "outward reach of empire," the United States becomes "internally foreign" and "unrecognizable to itself." Accordingly, World War II and its memorials serve as a cultural text in search of national unity, a text that explains what it means to be an American. Being a good citizen, observes Barbara Biesecker, means disregarding rather than seeking to dismantle "the inequitable power relations" of class, race, ethnicity, sexuality, and gender "that continue to structure collective life in the United States."[2]

Writing in the *Southern Review* in 1939 about Hitler's recently translated political autobiography, *Mein Kampf,* which revealed the dictator's racist ideology and plan for transforming Germany into a warfare state, Kenneth Burke warned American readers that "Hitler's Battle" had cooked up a deadly brew. The book should be studied, not to dismiss it as the fascistic raving of a madman but "to forestall the concocting of similar medicine in America." Hitler had found a sinister snake oil, a crude magic, for effecting a fascist integration, "a grand united front of prejudices," in his own country. The basic Nazi trick was to cure the German people of their ailments by a "fictitious devil-function," which Burke cautioned had ominous "equivalents in America," especially in "Hitlerite distortions of religion."[3]

Burke's review of Hitler's battle was a cautionary tale. He warned Americans that they, too, had fascist tendencies—overly strong desires for unity in a troubled world. Those tendencies could be rallied against democracy and channeled into imperialistic drives by American politicians who would "perform a similar swindle," using "emotional trickeries" and selecting a scapegoat to "shift our criticism from the accurate locus of our trouble," which is the "accumulating ills of capitalism." Every movement that would unite a discordant and divergent people by suppressing the wrangle of their diverse parliamentary voices, Burke observed, must have its "devil" as "the symbol of a *common enemy,* the Prince of Evil himself." By the "projective device of the scapegoat," all the "bad" features of a given society can be "allocated to the 'devil.'" The external scapegoat is a projection that purifies a people and saves them from "battling an enemy within," of facing their "internal inadequacies." It provides a "noneconomic interpretation of economic ills."[4]

Exterminating Evil Savagery

Extermination of the perfect external enemy, the vessel of all that ails a society and that is the opposite of its self-perception, was the ultimate logic of world war. Total defeat and unconditional surrender became the bywords of America's fight against evil dictators. Machine gunning and gassing enemy soldiers, concentrating and containing civilian populations, firebombing and atomic bombing whole cities were escalating entailments of the rhetoric of total war, limited only by the state of technology. As the devil remarks, in George Bernard Shaw's *Man and Superman,* "In the arts of life man invents nothing; but in the arts of death he outdoes Nature herself. . . . His heart is in his weapons. . . . Man measures his strength by his destructiveness."[5]

Accordingly, in announcing that the United States had dropped an atomic bomb on its Japanese foe, Harry Truman was "grateful to Providence" that America had beaten the Germans in the race to harness the basic power of the universe. This "marvelous" achievement, "the greatest achievement of organized science in history," enabled the United States "to obliterate more rapidly and completely every productive enterprise the Japanese have above ground in any city." Japan must surrender or "expect a rain of ruin from the air, the like of which has never been seen on this earth." The rhetoric of "unconditional surrender," James Hikins argues, together with the invention of the atomic bomb, almost made the obliteration of Hiroshima and Nagasaki inevitable.[6]

This righteous attitude of utterly destroying an enemy was the product of half a century of chasing the devil in foreign lands and, before that, a history of clearing the adopted homeland of savage inhabitants. A culture of total war, premised on the trope of exterminating evil savagery, assured the now globally embattled nation of its exceptional virtue as a civilizing force. The trope was carried from nineteenth-century American Indian wars into twentieth-century world wars via the Spanish-American War.

The swift defeat of Spain in 1898 was heroically represented by the victorious charge of Teddy Roosevelt's Rough Riders up San Juan Hill (under cover of withering Gatling-gun fire) and Commodore George Dewey's destruction of the Spanish Pacific Squadron in Manila Bay (a lopsided victory of modern warships over an antiquated fleet). A war to liberate Cubans from Spanish concentration camps became, in President William McKinley's vision, a divine mission to uplift, Christianize, and civilize recalcitrant Filipinos. "White love," Vincent Rafael observes, was a promise to foster Filipino savages who, like "errant children," violently resisted the president's civilizing policy of "benevolent assimilation." McKinley's paternalistic vision extended manifest destiny into an overt quest for empire, which invested the United States in a long, brutal war in the Philippines. American democratic tutelage was turned into a mandate for imperialism.[7]

McKinley's vice presidential running mate, Theodore Roosevelt, compared the Filipino resistance to the American Indian wars of the previous century. Allowing Filipinos to govern themselves, he said, "would be like granting self-government to an Apache reservation under some local chief." Emilio Aguinaldo, the leader of Filipinos fighting for independence, was a "half breed" and "self-seeking dictator," in Senator Henry Cabot Lodge's view. As the war dragged on, US forces attempted to break the will of guerilla fighters by means of torture and executions and by looting villages, raping women, and rounding up civilians in concentration camps. According to Susan Brewer, "An estimated 200,000 Filipinos died from disease and starvation." American general Jacob H. Smith actually ordered his men to kill everyone on the island of Samar over the age of ten.[8]

What had been portrayed in the beginning as a valiant act of liberation quickly degenerated into a gruesome act of repression. Americans could ignore their own history of using concentration camps to contain and quell Indian populations by expressing outrage over Spain's concentration camps in Cuba, but they had to blame the victim in order to rationalize US concentration camps in the Philippines. Thus, Filipinos, like Indians before them, were dehumanized and demonized. Senator William Howard Taft spoke of them as "nothing but savages, living a savage life . . . without the slightest knowledge of what independence is," while Senator Lodge blamed American atrocities on the nature of the enemy, saying that Filipinos were "a semicivilized people . . . with the Asiatic indifference to life, with the Asiatic treachery and the Asiatic cruelty."[9]

Some of the same regiments that took part in the Great Sioux War of 1890–1891, culminating in the massacre at Wounded Knee of the "crazed" and "fanatical" Ghost Dancers, were also engaged in the Philippines against an enemy they regarded as Indians. The Filipinos were a "savage foe," which soldiers and officers alike stereotyped as sadistic, violent, shiftless, and fanatical perpetrators of "sneak attacks," an enemy they considered inferior to white men and a hindrance to civilization's advancement.[10] America was engaged in a race war, as Paul Kramer recounts, a "war of racial extermination" in which "colonial violence" was justified by "racial ideologies" that "Anglo-Saxonized" Americans and "tribalized" Filipinos. Thus, "race became a sanction for exterminist war," a war of "hunting," torturing, and killing "black devils," "niggers," and "the little brown man," but mostly Indians.[11]

As an expression of national identity, the racist theme of advancing civilization against barbarism was neither unprecedented nor incidental to an attitude of extermination, an attitude that advancing technologies of war enabled Americans to act on with increasing efficiency. The unifying myth of divine mission transformed war into a moral absolute in which the United States fought, with little or no restraint, against dehumanized enemies who were imagined in various decivilizing terms as vermin, reptiles, beasts of prey, primitives, monsters, hordes, mindless automatons, treacherous criminals, deranged tyrants, and, ultimately, devils.[12] America's foes were always envisioned as lesser beings in some essentially savage way, often with strong racist overtones, which diminished the value of their lives. Then as now, the language with which images of enemies were constructed was freighted with assumptions about race and violence to suggest the threat of infestation and moral corruption and to mandate extermination.[13]

The German Hun

Even the German enemy of World War I, whom Woodrow Wilson was determined to defeat in order to make the world safe for democracy, was reduced to the image of the Hun. Allusions to these medieval nomadic invaders of Europe from the East conjured a specter of Attila the Hun and his horde laying waste to the civilized West. Germany's Kaiser Wilhelm II, who compared his army (sent to quell the Chinese Boxer Rebellion in 1900) to the legendary might of Attila's merciless Huns, inspired the use of the term "Hun" by British, American, and Allied propagandists, who painted a frightful image of German barbarians in their spiked helmets.[14] The term even carried over in some measure to World War II, when Winston Churchill referred to "malignant Huns" who "bully and pillage" like a "swarm of crawling locusts."[15]

The Kaiser, who personified German autocracy and atrocity, became the projected symbol of imperial ambition—a deadly threat to democracy, a monster that aimed to conquer the world. Students in Wisconsin schools were taught that Germany considered itself to be "a race chosen by God to rule the world"—an image of the enemy that was reflected in war posters produced by the Wilson administration's Committee on Public Information.[16] Posters such as "Halt the Hun" and "Destroy This Mad Brute" brought the point home, with the latter showing an oversized ape in a spiked helmet, labeled militarism, baring its fangs while carrying a club, labeled Kultur, in one hand and a ravaged white woman in the other hand. White civilization would be raped by this dark and brutal symbol of militant expansionism and its oppressive attitude of superiority.[17] A war poster produced by the Women's National Committee of the American Defense Society (a society organized by Theodore Roosevelt and his wealthy Republican associates in 1914) featured the image of an Asian-looking German soldier holding a bloody knife in his right hand and a burning torch in his left hand. Its warning was to "remember this Hun who killed, burned and pillaged."[18] The profane Hun was accused of horrendous atrocities against defenseless Belgians, among other victims.

This Hun-at-the-Gate was the ubiquitous "devil-brute" of murder, rape, and pillage.[19] Many Americans feared that an invasion of the United States by the German Huns was likely and imminent. The film industry, according to Erik Van Schaack, persuaded the public that "America was vulnerable to invasion" from "the brutal 'Hun.'" Anxieties ran so high that the women of the Boston Auxiliary of Roosevelt's American Defense League were requested to register their cars so that "they could carry Boston's virgins to safety in the event of an invasion."[20]

"The Kaiser" himself was portrayed as "the beast of Berlin" in a blockbuster Hollywood propaganda movie released in 1918.[21] Standing in as America's opposite, he was the perfect target of President Wilson's crusade for democracy. Indeed, *Pershing's Crusaders* was the Committee on Public

Information's first feature-length propaganda film. Released in April 1918, it was promoted in a colorful lithographic poster that placed General John J. Pershing, commander in chief of the American Expeditionary Force (a man who had made a career of fighting Indians, Mexicans, Spaniards, and Filipinos), in the foreground on horseback leading his foot soldiers to battle. An ethereal image of horse-mounted crusading knights was imposed in the background.[22]

Much as the figure of the German Hun gestured to Attila's Asian hordes, the symbol of the crusading American expedition force invoked an image of the medieval Christian expeditionary war against Muslims in the Middle East. Even America's modern European enemy was racially marked with the sign of the alien, dangerous, backward, despotic, and unchristian East, or what Edward Said since has termed latent Orientalism. The Orient was the colonial counterimage of all things Western—in Sigmund Freud's terms, the unwanted, evil features of the self projected onto the image of the Other, the enemy becoming everything the self does not wish or dare to be; this inverse image of the self, Marja Vuorinen explains, is the scapegoat that leads to the witch-hunt. As Harold Lasswell observed in his retrospective analysis of World War I propaganda, the overriding theme of Satanism carried overtones of race, of thrusting back the infamous German hordes. These repulsive invaders were depraved, wicked, perverse, and monstrous. The war must be won to prove that God was on the side of America and its allies, to reassure the nation that "the Lord is working through us to destroy the Devil."[23] A relatively smooth transition from fighting nonwhite Filipinos to German Huns rhetorically transformed America's overt quest for empire into a crusade for democracy against an evil dictator.

Those who resisted the image of the evil Hun as a justification for world war were silenced and imprisoned. Eugene Debs (whom General Nelson Miles called a "dictator" during the 1894 Pullman Strike, a strike Miles characterized as a war of civilization being fought between the forces of good and evil) was a longtime labor leader and president of the newly formed American Railway Union, a union of unskilled and skilled railroad workers. Debs was sentenced to six months in prison for his role in the Pullman Strike. He became a Socialist during his incarceration and later ran as the Socialist Party's presidential candidate in the elections of 1900, 1904, 1908, 1912, and 1920. Again, under the oppressive Espionage Act of 1917, Debs was imprisoned. This time a sentence of ten years (of which he served three) was assessed against him for delivering an antiwar speech in Canton, Ohio, on June 16, 1918.[24]

In that speech, Debs mocked the claim that the United States was "the arch foe of autocracy," calling it "false pretense" to assert that the United

States was defending the holy grail of democracy against a murderous German emperor bent on world domination. The "ruling class" of the United States and Germany were equally opposed to the interests of the "subject class" of workers and to the development of real democracy. The capitalist master class was the modern-day descendent of "the feudal barons of the Middle Ages," who sent their "miserable serfs" to fight wars for "the profit and glory of the lords and barons who held them in contempt." Wrapped in the "cloak" of patriotism and religion, these capitalist tyrants, oppressors, and exploiters attempted to "deceive and overawe the people." The people had no say in decisions of war other than to be "slaughtered," as a matter of patriotic duty, at the command of the ruling class. "Corporate capital," which appointed federal judges who in turn imprisoned protesters, also controlled the press and the clergy: "When Wall Street says war the press says war and the pulpit promptly follows with its Amen." The so-called institutions of a free republic were under the thumb of American "Junkers," who "want our eyes focused on the Junkers in Berlin so that we will not see those within our own borders." Theodore Roosevelt was a member of the American ruling class who counted the German kaiser—the "Beast of Berlin"— among his friends. Roosevelt even said that if he had the kaiser's army he could conquer the world. Roosevelt was no "champion of democracy" but instead "a Kaiser at heart" in a country that suppressed the exercise of free speech, even as it called upon its citizens to fight in a war against the German hordes "to make democracy safe in the world."[25]

Debs's Socialist plaint collapsed the ideological distinction between capitalism and tyranny, on which the rhetoric of an apocalyptic war rested, to expose the projection of evil onto a foreign devil. The devil of oppression operated with impunity within the United States, according to Debs, disguised as the patriotic defender of democracy. The "Beast of Berlin" was a convenient fiction that masked undemocratic aspirations for global empire by America's greedy ruling class at the expense of its oppressed working class. The irony of suppressing dissent to make the world safe for democracy was symptomatic of a deep deceit by "aristocratic conspirators" promoting war in the name of "a free and self-governing people."[26] Viewed from Debs's perspective, war was a misdirection of, and diversion from, democracy.

Indeed, social critic Randolph Bourne argued in 1918 that war was at once the health of the state and the antithesis of democracy. The state came into its own with "the shock of war," allowing the executive to rule like an absolute monarch over the people. The commitment of the common people to peace and tolerance was sacrificed in a militarized state to the grasping interests of the ruling class. The people were reduced to an obedient and pugnacious herd. War, in Bourne's analysis, was akin to "an upper-class sport."[27] As the chief function of the state, it was rationalized for the public, and its economic motive was sublimated beyond critical reflection, by the call to defend civilization and democracy against an evil enemy.

Satanic Dictator

When the Great War turned out to be the first of two world wars, and the United States once again found itself at odds with Germany and its allies, the theme of civilization versus barbarism, Brewer notes, was portrayed as "an all out fight between democracy and dictatorship." Dictators were the sinister enemies of a nation fighting to defend freedom of worship and speech and freedom from fear and want. America's despotic enemies would enslave the world unless they were eliminated. As Franklin Roosevelt put the matter in his State of the Union address one month after the Japanese attack on Pearl Harbor, "We are fighting to cleanse the world of ancient evils." Only "total victory" over "the dictators" would suffice, he insisted, for these dictators, led by Hitler, harbored "dreams of empire," "gargantuan aspirations," and "schemes of conquest" and "domination" over "the whole world." To "crush the enemy" would be a "victory for freedom" and a "victory for religion" against the "German, pagan religion." The "Nazi hordes" meant to displace the "Holy Bible and the Cross of Mercy" with "Mein Kampf and the swastika and the naked sword."[28]

In the interim between world wars, before Pearl Harbor and while the United States was officially still at peace with Hitler's marauding Germany, Charlie Chaplin had written, directed, produced, and starred in *The Great Dictator*. The film, released in October 1940, was a comedic drama that satirized Hitler and his fascist ally, Mussolini. It was Chaplin's first talking movie and also his most overtly political film. Its explicit politics were controversial with film critics, but the film was popular with the American public and proved to be a large commercial success. While it is mostly remembered as a condemnation of Hitler's fascist militarism and anti-Semitism, *The Great Dictator*'s critique of war was similar in certain ways to the arguments against economic greed, and on behalf of real democracy, that had been advanced previously by Debs and Bourne. Chaplin's 1936 film, *Modern Times*, had already implicitly criticized capitalism. Four years later, *The Great Dictator*, more than a mere projection of evil onto a foreign enemy, suggested a tension within the American character that might be resolved by a turn to democracy.

Born into poverty and raised in London, Chaplin found his way to the United States as a young performer in vaudeville, which led to a lucrative career in cinema. As a financially independent filmmaker, he produced *The*

Great Dictator before the extremes of Nazi atrocities were fully known but after the military advance of fascism was well under way in Europe. Reflecting on the film two decades later, Chaplin doubted he could have joked about Hitler if he had been aware of the extermination camps.[29] Yet, his 1947 film, *Monsieur Verdoux*, set in World War I France, compared the act of war to murder. A concern with war itself was at play in Chaplin's political films.

In *The Great Dictator*, war was the product of greed, which poisoned men's souls.[30] Hitler's caricature, Adenoid Hynkel, ruled Tomania (a pun on ptomaine), and his fascist ally, Benzino Napaloni, ruled Bacteria. Greed was a poison that made men "torture and imprison innocent people." War turned men into regimented brutes, "unnatural men—machine men with machine minds and machine hearts"—whom dictators enslaved and used as cannon fodder. Greed made people hate and despise one another. Democracy was the antidote. The "goodness in man" could be recovered and "universal brotherhood" achieved only when the power that dictators had taken from the people was returned to the people. Only "in the name of democracy" could humankind unite "to do away with greed, with hate and intolerance" in full knowledge that, as written in the Gospel of Luke, "the Kingdom of God is within man." There was room for everybody in a democratic world where no one would be conquered and everyone might be helped, regardless of race or religion—"Jew, Gentile, black men, white." Chaplin was strongly opposed to racism.

The tension that the film struggled to transcend was manifested not only in the similarity between Chaplin's toothbrush mustache and Hitler's dictator mustache but also the dual roles Chaplin played as victim and victimizer. By repeatedly switching between the roles of Jewish barber and heartless dictator, Chaplin comedically enacted a measure of critical reflexivity in which it was possible to see a certain, even odd, similarity in two otherwise diametrically opposed characters. "He looks strange," Garbitsch-the-Minister-of-Propaganda remarks to Herring-the-Minister-of-War, as they saluted the barber-dressed-like-Hynkle passing in front of them. Indeed, this strange barber-mistaken-for-Hynkle was about to announce to the world, after the invasion of Osterlich (Austria), that he did not want to be emperor, nor did he want the world to descend into the darkness of the killing fields. He called on soldiers not to give themselves to brutes that despise and enslave them, regiment their lives, tell them "what to do, what to think, and what to feel." He wished to promote kindness and respect for all humanity. He wanted to rid the world of violence, to bring about the Kingdom of God on earth where a socially just and peaceful life would supplant greed and the misery of war. Just as Hannah, the young maiden to whom the barber was romantically attached, professed her faith in God, the barber, now posing as a transformed dictator, professed his dream for mankind "in the name of democracy." "Look up," he called out to Hannah, as she lay prostrate in an Osterlich vineyard that had been overrun by Hynkle's invading storm troopers. "The clouds are lifting, the sun is breaking through. We are coming out of the darkness into the light. We are coming into a new world, a kindlier world, where men will rise above their hate, their greed, and brutality. Look up, Hannah. The soul of man has been given wings."

The film and its concluding speech, Adrian Daub argues, was a "desperate attempt at making sense" out of insanity, to "drive out the devil." The central theme was Hynkle-the-dictator symbolizing the "failure of vision." The film would "recuperate communication" and thereby "release the masses from Hynkel's spell" in order to "exorcise the demon of Fascism." As Robert Cole notes, *The Great Dictator* was propaganda "warning against propaganda." Chaplain perceived Hitler as a hideous and grotesque dictator stirring up madness, but he also saw in Hitler some of his own qualities. The "arbitrariness of power" and similarity of all human beings are indicated, Jodi Sherman observes, by Chaplin's "liminal positionality" as "indistinguishable dictator and Jewish ghetto dweller."[31] Nor was capitalism Chaplin's good alternative to Hitler's bad fascism. He may have later agreed with critics who thought Hitler was too sinister for comedy, but comedy expressed Chaplin's ultimate concern for preserving the freedom and dignity of people, not for promoting a grasping capitalism by debunking a dehumanizing fascism.

After the war, Chaplin was accused of Communist sympathies, becoming the subject of investigation by J. Edgar Hoover's Federal Bureau of Investigation (FBI) and an object of interest by the House Un-American Activities Committee (HUAC). He took refuge in Switzerland after being informed he could no longer live or work in the United States. He had been deported and blacklisted, in his words, not because he was a Communist but because he refused to conform to anti-Communism, "to fall in line by hating them."[32] The frenzy of McCarthyism smothered any progressive or egalitarian suggestion that a victorious America should reflect upon its own undemocratic greed and warmongering tendencies.

Disney's Donald Duck, not Chaplin's Jewish barber, was the conventional voice of American virtue in World War II, complete with racist overtones. The six-minute animated propaganda film, *Spirit of '43*, a collaboration between Walt Disney Productions and the US Office of Wartime Information, was released on January 7, 1943, in Technicolor.[33] Donald Duck, who represented the "average worker" on payday, was torn between his "two separate personalities": an angel, "the thrifty saver," wearing a Scottish kilt and cap, and a "spendthrift" devil, "dressed in the zoot suit fashionable among urban African Americans and Mexican Americans."[34]

The zoot suit—consisting of high-waisted, pegged pants with narrow cuffs and a thigh-length coat with wide lapels and padded shoulders— became an emotionally charged symbol of wastefulness and disloyalty to the war effort. Wearing the zoot suit amounted to a bold public swagger by young people of color, often considered gangsters by the white majority. It suggested a rebellious attitude and raised questions of their allegiance. After the War Production Board established guidelines in 1942 to reduce the national consumption of wool, only bootleg tailors manufactured zoot suits to meet the high demand by Latino and black urban youths. Racial tensions continued to increase until the Zoot-Suit Riots, a battle between white servicemen and Mexican Americans, broke out in Los Angeles in 1943 and soon spread to cities across the country.

The zoot-suited devil figure in the *Spirit of '43*, which transformed into Hitler, urged Donald to spend his money on "good dates" at the "Idle Hour Club," its saloon doors shaped in the image of a swastika. Donald's choice was whether to "spend for the Axis or save for taxes." "It's your dough," the devil advised. "Aye, Laddie, it's your dough, but it's your war, too," the Scottish angel responded. Donald's good conscience urged him to save his money so that he could pay his income taxes "to defeat the Axis" and, as the film's narrator further explains, "to bring to earth the evil destroyer of free- dom and peace"—which was illustrated as a satanic figure, wearing a Nazi helmet, with horned ears and gunfire bursting from of its bat-like wings and mouth. Donald's income taxes were necessary to "keep democracy on the march" against this ominous enemy.

East versus West

Disney also had a hand in animating parts of the *Why We Fight* films, a se- ries of seven propaganda documentaries, released between 1942 and 1945. The films ranged from forty to seventy-six minutes in length.[35] They were produced by Frank Capra, whom General George C. Marshall assigned the task of explaining the goals of the war to soldiers and, by order of President Franklin Roosevelt, to the general public. They were a "paean to democracy" and an "indictment of oppression" that proved to be a powerful public rela- tions weapon viewed by an estimated fifty-four million Americans.[36] Capra, like Chaplin, was moved to respond to Leni Riefenstahl's stunning Ger- man propaganda film, *Triumph of the Will*, which had been commissioned by Hitler and released in 1935 to celebrate the rise of the Nazis and the re- turn of Germany to the status of a world power. While Chaplin laughed at the film, Capra counterattacked, describing *Triumph of the Will* as "terrifying." In Capra's view, "Satan couldn't have devised a more blood-chilling super-spectacle."[37]

The clash, as portrayed in *Prelude to War* (the first *Why We Fight* film), was a "life and death struggle" between opposite worlds, one light and the other dark, one free and the other slave, one democratic and the other tyrannical, one Christian and the other satanic.[38] The dark, slave, pagan world of the Axis powers used brute force to destroy freedom and to turn humans into a herd. They reversed the march of history. They destroyed churches, replaced the cross with a swastika, sang of Hitler in Germany as Lord and Savior, and fanatically worshipped the emperor of Japan as God. Hitler mustered the German "inborn natural love of regimentation." He intended to conquer the United States and enslave the free world with the aid of his militarist "buck-toothed pals" in Japan and the fascist "demagogue" of Italy. In the meantime, the democratic world had disarmed after World War I in a quest for peace. While American children innocently romped in playgrounds, the children of Germany, Japan, and Italy earnestly trained for war, their lands run by "gangsters" who embodied "freedom's oldest enemy: the passion of the few to rule the many." The slave world goose-stepped to the throb of war drums. The free world eventually responded to the call of "Onward Christian Soldiers."

Hitler's Germany sent Protestants, Catholics, and Jews alike to concentration camps. In *The Nazis Strike*, the "maniacal will" and "insane passion" of the pagan führer conjured images of Genghis Khan, the Mongol conqueror of the Middle Ages. "The plague of slavery descended on the world" when "barbarian hordes" swept across Asia and eastern Europe, "burning, looting, pillaging," on their way to conquer "most of the world of the 13th century." Adolf Hitler was determined to best Genghis Khan by subduing "all of the world of the 20th." Hitler and his "fanatic followers" had inherited from Kaiser Wilhelm II, himself a modern Attila the Hun, "Germany's maniacal urge to impose its will on others," a barbaric desire for world conquest mixed with a righteous belief in a civilizing mission. "God has made us for civilizing the world," proclaimed the kaiser. "Woe and death to all who resist my will." With "Nazi pageantry," Hitler "hypnotized" the German nation into believing they were a "master race" destined to rule the world by terrorizing it into submission. The image of the enemy horde was reinforced by scenes of countless German soldiers marching through streets and amassed in public squares. The enemy masses were visually contrasted, as Kathleen German observes, with American individualism.[39]

Divide and Conquer drove home the point that Hitler's Germany was savage and satanic. Vividly chronicling the bloody blitzkrieg of Norway,

Holland, Belgium, and France to reveal "the coming hurricane of terror," the film underscored the price to be paid for believing the "voice of the dictator," whose campaign of lies, deceit, and propaganda undermined the morale of the European democracies, softening them up prior to launching a surprise invasion. "When a people loses its faith in its own ideas," narrator Walter Huston intoned, "it is ripe for the insidious words of the devil." The obliteration of Rotterdam, after its unconditional surrender, was "one of the most ruthless exhibitions of savagery the world has ever seen." Repeated assurances of nonaggression aside, Hitler ultimately proved to be a "gangster" bent on enslaving the world. There was no alternative but to exterminate this fascist plague on humanity. "Victory of the democracies," in the words of American chief of staff, General Marshall, "can only be complete with the utter defeat of the war machines of Germany and Japan."

In *The Battle of Britain*, the Nazi war machine prepared to cross the English Channel but first had to subdue the Royal Air Force, which it failed to accomplish. Hitler intended to "crush the spirit of democratic life itself" by bombing England into submission. The "savage destruction of London," including a devastating firebombing raid on Christmas in 1940, left the free British people undaunted. This was the "people's war" against a dictator bent on world conquest. "The German mind has never understood why free people fight on against overwhelming odds." The Germans lost the Battle of Britain because "a regimented people met an equally determined free people," a lesson repeated in *The Battle of Russia*.

The Russian defenders were European to the eye, with rare and brief exception, and never Communists. They were a diverse people, pioneers who had tamed a wilderness and built a modern civilization in a rich land—skilled and hard-working professionals of every kind, homemakers, artists, craftsmen, and more—individuals, very much "like us." These Russians, "like ourselves," celebrated Christmas, "just as in our home towns," even when their cities were besieged and bombarded. They were "men of God," with "faith in the inevitable power of light over darkness, of justice over evil and brutal force, of the cross of Christ over the Fascist swastika." The invaders were "the German hordes," raping, burning, and murdering countless civilians. The Russian people, who had been defending their land for over seven hundred years against "would-be conquerors," proved once again that "there are no invincible armies against the determined will of free and united people," even in "total war."

Similarly, *The Battle of China* westernized the Chinese, who were now America's "fighting ally" moving "westward to freedom" to escape Japanese "slavery." The Chinese were a historic people of great inventors who developed the art of printing from moveable type, devised the mariner's compass to navigate the seas, and advanced the science of astronomy "to make possible the accurate measurement and recording of time." Taking from "our Western civilization" the inspiration for self-rule, they overthrew their ancient imperial government in 1911 to enter "a new era as a modern republic." Sun Yat-sen, the father of this revolution, was the George Washington of China. Following his vision, and echoing Abraham Lincoln's belief in "democracy," in government "of the people, by the people," the Chinese built schools and sent their young men and women to universities in the United States and Europe so that they could bring back to their country "other Western ideas," including new techniques of industry, architecture, science, and medicine. In the image of Christ upon the cross, their new republic guaranteed freedom of religion and speech. Chiang Kai-shek inherited the leadership of Sun Yat-sen's "disciples," who used "the best of Western civilization" to carry on the monumental modernization of China.

Unlike the Chinese, the Japanese aggressors appropriated Western technology to build war machines and to strike an "infamous blow against the civilized world." They were "modern barbarians invading" an ancient Chinese civilization of "art, and learning, and peace." Their "mad dream" was to conquer China as a first step toward conquering the United States and enslaving the world. The Chinese were a peaceful people with democratic aspirations, a people who never in four thousand years had "waged a war of conquest." No Chinese Communists were mentioned—no Mao Tse-tung—only a great unification of the Chinese people, under the leadership of Chiang Kai-shek, defending themselves after the Rape of Nanking. In "one of the bloodiest massacres in recorded history," the "blood crazed Japs" had raped, tortured, killed, and butchered the "helpless populace" of Nanking. Japan's "military dictatorship," with its "God-Emperor and fanatic warlords," had prosecuted a new kind of war against their Chinese victims, a war of "deliberate terrorization, of deliberate mass murder." A heroic Chinese people were fighting for "freedom" in an epic struggle of "good against evil."

That was "the story of China—a story of murder, of pillage and sacrifice." A "miracle" happened in China. The Japanese were stopped just short of the gates. "The yellow flood that seemed irresistible was stayed," just as "Hitler's barbarians" were "thrown back" in Russia. But "the little yellow men" of Japan, who fanatically worshiped their "God-Emperor," still threatened America's peace. They were a "slimy" enemy that held much land and many people captive in their "tentacles," an enemy the United States must remain determined to "finish" as "completely as any effort of ours can determine." This was a righteous war against a yellow peril. Victory would re-deem a nation that had been wronged. "History will declare us guiltless of any animus against any people."

Accordingly, *War Comes to America* recounted the story of an exceptional nation, as Peter Rollins notes, a nation that would live up to its "historic mission."[40] The story opened with a scene of children pledging allegiance to the flag in a time of world war. A panorama of the nation's fields, forests, and cities accompanied images of citizens of all kinds—mechanics, doctors, college students, merchants, lawyers, rich men and poor—all fighting for their country and its integrating idea of liberty, freedom, democracy. This story of liberty began with Jamestown in 1607 and Plymouth Rock in 1620, a people searching for freedom and determined not to bend to tyranny. They built homes and churches in the green wilderness of this "virgin continent." Their colonies grew into a nation set on the idea of self-rule. The words of James Otis, Thomas Jefferson, Thomas Paine, and Patrick Henry inspired their Declaration of Independence and their "sacred charter," the Consti-tution. Americans were pioneers who carried freedom with them as they settled the continent. Humanity made "a clean fresh start from scratch" in this new land.

The new beginning, in "a land of hope and opportunity that had arisen out of a skeptical world," attracted immigrants from every corner of the earth, working side by side. In America, "a light was shining" for freedom as a united people farmed together and built industry and transportation systems, skyscrapers, and great cities. They were a working people and an inventive and industrious people. Their long list of inventions ranged from the lightning rod and incandescent bulb to the telegraph, the "blessed an-esthesia of ether," and the X-ray tube, submarine, motor-driven airplane, sewing machine, and television. They lived by the "democratic ideal of the greatest good for the greatest number" and "created for the average man the highest standard of living in the world," with the most automobiles, the highest standards of sanitation, purity of food, and the best of health care.

Americans lived the good life, eating well, taking two-week annual va-cations, enjoying music and sports, and exercising freedom of religion. Ev-ery religious denomination on earth could be found in the United States. Americans elected their neighbors to political office. They believed in "in-dividual enterprise and opportunity for men and women alike." When they made mistakes, like Prohibition, they corrected them, never losing their faith in the future. "That's the kind of people we are"—outwardly easygoing but underneath "passionately dedicated to the ideal our forefathers passed down to us, the liberty and dignity of man." They were spiritually a pio-neering people committed to progress and guided by "a great yearning for peace and goodwill toward men." These were the kind of people the Japanese attacked without warning on Sunday, December 7, 1941, during worship services, "a date which will live in infamy."[41]

Last Stand

Pearl Harbor, in the mythic legacy of Little Bighorn, was another last stand, which both proved the nation's innocence and demonstrated the savagery of its evil enemy. It made the presence of the devil palpable, undeniable, and inexorable. The 1942 newsreel *Bombing of Pearl Harbor,* produced for the home front, portrayed the "cowardly strategy" of the "sneak" attack that was "grim and positive evidence of Jap treachery." The film showed a panorama of dead warships and military aircraft in the aftermath of the battle, black smoke billowing from the mortally wounded battleship USS *Arizona,* which had been destroyed by a single "lucky hit" by a Jap bomb tumbling through one of the ship's funnels to explode its engine room and set tons of fuel oil on fire. "The Arizona's courageous crew stuck to its guns until the very end," leaving behind a saga of "heroism that will live forever in the glorious annals and traditions of the American Navy." The sunken battleship's control tower still stood above the water, "a defiant beacon that in days to come will cast its shadow on Nippon's very shores." Americans would "never forget" the "cunning deceit of the Japs." Already, an American light cruiser was seen heading bravely out to sea to "avenge Pearl Harbor."[42]

The last stand at Pearl Harbor, as a frontier myth, was a determined and redemptive confrontation with death. The defenders of civilization sacrificed themselves in a valiant struggle against savagery and tyranny. A blameless nation was victimized by the treachery of an unholy enemy. Only by the wiles of deceit could barbarism prevail on that infamous day over civilization's heroic defenders. The death of these brave men would be avenged, the power of the nation restored, and its divine mission reaffirmed. As Franklin Roosevelt proclaimed, in his declaration-of-war speech the day after the attack, "The facts of yesterday and today speak for themselves." Americans understood "the implications to the very life and safety" of their nation from this "unprovoked and dastardly attack by Japan." The American people "in their righteous might" would "win through to absolute victory" and make certain that "this form of treachery shall never again endanger us."[43]

An eighth film, *Know Your Enemy—Japan,* was produced for Capra's *Why We Fight* series, in anticipation of a costly invasion of Japan, but it was not finished in time for distribution. Just as it was completed, the war ended abruptly, without an invasion of the Japanese island nation, when the

United States dropped an atomic bomb on Hiroshima and another on Nagasaki.[44] The logic of total war, unconditional surrender, and extermination came to a head in the mushroom cloud hovering over each of the obliterated cities.

Capra's film, designed to prepare Americans for the sacrifice of the lives of perhaps a half a million of their own soldiers and sailors, reduced the image of the enemy to a race of "fanatics," instilling hatred and fear of the Japanese, Claudia Springer notes, by focusing on their "evil fanaticism" and "desire to dominate the world."[45] The "Japs" were "an obedient mass with a single mind." They were like "photographic prints on the same negative." They followed blindly their sun god, the God-Emperor Hirohito, "willing prisoners in a system of regimentation" ruled by a "supreme dictatorship." Their children were "hammered into fanatic samurai," who understood that the greatest honor was to die in battle. The national religion, Shinto—a "nice, quaint religion for a nice, quaint people"—had been transformed into a "fanatic doctrine of war and world conquest." Christianity—the religion of peace, social justice, and tolerance—was oppressed in Japan. The sword was their "steel Bible," ambush and treachery their "national code." They were a barbaric foe, a "bloodthirsty people," an impure race, a "plasma cocktail" of Mongolians and other "quarrelsome tribes." True to Said's conception of Orientalism, the Japanese were rendered a lesser people—exotic, alien, backward, and unchristian—an enemy small in stature, but dangerous and undesirable. This was an image of race war, as John Dower observes, "a potpourri of most of the English-speaking world's dominant clichés about the Japanese enemy."[46]

Projection

What was the meaning of the composite picture of evil—the amalgamated figure of the dictator-devil—projected by Capra's and other propaganda films? "By killing the constructed enemy," Steuter and Wills observe, "we are being intrinsically virtuous."[47] What dark apprehensions did these films evacuate from the nation's collective self-image in order to purify and preserve the pretense of exceptional virtue? Could the United States be so worthy if its enemy were not so utterly evil? What terrible misgiving was projected and eradicated in order to cleanse and sustain the image of a chosen people on a sacred mission? What dark visage would have been reflected in the trickster's mirror of projected evil?

The dirt extracted from America's pristine self-image by projecting it outward was a dark, not white, dictator-devil. The enemy was America's imagined opposite: falsely proclaiming its racial purity, it was instead a barbaric, irrational, and undemocratic horde, an impure race ruled by tyrants bent on world domination, an enemy that slaughtered its victims indiscriminately. Thus, when our side bombed cities, the cinematic perspective was from high above the ground looking down; when they bombed cities, the perspective was from the ground witnessing the carnage.

Even "our" concentration camps were models of democracy, unlike theirs. Rather than calling them "concentration camps," as did Franklin Roosevelt and other government officials in moments of candor, they were euphemistically labeled "relocation" and "internment" camps. People of Japanese descent living in the United States, most of whom were US citizens, were forced from their homes on the Pacific coast and moved to camps in the nation's interior, where they could be safely contained and systematically transformed into real, more reliable Americans.[48] As Milton Eisenhower, director of the War Relocation Authority (WRA), explained in a 1943 propaganda film, *Japanese Relocation*, the Pacific coast had become a "potential combat zone" after the attack on Pearl Harbor. "No one knew what might happen" among the "more than 100,000 persons of Japanese ancestry" living there "if Japanese forces should try to invade our shores." America was determined to carry off this necessary "mass migration" humanely, however, "as a democracy should."[49]

The reality of the camps was one of dislocation and austere living conditions, consistent with a tradition of white supremacy.[50] The Gila River War Relocation Center, for example, was built by the War Relocation Authority in the Arizona desert in the middle of the Gila River Indian Reservation, despite the protests of tribal leaders, about fifty miles southeast of Phoenix. It was an internment camp within a reservation: a double layer of containment. Internees were subjected to open hostility and racial slurs by whites in Arizona: "whites reacted to them as they had to their Apache predecessors."[51]

Summer temperatures at Gila River averaged 104 degrees, reaching as high as 125 degrees. Two camps, built three and a half miles apart in less than two months, operated from July 1942 until November 1945, one named "Central" and the other "Butte." Together they housed nearly fourteen thousand internees from California and other parts of the country in facilities designed for ten thousand people. Some internees died from the harsh desert environment in route to, or soon after arriving at, the camps. Most lived in barracks, arranged in blocks of twelve, each barrack housing four families in separate small apartments. Thousands were housed in mess halls and recreation centers, using blankets for walls. Chronic water shortages, which reduced the use of evaporative coolers, as well as rattlesnakes and scorpions made life even more unpleasant.

Gila River, which was considered one of the least oppressive internment camps, included schools, a baseball field designed and built by internees to seat six thousand spectators, a theater for the performance of
plays and screening of films, a medical facility, post office, canteen, la-
trine and shower buildings, laundry and ironing rooms, shoe repair, barber
and beauty shops, and churches, mostly built by internees who also organized Boy Scout, American Legion, and other civic groups. Michi Nishi-
ura Weglyn, who was herself interned at Gila River, later published the first
book on these "infamous" facilities, which she called "America's concentration camps."[52]

In Eisenhower's narrative, however, these were "new pioneer communities" for people of Japanese ancestry, people who were "eastward pioneers," as Allan Austin ironically labels the victims of mass incarceration.[53] The WRA's new communities provided, Eisenhower intoned, for
a "nearly normal life." They were a place where internees could be transformed. With fences and military guards to keep inhabitants safely contained, the relocated Japanese relived a condensed version of the American saga. They inhabited "a new area, in a land that was raw, untamed, but
full of opportunity." They attended church services—Protestant, Catho-
lic, and Buddhist—issued their own newspapers (which, Eisenhower failed
to mention, were censored by government authorities), organized schools,
chose civic leaders, and received good medical care.[54] They went to "Ameri-
canization classes" and made "a rough beginning at self-government" while
irrigating, reclaiming, and farming the desert land. These camps set "a standard for the rest of the world in the treatment of people who may have loyalty to an enemy nation." They allowed America to protect itself "without
violating the principles of Christian decency."

Just as the perceived internal threat from people of Japanese ancestry living in the United States was eliminated by containing and Americanizing
them, the external threat from foreign Japanese "fanatics" was eradicated
by nuclear extermination, occupation, and ultimately reconstruction of their
society in America's self-image of a democratic and peaceful people. The
official goal of the occupation of Japan was to westernize and democratize
Japan, to remake it into a "peaceful and responsible" country that would
"support the objectives of the United States." The new Japan was to "become
familiar with the history, institutions, culture, and the accomplishments of
the United States and the other democracies." It would guarantee religious
freedom, secure civil liberties, and develop "organizations in labor, industry, and agriculture, organized on a democratic basis."[55] Militaristic Shinto
no longer would be the religion of the state. Oriental Japan would be paci-

fied and politically transformed, its dictator-devil exorcised and America's democratic virtue redeemed.

Externalizing the dictator-devil figure served the purpose of reassuring the nation of its special goodness as it transitioned from a post–World War I attitude of disarmament and isolationism into a mindset of militarization and internationalism. America emerged from World War II perceiving itself as an international peacekeeper determined to spread its ideals across the globe. It entered the brave new era of a triumphal "American Century," Henry Luce's missionary vision of US political, cultural, and economic domination.[56] America would be the Good Samaritan to the world, a world it was determined to control in the name of freedom and democracy. It had contained, exterminated, and transformed the barbarism of tyranny. The new civilized order would be a democratic and capitalist world in which, as Brewer observes, "the United States would be in charge."[57] Dictators symbolized the primitive motive of conquering and enslaving their victims. The ritual of sacrificing these satanic figures on the altar of God's chosen people cleansed American hegemony of any malfeasance or responsibility for past and future wars. Thus, the *New York Times* proclaimed the death of a "defiant dictator," one of recent history's "most brutal tyrants," when Saddam Hussein was hanged after being plucked out of a spider hole in 2003 and convicted three years later of crimes against humanity.[58]

The United States Holocaust Memorial Museum in Washington, DC, initiated by President Jimmy Carter in 1978 and dedicated in 1993, stands as a reminder of the Nazi extermination of Jews, a testimony to democracy and to the Allied forces who liberated survivors of the German concentration camps. It looks outward and eastward for the cause of genocide. Its "journey through the world of the Holocaust" was designed to remove visitors "from American ground," reports Edward Linenthal.[59] Its story focuses on "the evil of the Nazi perpetrators," observes Marouf Hasian Jr., an evil that could only happen because others—not Americans—had failed to venerate American principles and values.[60] Indeed, "the Holocaust is constructed as the most un-American of crimes and the very antithesis of American values," emphasizes Tim Cole. Americans are positioned as "bystanders, liberators, and ultimately a refuge" from this horror, this "nightmare of evil" physically juxtaposed in the nation's capital against the sacred story of America's founding and its monuments to democracy.[61] As Fath Davis Ruffins notes, the museum is a narrative of "American triumph over evil," an evil that "happened outside the U.S."; as such, it is a "living memorial to the cause of freedom," which reinscribes the mythic "power of the United States to resist, if not fully conquer, evil."[62]

Meanwhile, just a few blocks down Independence Avenue, sits the National Museum of the American Indian, established by Congress in 1989 and opened in 2004 as part of the Smithsonian Institution. It tells no story of genocide or holocaust in the West, at least not from the perspective of a colonized people. It is designed instead "to celebrate living Native cultures," those who survived. One of its permanent exhibits, "Our Peoples," highlights the "survivance strategies" of Native peoples who encountered European colonizing forces. Rather than telling a story of "victimization," "holocaust," or "genocide," it proclaims, *We Are Still Here.*[63] While it resists the myth of the vanishing Indian and challenges the stereotype of a generic Indian, there is no tragic tale told to teach America a lesson about the consequences of projecting evil. The "realities of genocide" are transcended in this "Native space" by a reassuring narrative of Indians transformed, Indians incorporating "the beliefs and tools of colonialism into their very means of survival."[64] Although a nuanced account, which hopes to prompt a degree of reflection, this story of Native American survival does not shift the gaze of the colonizer inward or disrupt the ongoing imperial hunt for external devils.

5

Reds

I am merely an honest American like yourself—and of the best descent—for, to tell the truth, Mr. Webster, though I don't like to boast of it, my name is older in this country than yours.

Stephen Vincent Benet, *The Devil and Daniel Webster*

The ritual drama highlighted by the American Indian wars of the nineteenth century—Last Stand versus Ghost Dance; protagonist hero versus native devil antagonist—continued unabated through the twentieth. As justification for every land-grab, quest for gold, or effort to conserve military power, the bloody flag of the Last Stand was waved and its call to war sanctified as a Christian, patriotic necessity. The country followed successive Last Stand scenarios: remember the Alamo; the first scalp for Custer; remember the *Maine*; remember Pearl Harbor. There was always an outrage to be avenged and another war to be fought. In opposition stood a recurring myth of eternal return: the Ghost Dance, through its magical alchemy, would create a revolution led by an avatar—a devil hero that would free the defeated and dispossessed from oppression, make the earth holy, and bring the dead back to life.[1]

Anarchy's Red Hand

Eugene O'Neill, during his early career, considered himself an "active socialist" and later a "philosophical anarchist." In *The Hairy Ape* (1922), Yank the stoker wants to join the Industrial Workers of the World. He asks the Wobblies to give him a job blowing up steel: "Dynamite! Blow it offen de oith—steel—all de cages—all de factories, steamers, buildings, jails—de Steel Trust and all dat makes it go." Steel was the symbol of Yank's world; it formed the structures that perpetuated the unequal conditions of his society. Ghost Dancers prayed for a tornado and an avalanche to rub out the white hegemony; anarchist revolutionaries counted on dynamite as a "sublime substance" to raze the state.[1]

Months before the final surrender of Geronimo and years before the death of Sitting Bull, the catastrophe prophesied by the Ghost Dance seemed to materialize with a bang in Chicago on May 4, 1886. On that day at a worker's rally in Haymarket Square, in the wake of a general strike in support of the eight-hour workday, a dynamite bomb thrown by an unknown assailant killed several policemen. In the ensuing firefight and chaos, dozens of other policemen, workers, and bystanders were also injured. After the bomb, anarchist sympathizers "brought out at the window of their press, a red flag." The next day, headlines in the *Chicago Tribune* called the act "A Hellish Deed." The *New York Times* carried the news of "Rioting and Bloodshed in the Streets of Chicago" caused by "Anarchy's Red Hand." Eight anarchist leaders were tried for conspiracy in the bombing; seven were condemned to death. The day before the execution, two (Fielden and Schwab) had their sentences commuted to life in prison. One (Lingg) committed suicide in jail. Four (Engel, Fischer, Parsons, and Spies) were hanged on November 11, 1887.[2]

José Martí wrote a series of articles from New York in which he reported the story of the Chicago anarchists for Latin America. A great European migration of Germans, Swedes, Norwegians, Poles, and eastern Europeans had arrived at the shores of the nation after the Civil War. They brought with them the "hatred of the servant, the appetite for the wealth of others, the rebellious fury that is unleashed periodically among the oppressed." Along with them came the anarchists, preaching a "war of fire and extermination against wealth and those who possess and defend it, and against the laws and those who maintain them."[3]

For nine days previous to the Haymarket rally, Chicago had been a battlefield in which policemen fought mobs of workers with clubs; women threw rocks, bottles, and pails of hot water out their windows to support their husbands; policemen fired revolvers at workers and workers returned fire point blank. A sybil of "tempestuous eloquence" led marches "waving a red flag with the gestures of a possessed woman." (This was Lucy Parsons, the civil rights leader and wife of condemned anarchist Albert Parsons.) Revealing the intrinsic wariness of the nation toward democracy as a political system, contemporary newspapers and the general public saw the ghosts of leaders of the French Revolution in the faces of Chicago anarchists: Spies, Engel, and Parsons were Robespierre, Marat, and Danton, "who want to pour the old world down a gutter of blood and fertilize the earth with living flesh."[4]

Anarchists were seen as shadowy, vociferous foreigners waving red handkerchiefs and rejoicing as they spread chaos with lit bombs in hand. This projection of evil had genealogical precedents in the demonic figures of Medieval drama and parallels in the Native American Ghost Dance movement. The extant text of the Anglo-Norman mystery play *Jeu d'Adam* (twelfth century) contains the following stage directions: "Then shall the Devil come, and three or four other devils with him. . . . And certain ones shall push [Adam and Eve] on, others shall drag them toward Hell . . . and thereupon they shall cause a great smoke to arise, and they shall shout one to another in Hell, greatly rejoicing; and they shall dash together their pots and kettles, so that they may be heard without. And after some little interval, the devils shall go forth, and shall run to and fro in the square." Sitting Bull, the Arapaho apostle (not the Lakota medicine man) of the Ghost Dance believed that the avalanche of new land would be preceded by a "wall of fire."[5]

Red was the color of Satan, the devil dragon of the book of Revelation (12: 3–9) that had cast the stars of Heaven upon earth and that had been defeated, along with his rebellious hosts, by Michael and his angels. Red was also the prime ceremonial color of Indians, and the color of the sacred paint Wovoka distributed to his disciples. The apocalypse prophesied by Ghost Dancers was an epiphany also desired by anarchist revolutionaries. A portrait of ritual secular fervor that ached to bring about the anarchist millennium was penned in luminous prose by Martí: "A handsome youth, who had his portrait drawn with clouds behind his head and the sun on his shoulder, sits down at a table to write, surrounded by bombs, crosses his legs, lights a cigarette, and like a man fitting together the wooden parts of a dollhouse, explains the just world that will flourish upon the earth when the explosion of the class revolution in Chicago, symbol of the universal oppression, smashes it into atoms."[6] It was the dream at the core of the Ghost Dance, and the sorrow in the heart of Sitting Bull.

In 1893, seven years after the incident, Governor John P. Altgeld of Illinois granted a full pardon to the three remaining anarchists (Fielding, Neebe, Schwab) languishing in jail. The case made for a gigantic anarchist conspiracy was false. Anarchist meetings had been attended, before the May events, by fewer than fifty people per meeting; anarchist newspapers boasted only a small circulation. Massive labor unrest had been confused by the state with anarchist conspiracy. "The soil of America," Governor Altgeld wrote, "is not adapted for the growth of anarchy."[7]

The devil who appeared in the guise of a Black Man had turned Indian in Salem. With the explosive appearance of anarchists, the devil—now dressed in red anarchist garb—had shape-shifted within the bounds of the nation and burst into the ranks of the Euro-American community.

Red Scare

In 1840, Karl Marx and Friedrich Engels declared in *The Communist Manifesto*: "A spectre is haunting Europe—the spectre of Communism. All the

Powers of old Europe have entered into a holy alliance to exorcise this spec-tre." Marx believed that societies were based on a perennial antagonism be-tween "oppressing and oppressed classes." The nineteenth century—"the epoch of the bourgeoisie"—had simplified this agon into the struggle of "two great classes directly facing each other: the Bourgeoisie and the Pro-letariat." The Industrial Revolution was producing the "grave-diggers" of bourgeois society. By bringing workers together in urban settings to com-pete for wages, it had created the opportunity for revolutionary associations. The aim of the Communist Party was to overthrow the existing social order by organizing the proletariat and conquering political power.[8]

Marx correctly anticipated the central economic tension of the Ameri-can Indian wars of the late nineteenth century: bourgeois society compelled all nations, "on pain of extinction," to introduce "what it calls civilization into their midst, i.e., to become bourgeois themselves." Several parallels can be identified between Marxist thought and the Ghost Dance movement. Marx believed in the abolition of private property; Tenskwatawa, the Sha-wano Prophet (brother of Tecumseh), had preached that "all property must be in common, according to the ancient law of [the] ancestors." Marx pro-posed an assumption of power and control of the social order by the pro-letariat; Tenskwatawa and Tecumseh had spoken in favor of a confederacy against Europeans, seeking the revival of "aboriginal sovereignty." Marx predicted that both the victory of the proletariat and the fall of the bour-geoisie were inevitable. Both doctrines shared with Christianity a proph-ecy of the end of days, but Christian belief held that the living and the dead would be raised, that "the first heaven and the first earth" would pass away, and that the worthy would "enter in through the gates into the city" of the New Jerusalem. Communism and the Ghost Dance—at odds in this with Christianity—declared that the kingdom would come to us, *here and now*, and replenish the earth.[9]

The Marxist "spectre" became a living reality on the world's stage with the 1917 Russian Revolution. In 1919, the US Senate repeated a tradition of witness examinations that dated back to the Puritans. The Overman Sub-committee of the Committee on the Judiciary (investigating Ameri-can breweries and German propaganda) was urged to expand its scope of inquiry to include Bolshevism. The Overman Subcommittee was the first of subsequent congressional committees to investigate Communism.[10]

In the 1930s, both the natural catastrophe prophesied by the Ghost Dance (the avalanche of earth took the form of dark storms and whirlwinds of dust) and a Great Depression combined like a two-headed monster to ravage the heartland of the North American continent. John Steinbeck's novel of the Great Depression, *The Grapes of Wrath*, begins in Oklahoma—

the Indian Territory to which Indian tribes were sent in relocations. The Joad family and their neighbors had engaged in a profanation of the earth by farming it, but had retained an Indian sense of land: "That's what makes it ours—being born on it, working it, dying on it." For Chief Seattle the earth was the ashes of his ancestors; Muley Graves could not leave his Oklahoma farm because it was the sacred place where his father was gored by a bull: "I put my han' on that groun' where my own pa's blood is part of it."[11]

But time, which had run over the vanished tribes, had also caught up with the Joads. The margin of profit from farm crops had gone the way of the buffalo herds. Banks owned the land, giant complexes that produced a deep alienation from the earth and its fruits. Metal tractors ("like locusts upon the earth," Rev. 9:3) ravaged the land, tore down the houses of indebted tenants, and ploughed the fields. When the Joads decide to emigrate, a former preacher and Burning Busher by the name of Jim Casy is compelled to join them. Casy has lost his Christian theology and has begun to wonder—like an Indian discovering the Great Spirit—whether a different kind of soul exists in the world, an all-encompassing divinity that permeates all human beings: "Maybe that's the Holy Sperit—the human sperit—the whole shebang. Maybe all men got one big soul ever'body's a part of." The hundreds of families driving down Highway 66 look to Casy "like they was runnin' away from soldiers." Casy had always thought the devil was the enemy, but now he figures differently: "Somepin worse'n the devil got hold a the country, an' it ain't gonna let go till it's chopped loose." The devil that was projected forward onto the face of the Indian has disappeared; the banks are empty, soulless entities. But for the big farm owners in California—worshippers of Mammon—the devil exists, and resides in "reds" who threaten their power and wealth. Reds are driving the country to ruin because they demand thirty rather than twenty-five cents an hour. Okies are content with the farm owners' characterization of their evil nature: "If that's what a red is—why I want that thirty cents an hour. . . . We're all reds."[12]

There is an intimation of revolution in *The Grapes of Wrath*, crying out from the parched land, burning in the breasts of Okies, lit by the hunger "in the wretched bellies of his children." The unjust economic system has made them "outlanders, foreigners" in their own country. Landless, migrant, and poor, their plight is a remembrance of the fate of Indian tribes. The first edition of the novel (1939) carried Julia Ward Howe's "The Battle Hymn of the Republic" printed on the inside cover. Ward Howe's poem—written in the first year of the Civil War—is a witnessing of the Lord's second coming, who has sounded the trumpet of the final days and loosed the lightning of his sword, and who will crush the "serpent with his heel." Steinbeck's novel syncretizes Christian apocalypse, Native American renewal, and Communist Revolution. The Reverend Casy, who gave up his gospel meetings for social activism, will be prophet and arch-priest of the new religion. One day, when the grapes grow big for the vintage in the souls of devils, Indians and Reds, "the armies of bitterness will all be going the same way. And they'll walk together, and there'll be a dead terror from it."[13]

Red Harvest

In 1949, Mao Tse-tung and the Red Army declared the birth of the People's Republic of China. In the early 1950s, the United States battled North Korean and Chinese Communists in the Korean War, which resulted in an unsettled peace agreement. In the words of Yunte Huang, "It seemed as if the whole continent of Asia had just been swallowed up by a Red Sea."[14] Within the United States, the House Un-American Activities Committee (HUAC) became a permanent committee of Congress in 1945 for the purpose of investigating citizens with Communist histories and associations.

In the 1920s and early 1930s, Dashiell Hammett had transformed American detective fiction. Hammett joined the Pinkerton's Detective Agency in 1915. During World War I he contracted pulmonary tuberculosis (an ailment that would plague him throughout his life) in the army during the Spanish Flu pandemic of 1918. Discharged honorably from the military in poor health, Hammett moved to San Francisco where he quit detective work and wrote short stories that were published in H. L. Mencken's *The Smart Set* and *Black Mask*. Between 1927 and 1933, Hammett wrote the five novels that constitute—along with his Continental Op short stories—his main body of work. In the mid-1930s he lent his active support, along with other American intellectuals, to the antifascist (Loyalist) cause in the Spanish Civil War. At the height of his career at age forty-eight (shortly after the release of John Huston's film of *The Maltese Falcon*), he rejoined the army as a private during World War II. By this time, the FBI considered him "to be among the upper echelon of the Communist Party in the United States."[15]

Hammett was a Marxist by his own admission, an ex-strike-breaker for Pinkerton who came to believe that "nothing less than a revolution could wipe out the corruption" in US society, and a sharp critic of the Soviet Union and the American Communist Party who remained in the end—according to his life-long friend Lillian Hellman—"loyal to them." In 1946, he was elected president of the Civil Rights Congress (CRC) of New York, an organization that maintained a bail fund for the release of defendants in political trials.[16] In 1949, four defendants convicted under the Smith Act for "criminal conspiracy to teach and advocate the overthrow of the United

States government by force," jumped their bail (secured by the CRC) and failed to surrender to federal authorities. As chair of the committee of trustees who administered the fund, Hammett was called to testify before the South District Court of New York.[17] Firmly and repeatedly, Hammett invoked the Fifth Amendment and refused to answer questions. The night before his sentencing, he explained his stance to Hellman: "I hate this damn kind of talk, but . . . if it were more than jail, if it were my life, I would give it for what I think democracy is and I don't let cops or judges tell me what I think democracy is." When asked by the judge if he had anything to say, Hammett replied: "Not a thing." Like Giles Corey from another age and in a previous court, he stood mute before his examiners. He was sentenced to six months in prison for contempt of court. Hammett's health never recovered from his stint in jail. He died in 1961.[18]

A long line of artistic luminaries like Hammett (especially Hollywood actors, screenwriters, and directors) were investigated for Communist ties by HUAC in the 1950s. Some (Ronald Reagan, José Ferrer) pledged their allegiance to the anti-Communist cause like Indians seeking Christian baptism. Others (Elia Kazan, Jerome Robbins) named names, like Salem witnesses accusing witches, and received approval and exoneration. Still others did not acknowledge the legitimacy of the committee (the Hollywood 10, Lillian Hellman, Arthur Miller, Paul Robeson). Bertolt Brecht (who fled Hitler's Germany as a Communist and spent the war years in California) was subpoenaed and left this observation of persecution in the United States during the McCarthy years: "The State does not put in an appearance but the execution does take place. One could call it Cold Execution—a certain form of peace is called Cold War there. This Cold Execution is carried out by the industry: the delinquent is not deprived of his life, only of the means of life. He does not appear in the obituary column, only on the blacklists. Whoever has witnessed the horrors of poverty and humiliation which, in the land of the dollar, fall upon the man without a dollar, will not prefer the punishment of unemployment to any punishment that the State could inflict." Garry Wills explained the source of HUAC's power: "The Redhunters were so dangerous precisely because they considered themselves saviors of the country from a diabolical plot."[19]

Red Sea

Eugene O'Neill's *The Emperor Jones* (1920) is a dramatic poem and an American fable. Bringing to mind Shakespeare's *The Tempest* and Conrad's *Heart of Darkness*, it tells the story of an African American ex-Pullman porter who becomes emperor of a Caribbean island. Brutus Jones and his commercial empire are overwhelmed by natural and magical island forces. Eerie spirits dwelling in the jungle, tom-tom beats from distant drums, ritual dances performed in the mountains by native inhabitants, memories of past crimes and ghosts from America's racial history—"haunts" as O'Neill would call them—all conspire to overwhelm the rootless Jones before he can escape to the sea, fleeing from a slave rebellion. In his stage directions, O'Neill wrote that the play takes place "on an island in the West Indies as yet not self-determined by White Marines." This was an allusion to the North American military occupation of Haiti in 1915.[20]

Such a "self-determined" island was Cuba, which was acquired along with Puerto Rico in the Caribbean as spoils of war in the 1898 Spanish-American conflict. The veteran commanding officers of the US expeditionary force had been young officers during the Civil War, and had climbed up to senior ranks through the crucible of the American Indian wars. General Nelson Miles, commander in chief of the US Army in 1898, had maneuvered Geronimo's last surrender in 1886 and was the officer in charge of army operations during the Sioux Ghost Dance rebellion. In Cuba, American officers engaged the defeated Spanish officers as equals but were disparaging and contemptuous of their allies. Ragged and exhausted after three years of brutal warfare, General Calixto García's Cuban troops (mostly black) were characterized by US Brigadier General Samuel M. B. Young as "a lot of degenerates, absolutely devoid of honor and gratitude. They are no more capable of self-government than the savages." Governor Leonard Wood, sounding the recurrent "civilizing" theme of the nineteenth century, wrote to President McKinley in 1901: "We are dealing with a race that has been steadily going downhill for a hundred years and into which we have got to infuse new life, new principles, and new methods." The "savage" populations of Cuba and Puerto Rico were considered Indians; the islands were treated precisely as Indian reservations. Henceforth, the United States would consider the Caribbean Sea a *mare nostrum*, to be invaded or occupied militarily at the first sign of threats (real or imagined) against its political hegemony, its economic interests, or the Panama Canal. Looking through the lens of a revivified Cold War against Communism's evil empire, President Ronald Reagan set out in the 1980s to stop "the red tide of revolution" in Central America before it could "roll north."[21]

The Circum-Caribbean area (circling counterclockwise from the Yucatán Peninsula, to the shores of Colombia and Venezuela, to the islands of the Antilles) included the classic domain of the ancient Maya. Except for the islands, the *Tierra Firme* retained large numbers of indigenous populations. During the first half of the twentieth century, the United States intervened, on different occasions and for varying periods of time, in Panama, Colombia, the Dominican Republic, Honduras, Mexico, and Guatemala, carried out extended military occupations in Cuba (1898–1920), Nicaragua (1926–1933, during the Augusto Sandino rebellion), and Haiti (1915–1934), and established political sovereignty over Puerto Rico to the present day.

Post–World War II, the new Indian Wars in the Americas were the old ones, with new masks but whipped by the same demonology. It was the eternal return of the perennial agon: good versus evil, Christian versus pagan devil, Indian versus European. Territorial acquisition was no longer represented as a crusade for civilization but as a fight for freedom and democracy. Behind Socialist movements in the central and southern hemisphere there was the spiritual world of the great American Indian civilizations, the immanent sacrality of the land in agricultural regions, and a mystic sense of the people ("those who did not arrive and those who will come") comparable to that of the "great soul" of Okies in *The Grapes of Wrath*. [22]

By the early 1950s, the Soviet Union had acquired atomic weapons. Open military confrontations between the United States and "red" forces now ran the risk of escalation leading to a mutually assured destruction. The result was a decided commitment—after the dangerous encounter between the United States and China in the Korean War—to covert intelligence operations, and to a shadowy, geopolitical chess game of clandestine wars. In 1954, President Eisenhower gave his final approval to a CIA-sponsored toppling of the democratically elected government of Jacobo Arbenz in Guatemala. Committed to a policy of land reform, the Arbenz government had expropriated 234,000 acres of arable land from the United Fruit Company between 1952 and 1953 and an additional 173,000 acres in 1954. United Fruit resisted these reforms; its chief executives believed "that the people of Guatemala were not entitled to the same freedoms as the citizens of the United States." One of Fidel Castro's closest associates witnessed Arbenz's resignation from the presidency and the succession of a military regime. The experience would leave Ernesto Guevara with a "profound distrust of the United States that was to grow with the years." For Latin America, the fate of Jacobo Arbenz was prima facie evidence of US hypocrisy: its vaunted worship of democracy was a fraud. With good reason Mark Twain had "brought down to date" "The Battle Hymn of the Republic" in 1901:

In a solid slime harmonious, Greed was born in yonder ditch,
With a longing in his bosom—and for others' goods an itch—
As Christ died to make men holy, let men die to make us rich—
    Our God is marching on.

John Foster Dulles declared the Guatemalan coup "the biggest success in the last five years against Communism." Eisenhower referred to it as "the model of its kind."[23]

Land and agrarian reform—a veritable avalanche of the earth—were at the heart of the southern insurgency led by Emiliano Zapata in the 1910 Mexican Revolution. A defense of Indo-Hispanic sovereignty was a moving force behind Augusto César Sandino's guerrilla war against US Marines in Nicaragua from 1927 to 1933. The success of the 1959 Cuban Revolution—a Caribbean, Antillean Ghost Dance—in an overseas possession close to home (a presumptive Indian reservation) presaged once again the final days, the arrival of the ghosts and a renewal of the earth.

Castro's Cuban guerrillas began operations in 1956 in the Sierra Maestra of the Oriente province, the legendary mountain stronghold of Cuban rebels for over a hundred years. In the mythology of Cuban insurgency the Sierra Maestra was a sacred realm, as the Black Hills were for the Lakota. It was the mountain range to which Hatuey had escaped from Hispaniola to flee the Spaniards in the fifteenth century. Oriente was also the province of the Great War of Independence (1868–1878) and where Martí began his war of 1895. Castro's 26th of July Movement began with an urban attack against the Moncada Barracks (also in Oriente) in 1953, but three years later in the mountains his revolt became land-based, peasant, and agrarian. In his manual of guerrilla warfare, Guevara explained: "The guerrilla fighter is above all an agrarian revolutionary."[24]

For the young guerrilla leaders that took power in Cuba, democracy was at best a dubious proposition. They were students of both the French and Russian Revolutions. Their generation of Latin American leaders had come of age in the wake of accounts by Spanish refugees of the fall of the Loyalists and the triumph of fascism in the Spanish Civil War. The United States, which had entered World War I to make the world safe for democracy, had refused to lend aid to the Spanish Republic. The lesson for the Hispanic world was clear: the United States was not only fearful of Socialism but also antagonistic to democracy. In 1959, Castro was not a Communist but a radical nationalist willing to use revolutionary means. His clear eloquence and urgent tone were received by the people as the signs of a messiah. Deliberately, performatively, like a messenger from a holy realm, he shared with mass audiences the sacred myth of the Revolution—the failed, unfinished effort that Cubans had waged against Spanish and North American colonizers for over a century: "In public, 'the Revolution,' that irresistible movement of men and spirits toward Utopia, is made to resemble an African deity, whose needs, sometimes wayward and inscrutable, are interpreted by Castro as *santero*, a worthy successor to others who aspired to fulfill this role in Cuba, from Carlos Manuel de Céspedes and José Martí onwards." "Revolution" was a concept that had been "indigenous" to Cuban history since at least 1868. And Revolution was not only an avalanche of the earth but also a summoning of the Cuban dead who had perished in past wars. In his patriotic speeches, Martí had conjured the dead martyrs of the Great War of Independence; on the first day of the Revolution's triumph, Castro also rendered homage to the presence of dead martyrs: "This time it will not be possible to say . . . that we will betray our dead, because this time the dead will continue in command."[25]

Black Operations

John F. Kennedy's "New Frontier" began, fittingly, with an invasion of Cuba. The Assault Brigade 2506 wrote its page in history as one of those lost armies of allied fighters—the Indian scouts and police forces of the reservations, the Army of the Republic of Vietnam (ARVN) in Vietnam—that were first used and then discarded by the United States and its war policies. Recruited, financed, and equipped by the CIA, the 1,500-strong force of Cuban exiles trained in the confines of coffee plantations near Retalhuleu, Guatemala. According to Richard Bissell, CIA deputy director in charge of undercover operations, the plan was simple: "The aim of the invading brigade was specifically to establish a beachhead. . . . A government could have been established, which the U.S.A. could have recognised." Kennedy approved the operation with a strict proviso: there would be no US intervention and no American air strikes in support of the invasion force. But brigade members, isolated in their training camp, and their CIA handlers thought differently. The exiles believed they were enlisting in a sort of "Rough Riders" regiment (as in 1898) that would form a part of a larger US expeditionary force; the CIA operatives were persuaded "the president might approve American military intervention if the alternative was defeat."[26]

The brigade's first mission was the bombing of Cuban airports by eight B-26 World War II airplanes on April 15, 1961. On April 16, at a funeral for victims of the air strike, Castro delivered a determining speech. First (and for the first time), he openly declared a "Socialist revolution" in Cuba. Second, he reversed the American penchant for Last Stands to fit the previous day's events: "If the attack on Pearl Harbor is considered by the American people as a criminal, traitorous, cowardly act, then our people have a right to consider this act twice as criminal, twice as cunning, twice as traitorous, and a thousand times as cowardly." Last, in trickster fashion, he paraphrased Abraham Lincoln to claim a democratic legitimacy for the Revolution: "This is the Socialist and Democratic Revolution of the humble, with the humble, for the humble." Following the international uproar caused by news of the bombings, Kennedy cancelled two additional air strikes by exile pilots scheduled to coincide with the invasion.[27]

On April 17 at dawn, the Assault Brigade landed on Playa Girón, a beachfront surrounded by impenetrable swamps on the southern coast of Cuba. By the second day, the brigade was surrounded by twenty thousand Cuban troops with tanks and artillery. Kennedy was urged by his advisors to approve an air attack from the American vessels off the coast of Cuba. He refused. Next day Castro's forces breached the brigade's defenses. The surviving invaders tried to escape through the swamps. Eleven hundred and eighty prisoners were rounded up and captured. Shortly after the defeat at Girón, Kennedy met with leaders of the Cuban Revolutionary Council (the civilian and political arm of the exile invasion, also recruited by the CIA) to explain his decision not to intervene militarily. Whatever the CRC or the brigade fighters "supposed" they had been told, "if the U.S. moved against Cuba, would not the USSR move against Berlin?"[28]

The Bay of Pigs revealed a contrast in competing mythologies. Kennedy's frame of reference (as well as that of his advisors) for a maritime invasion was that of D-Day in World War II. Arthur Schlesinger convinced Kennedy to meet with the CRC after the invasion's failure by insisting that "this is a Pearl Harbor! They're really upset!"[29] The United States still saw itself as good guys fighting evil dictators. Conversely, Castro evoked collective memories from Caribbean history by calling the invasion a pirate attack planned by imperialists and executed by mercenaries. The Cuban government would declare the victory at Playa Girón the *first* defeat of imperialism in America (in spite of Dessalines's nineteenth-century victory in Haiti against Napoleon's invading army).

The fate of the Cuban brigade on the shores of Girón in April 1961 had all the makings of a Last Stand. For three days the exile volunteers faced overwhelming odds unaided by the full military might of the United States in nearby waters. Bay of Pigs would be the last viable chance to free Cuba from Castro and change the course of history. There would be future attempts (all futile) by the Kennedy administration to topple the Castro regime, but no bugle call ever sounded (except by Cuban exiles in the United States) to "Remember the Bay of Pigs!" After the humiliating defeat at Girón by a small country, the embarrassing discovery of direct US participation in the invasion, and notoriously clumsy attempts to deny involvement, it was not expedient to wave a bloody flag of martyrdom based on the brigade's heroism and imprisonment. It was a Last Stand provoked, and then refused.

The Last Stand is never an objective reality but always an expressly manufactured myth for the purpose of conjuring war. The sacrifices of heroes—heroism itself—are embraced or ignored according to the wishes of a ruling order. Without a reasonable assurance of power acquisition, without profit—human or monetary—societies are content to let sleeping heroes lie. It was in this knowledge that General Smedley Butler—with tours of service in the Philippines, China, Central America, Mexico, and Haiti during the early twentieth century—advised American mothers: "When you listen to some well-worded, well-delivered war speech, just remember that it's nothing but Sound." The olive-green-clad guerrillas had won. The ghosts had returned and the land was renewed. A question posed by Schlesinger to Kennedy in the wake of the invasion still remained unanswered: "Why was Cuba such a threat to you?" Years later, unknowingly, one CIA official would provide the reason: "The bearded devil had won the war."[30]

During the Cuban missile crisis of October 1962, the United States renounced future invasions of Cuba in exchange for USSR removal of nuclear missiles. Elsewhere in the world, it reaffirmed its commitment to stop the spread of Communism. In 1965, the United States returned to its former policy of direct intervention in Latin America with an invasion of the Dominican Republic to prevent a leftist government from taking power. By then, it had stationed hundreds of thousands of troops in the Asian nation of Vietnam.

Red Devil

The devil that the United States feared in our time was born in Argentina and lived during the rule of Juan Perón. The devil—studious and well read—attended the University of Buenos Aires. Wishing to discover his world, he rode a motorcycle on a journey through Chile, Colombia, and Venezuela. He discovered the hunger of peasants, the poverty of miners, and because he was a kind devil, he stayed for a time to tend the sick at a leper colony in San Pablo, Perú.

When he completed his medical degree he set out for Guatemala. There the devil met the great octopus of the Americas—the United Fruit Company—and supported the land reform efforts of Jacobo Arbenz. This was his first defeat. He fled to Mexico, where he met a kindred fallen angel who was organizing an armed insurrection in Cuba. He was instructed by Alberto Bayo, a veteran Republican guerrilla fighter from the Spanish Civil War, and sailed with Fidel Castro's small band of rebels on the fabled yacht Granma. In the mountains, the devil became a fierce guerrillero despite his childhood asthma. He rose to the highest rank in the Rebel Army, and as the comandante of a rebel column, took the city of Santa Clara just before Batista's fall.

When Castro assumed power, the devil took command of La Cabaña, an old Spanish military fortress in Havana harbor that was also used as a prison. He set up revolutionary tribunals to judge former torturers, policemen, civil servants, and suspected criminals. Ruthlessly, he carried out their death sentences. US congressmen protested the executions as a "bloodbath." Typically, Castro pointed out US hypocrisy and denial of its own crimes: "What was done at Hiroshima and Nagasaki? . . . They said it was to obtain peace. They also said it was to prevent the death of many North Americans in battle. . . . We are executing the tyrant's henchmen to obtain peace, and we are executing the (butcher?) so that they cannot murder our children again tomorrow." In March 1960 the French ship *La Coubre*, bearing weapons bought from Belgium by the Cuban government, blew up in Havana harbor, stirring memories of the explosion of the USS *Maine* in 1898. On March 5, 1960, at a mass funeral for the victims of the explosion, Alberto Korda saw the devil *"encabronado y dol[i]ente"* (furious and in pain). Korda snapped two shots with a Leica camera. One negative revealed the devil in front of a light background, between the right profile of a bystander and palm tree leaves. A cropped print of the negative—a solitary head shot of the devil against the white heavens—appeared for the first time in the Cuban newspaper *Revolución*. Korda would refer to the photograph as "Ché in the sky with jacket."[31]

After the Cuban missile crisis, as in the book of Job (2:2), the devil went "to and fro in the earth," and walked "up and down in it." He represented Cuba in the United Nations. He traveled to China, France, the Soviet Union, and Africa. He resigned his tasks in the Cuban Government and joined Marxist guerrillas in the Congo. He returned to Cuba, wrote a farewell letter to Fidel Castro, and left to begin a guerrilla war of liberation in Bolivia. Discerning the enormity and mythical importance of his task he kept a diary, as José Martí had kept a *Campaign Diary* (a masterpiece of minimalist literature) in 1895.

From the jungle and Andean mountains where Incas had fought Spaniards, the devil sent a message to the Tricontinental Conference in Havana. And his message was like the sound of angel trumpets, or like a wonder in Heaven. "The United States," he declared, "is the enemy of mankind." The future of the world would be bright if "two, three or many Vietnams flourish throughout the world." And the devil's call was also like a prophecy of Armageddon at the end of days: "Imperialism is a world system, the last stage of capitalism—and it must be defeated in a world confrontation."[32]

An Italian publisher by the name of Gian Giacomo Feltrinelli reproduced thousands of copies of Korda's photograph in book covers and posters. His intent was to protect the devil through an "international awareness of his vulnerability." By then, after Cuba and the Congo and the Bolivian jungle, the face of the devil had transformed. It was no longer the portrait of a man in pain. Now it shone with the splendor of an alluring presence: "He was unbelievably beautiful. Before the era of the obsessive adulation accorded to musicians, he had the unmistakable aura of a rock star. People stopped whatever they were doing, and thus stared at the Revolution made flesh." So did Lucifer, Son of the Morning, shine before the fall.[33]

On July 24, 1967, the devil wrote a cryptic, satiric note in his diary: "Friends call me a new Bakunin, and lament the spilled blood and that which will be shed in the case of 3 or 4 Vietnams."[34] On October 8, the devil was ambushed by Bolivian troops trained, equipped, and advised by the United States. He was captured and taken to a makeshift prison in a rural schoolhouse. He was shot the next day. Photographs of the devil's body on a stone slab were distributed to the world. As in the case of Osama bin Laden, the threat had been erased.

Writing about a photograph of the dead Ché, John Berger commented that Guevara's "envisaged death" was an act of commitment to a choice that freed him from the circumstance of fact. The Caribbean poet Derek Walcott foresaw the future:

The corpse glows candle-white on its cold altar—
its stone Bolivian Indian butcher's slab-
stare till its waxen flesh begins to harden
to marble, to veined, white Andean iron;
from your own fear, *cabrón*, its pallor grows.

No one heard the rumble of the stone that rolled away from the sepulcher. The Cuban graphic artist José Gómez Fresquet (Frémez) worked through the night of October 17–18 on a poster to honor the memory of Guevara at a mass meeting in Havana's Plaza de la Revolución. Based on a copy of Korda's photograph, Frémez used only one color for the poster: "Only red paper was available." He printed the image as a ghostly black shade against a vast red background, and the portrait became the mystic symbol of an eternally recurrent myth.[35]

Black was the color of the devil in Salem; black is the color—in Frémez's poster—of the devil's shoulder-length hair. Terrifying are his dark moustache and beard, like those of anarchist revolutionaries, and arrogant is the tilt of his black beret—the enduring icon of the Spanish Republic. The lone star of Caribbean rebels shines on his brow. Faintly perceived under a sea of red (the sacred color of the Ghost Dance), awash in a red flood of Socialism, the apparition stares with haunted eyes at onlookers. Underneath the photo there is a caption, the devil's parting words to Castro, which could have been Crazy Horse's last farewell to Sitting Bull: "Until Victory Always, Ché." And his visage was the guidon of a distant prophecy of renewal of the earth led by ghosts and a messiah.

Sometimes in black and white, often in black against red, the face of the devil appeared in myriad places not only to honor the fallen angel but also to infuriate the beast. It was adopted by French students during the protests of 1968 and by Irish rebels. American students against the Vietnam War hung posters of the devil on their walls. Black Panthers wore his black beret. And the greater the anger of the beast at the sight of the *Guerrillero Heroico*—the "Heroic Guerrilla" was the name the portrait acquired—the greater its proliferation. It became like an avatar created by Tom Joad's warning: "I'll be ever'where—wherever you look. Wherever they's a fight so hungry people can eat, I'll be there." Amplified by inner fears, the power and intensity of the devil's image grew. In time, the aspect framed by Korda's photograph— a projection of the Jungian shadow—became "the most reproduced image in the history of photography."[36]

Portrait of the Beast

Upstream the river's labyrinth, at the source and end of time, lives the monster in his house of shadows. His Cambodian temple is surrounded by jungle, and beyond it there is only jungle. Tropical Golgotha, his garden is a desert of solitude and pain. The skulls of victims oversee steps leading to his palace. Tiger cages constrict tortured prisoners. Disemboweled bodies hang from aching trees like bitter fruit. And the legion of the beast awaits him in the garden: Montagnard guerrillas, former North Vietnamese Army and ARVN soldiers, outlaw Green Berets.

Malaria walks unimpeded through his halls. His voice is soft and clear, far and very near, speaking memories of a plantation of gardenias like a piece of Heaven fallen on earth. The beast dreams and remembers but does not yearn for home—the paradise from which he was exiled. He peeps through shadows like a figure in dreams, like a phantom bubbling up from the unconscious. He washes his face and bony head with swamp water. By the light of a single candle he reads Eliot's *The Hollow Men* and writes a postscript in red ink on the pages of his report: "Drop the Bomb Exterminate Them All!"

Francis Ford Coppola's *Apocalypse Now Redux* (2001) is a mythical compendium of US wars. The film is based on two masterpieces: Joseph Conrad's *Heart of Darkness* and Werner Herzog's *Aguirre: The Wrath of God*. Conrad's novel tells the story of a company man who goes into the heart of Africa to find ivory for his Belgian employers. Herzog's film is about a Spanish conquistador who revolts against his officers in the Amazon forest to lead an expedition in search of El Dorado. Both heroes at the end of a river journey, like Dante at the end of his *Inferno*, find the beast.[37]

The original title was "The Psychedelic Soldier," and some truth of this remains in the film. Lee Benjamin, a Vietnam veteran who was a marine at Khe Sanh, used to baptize young soldiers in river waters to dispel their fears of damnation. Benjamin was wounded and spent ten months in a veterans hospital. He gave this critical assessment of Vietnam War films: "*Platoon* is what happened to me; *Apocalypse Now* is what I experienced trying to sleep in the jungle with the runs, surrounded by snakes and spiders the size of a quarter coin, while it's raining hard in one-hundred degree heat. It was surrealist, like the movie."[38]

The assassin is given his mission "for his sins." Ben Willard—a specialist in black operations—escapes from the whited sepulcher of Saigon. His commanding officers believe that Colonel Walter Kurtz's methods have become "unsound." The Patrol Boat, River (PBR) called *Erebus* (son of Darkness and Chaos, a dim, cavernous passage leading to Hades), code-name "Street Gang," will take him to No Man's Land, Indian Territory. Cambodia is the mythic realm of primitive cultures: a world of dreams and images where time and space exist all at once. The boat is a mystic canoe, an emblem as old as Jason's *Argo* from Greek mythology. The Captain (Chief) of the PBR has "pulled a few special ops" but is untouched by Ahab's madness. The Argonauts are children caught in war, "food for powder" in Falstaff's words, who can "fill a pit as well as better [men]." Willard is guided not by Virgil but by a simulacrum of Kurtz constructed from military files, newspaper clippings, and interceptions of ghostly radio broadcasts. He opens Kurtz's dossier as if it were the book from Revelation, sealed with seven seals. Willard's journey up the river will be a confession, as if Theseus needed to explain his slaying of the Minotaur.

Colonel Bill Kilgore is the symbolic representation of American war heroes since the Civil War. Robert Duvall's blue Union Cavalry hat and golden neck scarf are reminiscent of Errol Flynn in *They Died with Their Boots On* (1941) and John Wayne in John Ford's *The Horse Soldiers* (1959). Kilgore, like George S. Patton, wears a handgun with an ivory handle. He believes, with Patton: "Americans love to fight—traditionally. And real Americans love the sting and clash of battle." The Air Cav ("an old cavalry division that had cashed in its horses for choppers") attacks a Viet Cong (VC) village to drop the *Erebus* at the mouth of the Nung River. Custer and the Seventh Cavalry attacked Indian villages at dawn while the regimental band played "Garry Owen"; Kilgore's Hueys lift with the rising sun at the sound of a cavalry charge and attack on the wings of Wagner's "The Ride of the Valkyries" (Hitler's favorite opera composer). The attack on Vin Drin Dop is a graphic sequence of what James William Gibson has called *Technowar* or the *production model of war*: "the military mode of strategy and organization in which war is conceptualized and organized as a high-technology, capital intensive production process." It is the war dynamic unleashed by the Last Stand. All reason for war has been lost, and only the commanding voice of the pilot ("Shoot to kill!") is discerned in the frenzy. This Custer brings napalm to the war, affronting the earth, scorching the natural world, and harbors old perspectives: when a young female VC (a "dink bitch") throws a grenade into one of Kilgore's helicopters, he exclaims: "Fucking savages!"[39]

When Marlowe's Dr. Faustus begins to doubt his pact with Mephistopheles, Lucifer rewards him with a pageant of the Seven Deadly Sins. At Hau Phat, the crew of the *Erebus* meets the Playboy Bunnies. Phallic rockets surround the USO stage. The Playmates jump out of a helicopter appropriately dressed as Cowboys and Indians—a faint echo of the martial affirmations of Buffalo Bill's *Wild West*. They are Graces, Hours, illusory Sirens casting a spell of sex and merriment upon the soldiers. To Flash Cadillac's *Suzie Q*, they dance a number that expresses the erotic submission of North Americans to guns and rifles. But the assassin who escaped the tiger burning in his natural environment remains unmoved: "Never get out of the boat."

Since the story of *Apocalypse Now* takes place between 1968 and 1969, members of the cast and crew suggested that "something approaching the My Lai massacre" should be part of the film. The result was the sampan massacre sequence. The My Lai revelations after the Tet Offensive produced a defining moment of clarity for the United States. Much like the conquistadores of Spain and Custer's troopers, US soldiers had engaged in the pillaging of villages and the execution of native populations. In 1968, Arthur Kopit's play *Indians* upheld the premise that American Indian history predicted the horrors of the Vietnam War. My Lai was an echo in the spiral of time that conjured Wounded Knee. The armed contingent of the *Erebus* shoots a band of unarmed civilian detainees (an M60 being the modern version of a Hotchkiss gun). The assassin delivers the PBR from consequences by killing the last surviving boat person.[40]

There were no weapons in the sampan; few VC—if any—were found in My Lai and only old rifles at Wounded Knee. We are not content to fight the devil; we also hunt, suspiciously, the imagined marks of his hoof. The devil's presence is always spectral—a phantom, a shadow, a ghost. The very emptiness of the object (the devil's absence) heightens our warring intensity in order to reassure our constructs. Then we address My Lais and Wounded Knees with "band aids." Take the wounded baby to the hospital and carry the woman we just shot to the ARVN station.

Lance, champion surfer of the *Erebus*, drops a tab of acid as the PBR approaches the last army outpost on the Nung River. There are night flares, missiles exploding, and garish festival lights. There is Charlie calling out GIs, the roar of machine guns, and Jimi Hendrix riffing on his guitar. There is no order or chain of command. The bridge is destroyed every night and rebuilt during the day. The Do Long Bridge is a metaphor for the destruction of the Jungian *persona*. It is a psychic and mythological threshold for the hero—beyond it lies "the sacred power of the universal source."[41] Colonel Kurtz lived in the world before the Do Long Bridge; past it lives only the beast in Cambodia.

Through a bank of clouds on the river, the *Erebus* journeys into the past and meets the "Lost Soldiers" of the French rubber plantation. The French claim the pose and fury of the Last Stand: "This piece of earth we keep it." The French plantation is a mirage of the American slave empires of the nineteenth century and the United Fruit Company landholdings of the twentieth. Willard listens to lessons learned by the previous European colonial power in Indochina: "We want to stay here because it's ours, it belongs to us. It keeps our family together. We fight for that! While you Americans, you are fighting for the biggest nothing in history." Americans are foreigners in Vietnam, without connection to the earth. Given their past, the French are immune to hypocrisy: "Freedom? Bullshit. French bullshit. American bullshit."

Roxanne is a representation of the Jungian anima. She notices that Willard has the same look in his eyes that French soldiers once had: "She is the great illusionist, the great seductress who draws him . . . not only into life's reasonable and useful aspects, but into its frightful paradoxes and ambivalences where good and evil, success and ruin, hope and despair, counterbalance one another."[42] The Sybil, with a ritual pipe of opium, presents the assassin with his quest: "You are both a loving and a warring animal." In its final sequence, the film moves into a surrealist dream world—apocalypse truly now—in which the beast is faced, projections are retrieved, and opposites are reconciled.

In the Aztec legend, the enemy sorcerer with his dark mirror arrives to visit the monarch. The feathered serpent sees his monstrous image in the looking glass and is "filled with fear." Eventually, the ruler resigns his throne, discards the trappings of power, and begins a journey to the sea.

Apocalypse Now is a modern version of the legend of Quetzalcoatl. The beast conjures the assassin, who announces his presence with the blast of a boat siren. The assassin has experienced in his journey outer aspects of the beast: cruelty and savagery, sensual dissolution, technological insanity, and chaotic delirium. Now the naked beast shows his visage, holding a mirror without a glass up to Willard's nature: "Fancy thinking the Beast was something you could hunt and kill! . . . You knew, didn't you? I'm part of you?"[43]

John Wayne—a worthy heir to the mantle of Buffalo Bill—glorified last stands in *The Alamo* (1960) and *The Green Berets* (1968). Marlon Brando was the image of John Wayne through the looking glass. He played the role of Mexican revolutionary Emiliano Zapata—with script by John Steinbeck—in *Viva Zapata!* (1952); in 1963, he produced and starred in *The Ugly American* (1963), based on the bestseller novel that first brought attention to US involvement in Southeast Asia. All of Brando's performances of counterculture heroes contributed to his shaping of Kurtz: "It was probably the closest I've ever come to getting lost in a part."[44]

The beast walks in a reptilian mask through the jungle and cuts off an Argonaut's head. He has discarded all trappings, for he hates lies and emblems of hypocrisy: "Horror and moral terror are your friends. If they are not, then they are enemies to be feared." The beast was not immune to the touch of evil, and like Orson Welles's Hank Quinlan, rules in the swamp of his own savagery. The face of the beast is reflected on a dark mirror, explaining his need for severance from natural instinct: "To kill without feeling, without passion. . . . Without judgment. Because it's judgment that defeats us." Like Conrad's Kurtz, he dies evoking the horror that transformed him.

The beast is the personification of our metamorphosis when we hunt the devil. When Willard emerges from killing Kurtz, he is dragon—both man and beast. The assassin has retrieved the contents of his projection. But the function and presence of the shadow remain. For those condemned to live between Heaven and Hell, devils and avenging angels, are fated to agonic torment in the perpetual caverns of the soul.

6

Tricksters

The devil myth, as revealed in its genealogy, is a recurring cultural dynamic of projecting evil to justify warfare. It is embedded in the national identity, articulated in dramatic narrative, and memorialized in heroic iconography. Archetypal evil is a dark presence that defines and legitimizes the nation in violent opposition to the enemy-image it invokes. America imagines itself as the opposite of the wickedness it habitually attributes to the figure of the enemy.[1] The projected image of evil savagery adapts, evolves, and reconstitutes itself in each mythic cycle of redemptive violence.

This devil myth is a pernicious cultural formation but also an unstable assemblage held together somewhat precariously by the impetus of political ritual. Its very instability is a constant pressure on believers to conform. Yet, conforming can create its own complications, enough to strain the credulity of a distressed people when the violence of projected evil threatens to consume saints and sinners alike. The tragic narrative of good versus evil invites a comic corrective to escape unwanted consequences at such discomforting moments.[2]

To slip the trap of the devil myth's lethal polarities and circumvent the severe boundary between good and evil, if only momentarily, is to invoke the mythic figure of the trickster. Trickster is the archetype of fluidity and ambivalence that disrespects the authority of petrified archetypes.[3] The figure of the trickster, which "continues to make its influence felt on the highest levels of civilization," becomes useful and sensible, Carl Jung observes, as it manifests the "undifferentiated human consciousness" so that the "conscious mind is able to free itself from the fascination of evil and is no longer obliged to live it compulsively" or to project it "upon one's neighbor."[4] This shape-shifting, boundary-crossing figure of comic amorality is a clever escape artist bringing the ambiguities of circumstances into the forefront of consciousness. Trickster's mischief can disturb established truths, upset honored conventions, and confound the essence of categorical opposites to create new possibilities in an imperfect world of contingencies.[5] Trickster, as William Hynes puts the matter, "reminds us that every construct is constructed," that "life is endlessly narrative, prolific and open-ended." In Romand Coles's view, "Trickster politics" is a "construction of democracy-in-tension," which "promises a responsiveness, suppleness, and mobility that just might develop the power to bring forth a significantly better world."[6]

Tweaking paradigms avoids impending catastrophe by allowing for novel ways of seeing and understanding. Thus, the mythic life of a people disrupts the sobriety of social order with occasional episodes of unruly intoxication to make the worldview of the body politic pliable and more viable. Without order, there is no role for trickster to play, no boundaries to cross. Without trickster, there is no medium of cultural adjustment to a recalcitrant world. Obstinate, self-destructive violence is the only option absent the disruptive, reorienting intervention of trickster to allow society an escape from a looming calamity.

Changing perspective is seeing double, which is an initially confusing and vertiginous experience that subsequently resolves into a stereoscopic gaze. This is trickster's annoying gift of reflexivity and uncanny capacity for refracting demonizing images. The stereoscopic gaze is a way of glimpsing oneself in the reflected image of a despised enemy and seeing the irony of displaced evil. Recognizing and acknowledging such a reflection is requisite to retrieving and integrating projected evil into a more democratic conception of the self.

The stereoscopic gaze, as an enactment of critical reflexivity, recognizes demonizing projections through a shift in language. This rhetorical turn can produce what Kenneth Burke called "perspective by incongruity": a clash of terms, a corresponding sense of strangeness and disorientation followed by an altered angle of perception, a flash of insight, and reorientation. Burke thought of it as a kind of introspective verbal atom-cracking, metaphorically placing a word that belongs customarily in one category into a different category. This impious act of linking previously unlinked terms against the dictates of linguistic convention is a positive attempt, after "virtue itself turns vice," to rename and "remoralize" a situation that has become demoralized by inaccurate naming. Perspective by incongruity is a "salvation device" for "liquidating the false rigidity of concepts," a mode of "convertibility between . . . vocabularies," a shifting frame of reference that allows a new unity to emerge.[7]

Burke observed that when a culture faces a crisis an opportunity arises to shift its habitual frame of reference. Without such a shift, the culture suffers "decadence, neurosis, anger (expressing itself in either external war or internal antagonisms, the devices whereby a people 'projects' its uneasiness upon a scapegoat)." Metaphorically speaking, a planned incongruity is akin to an exorcist driving out demons by "call[ing] them by names unsuited to the nature that the sufferer attributes to them." This "exorcism by misnomer," or reorientation by reclassification, comes from "violating the 'proprieties' of the word in its previous linkages." The sense of piety, the prevailing attitude of what properly goes with what, is disrupted by juxtaposing incongruous words to reveal "hitherto unsuspected connections." Thus, the casting out of devils is "largely a linguistic product" of "incongruous naming."[8]

Trickster's stereoscopic gaze, prompted by the circumstances of a crisis, is a creative exercise in attributing human qualities to otherwise demonized enemies to allow for self-critique from the assumed perspective of the Other. It is an oblique deflection of the dark force of projected evil rather than a direct confrontation—an indirect act of self-critique by perspective taking. The first gesture of this double articulation elevates the image of adversaries above the base level of sheer evil by attributing subjectivity to them and speculating on their motives from what is postulated to be their point of view, thereby imagining from a constructed vantage point how one's rival might interpret the matters in dispute. The second gesture is to speak of oneself critically from the postulated perspective of adversaries (and of allies and bystanders by extension) as a hedge against self-deception. It can be easier to speak indirectly and tentatively of one's own shortcomings through the imagined voice of another than to condemn oneself straightaway. The stereoscopic gaze serves to humanize the parties in conflict by elevating the image of the damned enough to lower the conceit of the self-righteous.

Out of this perspective-shifting process can emerge a glimpse of points of interdependency between rivals to complicate the frame of good versus evil. Perceiving differences in complementary relationship to one another (rather than treating differences as inherently opposite and antagonistic) allows room to maneuver out of a tight corner and to muddle through difficult circumstances less violently. "To *muddle through*," Burke observed, "is to be not over-exact, to let events shape themselves in part, to make up one's specific policies as one goes along, in accordance with the unforeseen newnesses that occur in the course of events, instead of approaching one's problem with an entire program laid out rigidly in advance. Is not this the ideal equipment of the diplomat?" he asks.[9] Unique circumstances mandate diverse tactics of perspective taking. Trickster at his best invents various ways to see stereoscopically the trap of polarizing caricatures and to adopt the more flexible attitude of the savvy diplomat.

Democratic Tricksters

Trickster's cleverness is not always a reliable ally of the democratic ethos.[10] As a case in point, the voice of contrition that emerged out of the oppression of Salem proved to be a democratically empty gesture. The stern piety of this community of saints exacerbated their struggle in the wilderness. It insisted that they remain true and pure disciples of the received Word against the dark forces of a fallen world. The devil lurked in their collective nightmares of temptation. He was the betrayer, the demon that rented and haunted the souls of the weak. He was the alien source of the torment that demoralized the people. He was not of them but was instead the impure difference that polluted and threatened to possess them. His imminence was manifested in the dark image of the Indian, the personification of evil savagery, as the tormented faithful struggled through their violent anxieties. The most vulnerable among them were the first to be accused of consorting with the Evil One, but the public drama of accusation and confession of witchcraft inevitably escalated up the ranks until persons of power could no longer escape its reach without the aid of a salvation device. Trickster suddenly appeared to extricate them from their predicament.

This shape-shifting trickster adopted the disguise of a victim. Resistance to the witch-hunt by the accused initially took the form of denial. They withdrew their forced confessions, affirmed their Christian faith, professed their innocence, and admonished their accusers. Neighbors and friends petitioned on their behalf. Religious authorities challenged the procedural validity of accusations. All of this was to no avail until the web of allegations eventually ensnared the rich and powerful, who then declared the community of saints to be victims of an evil deception. The witch-hunters subsequently confessed their error but without acknowledging any fault. Their communal mistake was not of their making; it came from a force external to them. They had been duped by the devil himself. The projected darkness would not be integrated into a revised self-conception. The boundaries of good and evil remained sharply drawn, rather than obliquely breached, by a sobered yet stubbornly righteous people.

Trickster's escape in Salem was accomplished by a sleight of hand—by donning the mask of the contrite victim of evil deception—which was a ruse that yielded no basic reorientation or added depth of perspective. Satan remained the unquestioned source of trouble in a savage landscape where the alien face of the Indian personified the Evil One. This was not a democratic gesture of appreciation for the interdependency of differences. It was cleverness in the service of self-deceit.

An element of reflexivity missing from this hermetic drama of victimization was an attribution of subjectivity to the figure of evil.[11] The disorientation caused by a perception of incongruity—in this case, between the presumption of communal righteousness and accusations of witchcraft leveled against eminent members of the community—was ritually resolved by proclaiming a satanic deception. This undifferentiated category of evil supplanted any impulse to soul searching. Evil was assigned no quality, thought, purpose, motive, or aspiration other than to destroy virtue. One could not adopt the perspective of this figure of utter evil in order to reflect constructively upon one's own errors and limitations because it had no human qualities with which to identify. Tituba the Indian was a mere cipher of this undifferentiated satanic force, a vehicle of evil savagery.

Other dangerous encounters with the devil figure since Salem have revealed a cultural potential for critical reflection by perspective taking. Unlike the sleight of hand performed in seventeenth-century Salem, trickster's intervention in the Cuban missile crisis of 1962 took the form of a perspective-shifting double gesture. The projected image of evil was deflected enough to recognize its dehumanizing trajectory and in time to avoid a potential nuclear conflagration. Glimpsing the humanity of the enemy enabled a fitful collaboration between adversaries across the divide of good and evil. It even allowed for a fleeting moment of self-critique. As Jung notes, trickster comes to consciousness in the midst of calamity and impending disaster.[12]

The Kennedy administration, like its post–World War II predecessors, was obsessed with Cold War demonology. The National Security Council Report 68 expressed the nation's security doctrine as a confrontation with Communism, the antithesis of America. The leaders of the Soviet Union were "evil men" who ruled a "slave state" and professed a "fanatic faith."[13] After the United States discovered the Soviets had placed nuclear missiles in nearby Cuba, Kennedy wondered aloud how the "demonologists" (i.e., US Kremlinologists) might account for such a provocation. The president announced to the nation that "offensive missile sites" had been discovered on "the imprisoned island" of Cuba, an act by an enemy he characterized as deceptive, provocative, reckless, and aggressive; this was a threat to peace that could not be appeased by US "surrender or submission."[14]

As Steven Goldzwig and George Dionisopoulos observe, Kennedy's initial public response, characterizing the Soviet adversary as a moral pariah, was an exercise in brinksmanship that backed him into a tight rhetorical corner.[15] From that point forward, coming to terms with the situation short of nuclear warfare was a halting process of loosening the grip of Cold War stereotypes.[16]

The Kennedy Tapes show that even as Kennedy postulated that Khrushchev was guided by some unknown purpose, Secretary of State Dean Rusk characterized the Soviet leader as obsessing over Berlin, as bluffing in Cuba, and as "completely hypocritical." If the United States did nothing in response, Rusk advised, the Soviets would conclude that they could bully the president. The only way to deal with a bully was to push back. General Curtis LeMay, the Air Force chief of staff, advocated direct military action because "if we don't do anything in Cuba, then they're going to push on Berlin and push *real hard* because they've got us *on the run*." Anything but a firm response would be like appeasement at Munich. Despite this kind of pressure, and with the assistance of Robert Kennedy, the president kept probing the question of his Soviet counterpart's motivation rather than just presuming he was demonic. The Soviet "viewpoint" was "a goddamn mystery" to Kennedy. He pressed his ad hoc Executive Committee to consider how a purposeful Khrushchev might perceive and react to various possible US responses. The president addressed his Soviet adversary in private correspondence during the crisis as a "sane man" and eventually settled on a working theory that Khrushchev was operating rationally from his own perspective, that he was a "son of a bitch" who nevertheless could be reasoned with, that he should be given a way out of the confrontation, "a chance to pull back," and that he was a man with whom a compromise could be reached. Kennedy even allowed himself to acknowledge that he may have sent false signals inadvertently on which the Soviets based their decision to send missiles to Cuba and that America's European allies would consider a nuclear war with the Soviet Union over a few missiles in Cuba, which Kennedy acknowledged did not alter the balance of power, to be a "mad act" by the United States.[17]

Thus, rather than representing his Soviet adversary as demonically obsessed, manipulative, or hypocritical, Kennedy postulated that Khrushchev had acted cautiously and sanely with purpose and reason from some unknown perspective. Opening a space to speculate on the motive of an enemy allowed for consideration of what American miscues may have contributed to a Soviet miscalculation, how the Soviet leader might interpret US countermeasures, and whether there was a possibility of diplomacy short of appeasement. It enabled Kennedy to see the US position through Soviet eyes, or at least to suppose what their point of view might entail, and also to postulate from the presumed standpoint of America's European allies the insanity of risking nuclear war over inconsequential missiles. Within this speculative space, Kennedy could craft messages to his Soviet counterpart, which enabled a transaction of competing perspectives and ended in the coordination of plausibly coexisting narratives over whether the missiles were to be perceived as offensive or defensive in nature. A wider framework of interpretation allowed for an elevation of the image of the Soviet enemy above the level of sheer evil and a corresponding moderation of US pretensions, albeit slightly and tentatively.

Trickster's maneuver, in this instance, was to reveal a human subjectivity behind the mask of the demon and thus to insinuate an alternative rationality. Rendering an adversary purposeful and sane opens the possibility of one's own fallibility and contribution to the crisis at hand. It is an indirect act of self-critique advanced hypothetically as an exercise in role-playing. The oblique angle of the critique works a glancing blow to the ego, which nudges rather than confronts the self-image in order to slip through its defensive perimeter. How far it penetrates is another matter. Trickster's stereoscopic gaze is a tactical adjustment in a given situation to make a rigid perspective momentarily flexible. It glimpses, through cracks in the partition between self and other, a fleeting image of a common humanity. This stereoscopic troubling of monocular stereotypes occurs in an instant of opportunity. It is selective rather than comprehensive, temporary rather than permanent, situational rather than universal, and adaptive rather than transformative.

The trickster figure of Martin Luther King Jr.'s "Beyond Vietnam" penetrated more deeply into America's self-identity, challenging the nation's capacity for self-examination by questioning its democratic integrity.[18] King's call to conscience exposed the evil of racism hidden behind the bellicose façade of patriotism. The searing irony of oppressed black Americans being drafted in disproportionate numbers to kill (and to be killed by) a subjugated Vietnamese people disrupted the exceptionalist narrative of a democratic America battling the scourge of Communism. Trickster stripped away the veneer of patriotism to reveal the chauvinistic core of a racist war. Outwardly projected evil was reflected back to its point of origin, evoking a vexing image of America gone mad on war against poor people of color at home and abroad.

The Reverend King's penetrating gaze portrayed America, seen through Vietnamese eyes, as a strange liberator: a violent oppressor and exploiter with a poisoned spirit. Speaking from the vantage point of a world citizen, he pointed to the tripartite malady of racism, materialism, and militarism residing in the nation's soul, which put America on the wrong side of world revolution. Communism was a judgment against America's failure to make democracy real. King's trope of undemocratic oppression bespoke a demon within that contaminated the nation's self-image. Atonement for the sin of Vietnam required an admission of error and a reformed democratic spirit. This was a moral vision of compassion, fellowship, and brotherhood that reached beyond the boundaries of the nation.

The directness of King's frank critique made it hard to ignore but impossible to assimilate, at least in the short run. His prophetic eloquence lifted to the surface an inconvenient, yet culturally embedded, egalitarian ethic. He articulated a facet of the nation's ethos that was at odds with its actual conduct, a troublesome image that could not be erased entirely from public memory. His dissent not only tried the nation's capacity for critical reflection but also tested the limit of willfully denying one's own demons. To hear King's lament was to risk pondering the darkness of an impending spiritual death. Yet, not to hear it was to discount the nation's democratic integrity.

After a brief period of post-Vietnam malaise, the nation struggled to stifle the internal demons evoked by the war. The taint of wickedness was duly shifted back onto the image of America's Cold War enemy (the evil empire of Ronald Reagan's political theater) until the Soviet Union disintegrated. The United States then set out to kick the Vietnam syndrome for good (in the words of President George H. W. Bush) by dislodging Saddam Hussein from Kuwait and, after 9/11, (under the leadership of the second President Bush) by fighting a global war on terror. The outward projection of evil was never more absolute or explicit than in George W. Bush's vengeful rhetoric. The evangelical temper of his crusade against evildoers resonated with the religious fundamentalism of the Christian right, galvanizing a base of political support for a war of national redemption.

The religious investment of Bush's war rhetoric prompted its own kind of dissent. An evangelical trickster by the name of Jim Wallis appeared on the scene to trouble America's Christian conscience with the beatitude of peacemaking. He was a high-profile evangelical leader of the nation's progressive peace movement who spoke in the prophetic voice of healing and reconciliation to call to account the messianic militancy of the religious right.[19] He depicted the Manichaean heresy of good versus evil as bad theology and invoked the wider perspective of a worldwide church to critique the narrow nationalist religion of imperial warfare. He called on American Christians to break the cycle of demonizing rhetoric and to look for the devil in the darkness of their own souls so that, with the benefit of humility and compassion, they might reflect upon the interdependency of humankind in a world unsettled by social and economic injustice. This was the double optic of a transnational Christianity that contested the religious authority of jingoism. Wallis engaged God talk faithfully to dissociate the dehumanizing mindset of war from the moral sway of Christianity.

Wallis's prophetic call for an attitude of humility against the arrogance of redemptive violence confounded the Manichean division of good and evil by channeling the cultural value of modesty over vanity. It was a leveling gesture of acknowledging one's own fallibility. Peering downward into the darkness of America's soul lowered the angle of the outward gaze. Perceived from an equal rather than superior attitude, the face of projected evil appeared less alien and more human. To recognize the Other's subjectivity was to encounter a shared fate, to grasp the common plight of terrorism feeding on human poverty and social injustice, to see the shadow of rapacious greed in the image of a distressed world.

"There are dark places within us and our nation," Wallis observed, that we must muster the courage to confront and heal if we are not to "become the evil we loathe in our response" to the "evil we saw on Sept. 11." Terrorism, he insisted, is an evil of "perverted religious fundamentalism." It is an "ideological and fanatical force" that reaches for "regional and global power," rejects "the values of liberty, equality, democracy, and human rights," and is fueled by "grinding and dehumanizing poverty, hopelessness, and desperation." To respond to terrorism in kind is to play the "blame game." To respond to terrorism constructively is to look at the nation's "own sins" and to engage in a collective act of "genuine soul searching." To be "on God's side, rather than the other way around," is to find the courage to "drain the swamps of injustice that breed the mosquitoes of terror."[20]

The ironic similitude of two fundamentalisms cut to the quick of the matter. With evangelical license, Wallis associated the evil of terrorism with the vengefulness of fundamentalism, dissociated such violent rancor from the values of freedom, democracy, and human rights, and suggested a perverse symmetry of self-righteousness between fundamentalist rivals who blamed each other for the ensuing slaughter. Seeing this symmetry of competing fundamentalisms was tantamount to glimpsing the demon in the mirror. An inner darkness was reflected in the external visage of a reviled enemy, affording an opportunity to acknowledge the discomfiting likeness. Trickster's mirror cautioned the nation not to succumb to its fundamentalist inclination.

Besides warning against secular and religious fundamentalism, Wallis advanced an affirmative image in *God's Politics*. His best-selling book, published during the bloody occupation of Iraq, argued for a positive contribution of Christian values to political life. The Jesus Wallis revered was neither prorich nor prowar. This Jesus stood for healing and reconciliation. He was a reminder of "the people our politics always neglects—the poor, the vulnerable, the left behind." Wallis's prophetic vision of God's politics challenged the pursuit of "narrow national, ethnic, economic, or cultural self-interest" in a "wider world" of "human diversity." Made in the image of the creator, this world of rich diversity required good stewardship rather than exploitation, which meant resolving inevitable conflicts without resorting to war. Humility, reflection, compassion, and accountability in an "era aflame with war"—instead of closed-minded, polarizing partisanship, retribution, vengeance, and violence—was "the gospel vocation of peacemaking" that Wallis proclaimed as the moral purpose of bringing faith into "the public square" to exert a "presumption against war."[21]

Wallis's prophetic vision was "good theology" resisting the "bad theology" of President Bush's demonizing rhetoric. Bush's Manichean heresy misrepresented the ubiquity of evil in human affairs, falsely locating it exclusively "out there" without acknowledging its presence "in here." Denying the "deeply human" nature of evil, which was "embedded in our own attitudes, behaviors, and policies" as well as those of our adversaries, "[led] to dangerous foreign policy."[22] Evil existed on both sides of the equation.

Wallis's evangelical trickster evoked a potential for constructive "self-criticism and even repentance" by reminding Americans that Christianity was a world religion. Recognizing that the religious community was an "international community and not just an American one," he insisted, was good reason to "*listen to the different perceptions of Sept. 11 around the world.*" Minimally, Americans should consider "what other Christians around the world think about what the United States does." Prompting a transnational viewpoint, by way of the trope of the Sacrament, was a consciousness-raising maneuver to transcend the narrow attitude of imperial ambition. Thus, Wallis invited Americans to abandon their "easy certainty" and false "national theology of war" by taking communion with the "international body of Christ" and thereby to affirm the "global view of God's world." Confusing God's purpose with "the mission of American empire," he allowed, was "theologically presumptuous," "dangerously messianic," and "bordering on the idolatrous and blasphemous."[23]

The first loyalty of Christians living in a troubled world was to reject as false teaching the demonizing of enemies and to affirm the principal vocation of peacemaking.[24] From the Christian perspective on human nature and sin, Wallis observed, power corrupts everyone, and no one can be trusted to dominate others at home or abroad, but the image of God exists in every person, including one's enemy. Humility rather than self-righteousness was the spiritually appropriate trait of peacemakers; working for peace entailed working for social and economic justice while mobilizing international law enforcement, not invading armies, against the immediate threat of terrorists. Doing the right thing was doing the practical thing. Raising the nation's regard for the common good and respecting the humanity of others, as seen from the larger Christian perspective instead of the narrower nationalist religion of imperial warfare, allowed for a kind of "paradigm shift" from a Manichean rhetoric of evil to a pragmatic and ethical regard for the interdependency of humankind, including those who were recruited to terrorism out of desperation. Both the practical matter of increasing national and global security and the moral matter of adhering to the nation's deepest values were best served by ministering to the plight of the poor rather than succumbing to the arrogance of empire. President Bush, who symbolized the national myopia, was not the devil incarnate but, as Wallis allowed, a man of faith with a messianic vision, a man who had lost his way for lack of the broader and deeper perspective that comes from good theology.[25]

Wallis's trickster, like Kennedy's, attempted to finesse the demonology of war by raising the humanizing question of motivation to elevate the image of the adversary above a base level of sheer evil where no explanation other than inherent wickedness existed. Introducing the question of why prompted a discourse of perspective and an attitude of critical reflection— of looking back at one's own position from the imagined vantage point of others. While Kennedy expanded his vision by considering how allies and enemies might view the issues and weigh the mad consequences of his actions, Wallis sought a transnational perspective by repositioning Christian Americans via the trope of the Sacrament into a worldwide body of shared beliefs and interdependent aspirations.

Wallis, Kennedy, and King exposed in separate trickster moments an underutilized and underdeveloped cultural resource for slipping out of the trap of the devil myth. They adopted a stereoscopic gaze to reveal crosscutting ties that confounded outward projections of evil. Each proffered a humanizing gesture that attributed purpose to others to allow for self-critique and to turn from a position of alienation toward an attitude of interdependency.

The Limit of the Democratic Trickster

Barack Obama, in yet another trickster moment, revealed both the potential and the limitation of the democratic trickster when he briefly shifted the rhetorical trajectory away from the messianic figure of moral opposites and toward an image of the interdependency of differences. In the presidential election cycle of 2008, candidate Obama offered a vision of hope and change to a nation wearied of a global war on terror stalemated in Iraq and languishing in Afghanistan. He embarked on a campaign to change the "mindset" that had produced the now-unwanted war in Iraq.[26] His campaign featured the democratizing metaphor of partnership. This image of collaboration, rather than debunking or abandoning the myth of US exceptionalism and national mission, imbued an otherwise chauvinistic myth with a democratic spirit.[27] The heroic story of moral conquest over evil became in Obama's revised version a shared project and common quest for social justice. If not entirely devoid of evildoers, this democratized image of

American exceptionalism rendered terrorism a sign of the nation's neglected responsibilities in a challenged world.

The leveling gaze of Obama's perspective-taking rhetoric was evident in his trope of partnership. The nation could fulfill its purpose and pursue its dream in today's interdependent world, "not in the spirit of the patron, but the spirit of a partner—a partner that is mindful of its own imperfections" and that "recogniz[es] the inherent equality and worth of all people."[28] Collaborating, instead of acting unilaterally, he insisted, "forces us to listen to other points of view."[29] Toward this end, Obama would restore America's largely dormant democratic ideals and values. Partnership was expressed in the renewed democratic idiom of cooperation, discussion, negotiation, openness, transparency, civil society, community, human rights, rule of law, freedom of the press, bridging differences, and respecting diversity.[30]

Accordingly, Obama called for "finding a convergence of interests" and "solving problems as opposed to imposing doctrine."[31] Things get done, he insisted, by "bridging differences" rather than by "stand[ing] above the rest of the world."[32] He would "meet not just with our friends, but with our enemies."[33] This was not unlike the attitude he expressed in his speech on race after his former pastor, Jeremiah Wright, spoke out against the racial injustices of white America and its racist foreign policy.[34] Conjuring a spell of empathy, Obama reflected thoughtfully on solving the challenges of the times "together"; himself a mixture of black and white, Obama empathized with both black and white anger, which he described in some detail from each of their separate perspectives.[35] Likewise, achieving a "sustainable democracy" to defeat terrorism's message of hate required "global cooperation" based on mutual understanding in order to reduce poverty, promote education and health care, strengthen civil society, and develop representative governments.[36] By "promoting democracy" abroad, working "in concert" with allies, and engaging enemies in "direct talks," the United States would "mobilize the international community" to secure a just and peaceful future; democratic leadership was an exercise in perspective to "see around the corners" in anticipation of the challenges of the new century.[37]

The rhetorical import of this perspective-taking stance, within the context of the campaign, was to democratize rather than abandon the framing myth of US exceptionalism. It was trickster's gesture to hybridity by a man who represented himself as half black and half white—not as all black because he was part black, and not as black versus white.[38] This hybrid Obama would adjust (that is, augment rather than abandon) the mythic frame without losing the benefit of its mandate. America, he maintained, remained the "last, best hope of Earth." He would renew this "great promise and historic purpose" in a more democratically inflected myth of national mission to "reflect the decency and aspirations of the American people." His was at least a plausible articulation of change under the circumstances and within the cultural constraints of the dominant myth. He embedded a democratic appreciation for diversity in the story of mission to advance a revised vision, which drew from the past without being bound to "outdated thinking."[39] In this way, he tapped into what Cornel West termed America's "deep democratic tradition" of "justice and deeds of compassion" to turn the old story of moral conquest into a new expression of egalitarian hope.[40]

This democratizing turn on a traditionally messianic narrative of fighting foreign devils was remarkable for its use of the metaphor of partnership as a culturally legible expression of global interdependence. The language of partnership evoked a potentially transformative theme of collaboration, a theme based on a tacit image of complementary relations among differences, of the value of multiplicity over singularity. The presently "flawed" system of "free markets and liberal democracy," Obama insisted, was subject to "change and improvement" by moving it toward "greater equity, justice, and prosperity," thus serving "both our interests and the interests of a struggling world." To see the mutual benefit of a more equitable system, Americans would have to "look in the mirror" at a reflection of their harmful and self-serving foreign policies; they would have to improve their own example and perfect their own democracy to face up to pressing global challenges that could be met only by collaborating with others.[41] Partnership was a metaphor for the practicality of working cooperatively on the global scene to promote peace and security by augmenting social justice.

The metaphor's potential to transform an exceptionalist culture of redemptive violence into a more collaborative and less domineering mindset hinged on the kind of partnership envisioned, that is, whether a relatively egalitarian relationship was imagined in which differences complemented one another to the mutual advantage and for the joint empowerment of the partners. A shift of emphasis from subordination to coordination of differences would ground the logic of the situation on the premise of the whole being greater than its parts. Placing different parts in synergic relationship would underscore their interdependency while diversifying measures of worth and multiplying indices of importance. Although never fully realized, the pure or ideal form of a complementary partnership would put into play a multiplicity of valued qualities, each conditioned by and contingent upon the others, none absolutely superior or inferior, and all reliant in various ways for their own attainment on the fulfillment of the others. No single order of value (nationality, wealth, race, religion, or any other criterion of privilege) would place one party at the bottom of an upward progression or privilege another party at the expense of those below. Rather than abandoned, the principle of hierarchy would be deepened and broadened to accommodate the interplay of various orders of ideas, values, and interests.

Once seen, the devil in the mirror might be retrieved in the name of a revitalized democracy. Relations of power might be reimagined as hierarchies of equality, that is, as democratized hierarchies in which partnerships of mutually beneficial interdependencies are formed among parties with otherwise distinct and conflicted interests.[42] While the exceptionalist mindset of America's moral and material superiority draws on a thin conception of democracy to justify and perpetuate warfare against an evil enemy, a revival of the nation's dormant democratic ethos would prompt a perception of interdependency and an attitude of collaboration that acknowledges the nation's shortcomings. A strong sense of democracy is neither heroic nor radically individualistic in its commitment to equality and community. It does not contemplate a Manichean division between absolute good and utter evil. It is a comingling of competing political interests—an agonistic struggle of intersecting and diverging aspirations and aptitudes—that is not reducible to abject alienation and sheer antagonism. Thus, democracy expressed in the language of partnership might serve as a culturally evocative vehicle for pulling back from the rhetorical projection of evil in a messianic war on terror.

To retrieve the image of the devil in this way, however, would be to reach the limit of trickster's role, which is to befuddle the war-making culture short of actually transforming it. Juxtaposing the nation's latent democratic ethos with its compulsive sense of mission is an act of "egocide," which fractures the national identity.[43] It releases vital energy in an ironic turn that breaks up the unity of the exceptionalist national self, a unity that can exist only by treating democracy as a symbol emptied of political import. Trickster's ironic twist (the irony of dominating the world in the name of democracy, of patronizing instead of partnering) liberates the energy of the petrified exceptionalist myth. Yet, irony is not a trope of integration that reconciles opposites to reconstruct fractured identities. The ironic trickster is a necessary but insufficient agent of change. It is a trickster figure that can trouble an old vision by pointing to its contradictions, but a new vision must come from elsewhere. The mythic energy released by trickster's retrieval of projected evil either will be integrated into a revised conception of the national self or it will be projected anew onto yet another scapegoat.

Trickster's ironic maneuver, as a precursor to potential change, is an opening to acknowledge the devil within. Yet, while the projected devil might be retrieved via the vehicle of democracy, democracy itself is readily demonized when taken more seriously than a legitimizing gesture emptied of political import. An abiding distrust of strong democracy lurks within the nation's collective self—distrust so intense and exaggerated that it amounts to a political phobia. The mythic force of this "demophobia" compels the nation to contain the demos as if it were a dangerous demon.[44] Fear of strong democracy is foundational to the US Constitution and the republic it forms. In Robert Dahl's words, "A substantial number of the Framers believed that they must erect constitutional barriers to popular rule because the people would prove to be an unruly mob, a standing danger to law, to orderly government, and to property rights."[45] Thus, restoring an uneasy democratic tradition to reform a belligerent attitude of national mission and to arrest sanctimonious projections of the nation's internal demons presents a difficult challenge. Speaking up for democracy, other than in some thin and contained version, is readily perceived as a dangerously radical gesture.

The difficulty of transcending the demonology of US war culture by means of a democratizing metaphor was illustrated in the rhetorical trajectory of Obama's presidency. His guiding metaphor of partnership started well but foundered for want of a transcendent image with which to integrate a fractured national identity. The war culture was so ingrained, the messianic myth of American exceptionalism so strong, and the legacy of Manichean moralizing so intense that the most any trickster might achieve was to reveal the struggle facing the nation and point to the possibility of reforming itself.

During the early months of Obama's presidency, the spirit of positive change appeared strong and abiding when he traveled to Cairo to speak of peace and reconciliation to the Muslim world. "Assalaamu alaykum," peace be upon you, he began. He was both Christian ("I'm a Christian") and Muslim ("but my father came from a Kenyan family that includes generations of Muslims") in his devotion to respecting differences of perspective and resisting stereotypes in the search for common ground. He was "an African American with the name Barack Hussein Obama elected President" of the United States. Instead of appropriating religion to a rhetorical invocation of evil in a ritual of redemptive violence, the new president conjured a religious vision of a common humanity living in an interdependent world. He acknowledged the deep historical roots of the present tension between the United States and Islam but invoked a healing image of peacemaking. "So long as our relationship is defined by our differences, we will empower those who sow hatred rather than peace, those who promote conflict rather than the cooperation that can help all of our people achieve justice and prosperity," Obama observed. "God's vision," he professed, was that "the people of the world can live together in peace," and thus that "our work here on Earth" is to attain "God's peace." By working together, guided by the sacred command to "do unto others as we would have them do unto us," the people of all religions "have the power to make the world we seek." The world's problems can only be solved "through partnership." Indeed, "progress must be shared," he insisted, because the reality of "our interdependence" dictates against "any world order that elevates one nation or group of people over another."[46]

In this spirit, Obama called upon the Muslim world to partner with the United States to confront together the multiple tensions haunting humankind and preventing the realization of a true and just peace. There was important work to be done in partnership on each of six issues: violent extremism, Israel and Palestine, Iran and nuclear weapons, democracy, women's rights, and economic development.

On the matter of violent extremism, the United States was not at war with Islam. The word "terrorism" was never mentioned. All faiths, Obama insisted, reject the killing of innocent people. Thus, the United States partnered with a coalition of forty-six nations to target al-Qaeda in Afghanistan after nearly three thousand American civilians were ruthlessly murdered on 9/11. Al-Qaeda had killed innocent people of different faiths, including Muslims, in violation of the teaching of the Holy Koran. The United States would promote peace not just by combating al-Qaeda but also, in a spirit of partnership with Pakistan and Afghanistan, by committing billions of dollars to build schools, hospitals, and roads and to develop the economy. The United States had learned from its experience in Iraq that it must rely less on military power and more on diplomacy to build international consensus and resolve problems. America had learned, too, that to remain true to its principles it must abandon the use of torture. The United States would defend itself in partnership with the Muslim world.

The violent stalemate over a Palestinian homeland between two peoples with legitimate aspirations would never end until their conflict was seen from both perspectives. America would work with all sides to pursue peace. Similarly, the United States was ready to put aside a tumultuous history with Iran, to move forward in mutual respect on resolving the issue of nuclear weapons. The United States would also work to realize the promise of democracy throughout the world without imposing it on anyone. Religious diversity and freedom, along with all human rights, would be upheld as critical to the ability of peoples to live together. Respecting women's rights in the United States as well as Islam was key to advancing the world's prosperity. Educational exchange, business partnerships, scientific collaborations, and technology exchanges would deepen ties between the United States and the Muslim world to create new opportunities in a global economy. "All these things must be done in partnership," Obama concluded. "Americans are ready to join with citizens and governments, community organizations, religious leaders, and businesses in Muslim communities around the world to help our people pursue a better life" because "we can only achieve it together."[47]

Six months later, however, before the end of the first year of Obama's presidency, his ambivalence over the purpose of partnership—whether it was an instrument for building peace or making war—was indicated and largely resolved in two speeches given within nine days of each other in distinctly different settings. On December 1, 2009, in a televised address from West Point, he announced a military surge in Afghanistan. On December 10, in Oslo, he accepted the Nobel Peace Prize. In these speeches, his rhetorical posture was outwardly less militant than his predecessor's attitude of redemptive violence, but he fell short of his earlier commitment to transcend the mindset of war, at least in the foreseeable future. In the name of realism over idealism, the exceptionalist, even patronizing attitude of standing true to America's sacred mission overshadowed any expression of a democratic impulse to build a global partnership for true peace. Evil, in the image of an external enemy, still compelled the nation to win a final victory over terrorists.

At West Point, speaking to a divided nation in the presence of an assembled Corps of Cadets, the new president responded ambiguously to the old question of war or peace. He would move forward, ultimately toward a promised peace, by surging immediately the number of US combat troops in Afghanistan. The strategy was to increase the size of the US fighting force in order to end, over the next several years, America's direct participation in an ongoing war in Afghanistan. Rather than changing the basic mindset of war, Obama opted for a slow transition—a prolonged exit—from one theater of the war on terror. His rhetorical posture was sufficiently ambiguous to worry war supporters that he was insufficiently committed to stay the course and to upset peace advocates who wished to end the war.[48] Even though the president affirmed that "our nation is at war," former vice president Dick Cheney insisted that Obama's "dithering" projected weakness to the nation's enemies.[49] Tom Engelhardt, on the other hand, was one voice among those on the political left convinced that George Bush's war had become Barack Obama's war.[50]

The president's trope of partnership lost its trickster edge at West Point. It became more an image of collaborating with allies against a common enemy than working democratically toward a just peace in an interdependent world. The prospect of peace was at best obscured and deferred. Even if, according to reporter Ewen MacAskill, Obama did not want to be known as a "war president," Phyllis Bennis, a journalist specializing in US foreign policy and Middle East issues, was convinced that his actions in Afghanistan could not be portrayed in any way as a "commitment to global peace."[51]

The wavering image of partnership in the West Point speech did include a reference to breaking the cycle of war in an interdependent world. Military might alone would not be sufficient to realize a lasting peace. The nation needed to use diplomacy "because no one nation can meet the challenges of an interconnected world acting alone." A "new partnership" with the Muslim world must be forged, a relationship that "recognizes our mutual interest in breaking a cycle of conflict, and that promises a future in which those who kill innocents are isolated by those who stand up for peace and prosperity and human dignity."[52] This, however, was the last of twelve references to partnership in the speech.

The preceding eleven references to partnership were all about prosecuting the war: (1) The US military needed to "train and partner with Afghan security forces." (2) The president had consulted with America's "key partners" in his review of military strategy in Afghanistan. (3) The United States "must increase the stability and capacity of our partners in the region." (4) The thirty thousand additional troops would "partner" with Afghan security forces. (5) The United States would work with its coalition "partners" to "combat corruption" in Afghanistan. (6, 7) Obama would "seek a partnership with Afghanistan" and "forge a lasting friendship in which America is your [Afghanistan's] partner, and never your patron." (8) Success in Afghanistan was "inextricably linked" to America's "partnership with Pakistan." (9) The United States was "committed to a partnership with Pakistan." (10) A core element of the president's war strategy was "an effective partnership with Pakistan" to target terrorists. (11) "Where al Qaeda and its allies attempt to establish a foothold—whether in Somalia or Yemen or elsewhere—they must be confronted by growing pressure and strong partnerships."[53]

While the occasion of accepting the Nobel Peace Prize invited a less martial image of partnership, one of working collaboratively and nonviolently toward a just peace, the president deferred to the doctrine of just war. The concept of just war had emerged over the turbulent course of human history, he began, to "control the violence" and "regulate the destructive power of war." After the terrible destruction of World War II, America had taken a lead in "constructing an architecture to keep the peace: a Marshall Plan and a United Nations, mechanisms to govern the waging of war, treaties to protect human rights, prevent genocide, restrict the most dangerous weapons." But this "old architecture" was now "buckling under the weight of new threats." In reality, Obama proclaimed, violent conflict will not be eradicated "in our lifetimes" and nations will continue to find a re-sort to force "not only necessary but morally justified." The president un-derstood "the moral force of non-violence," but as the head of state "sworn to protect and defend [his] nation," he must "face the world as it is." War was necessary because "evil does exist in the world." The strength of America's arms and the blood of its citizens was the source of global security. Al-though tragic and never glorious, war is required to preserve the peace. Rather than hoping for a change of human nature, the world must direct its efforts toward "a gradual evolution in human institutions" through which international standards will develop to "govern the use of force."[54] War must be shaped into a better instrument of peace.

When the president turned next to the question of how to "build a just and lasting peace," he spoke of using strong sanctions to hold nations ac-countable when they "break rules and laws." He talked of upholding hu-man rights, without which "peace is a hollow promise." Only when the world becomes free and democratic, he suggested, would true peace some-day emerge. A just peace must be premised on economic security and op-portunity. The continuing quest for peace also requires an "expansion of our moral imagination" to cope with the "dizzying pace of globalization" and the "warped view of religion" that has allowed extremists to "kill in the name of God." Only by keeping faith in religion's "law of love," as the North Star of human progress, can humanity hope for "the world that ought to be." We should continue to dream even as we acknowledge in the "here and now" the reality of war: "Clear-eyed, we can understand that there will be war, and still strive for peace." As Robert Terrill has observed, Obama's Nobel Peace Prize address articulated an "unstable symbiosis" of "power and reason, realism and idealism, might and right" to envision a world in deli-cate balance.[55]

Yet, nowhere in the president's Nobel Peace Prize speech did the word "partnership" occur. The negative image of just war ultimately overshadowed the positive dream of a just peace. The dark presence of evil mandated the choice of violence over nonviolence and displaced a peace-building commit-ment in the here and now. All references to working together—which re-duced to the language of "agreements among nations"—were to the United States acting with "leaders and soldiers of NATO countries, and other friends and allies" to "secure the peace" through the necessary and proper use of force: "only when the world stands together as one" behind strong sanctions and armed intervention can it hope to hold rogue regimes ac-countable. America, as "the world's sole military superpower" and "standard bearer in the conduct of war," has "borne this burden" of world leadership out of "enlightened self interest" in the service of "freedom and prosperity."

While "America alone cannot secure the peace," America "will always be a voice for those aspirations that are universal."[56] Thus, American exceptionalism assumed the face, if not of the avenging angel, of the redeemer nation faithfully battling the reality of evil in order to bring about the eventual salvation of a fallen world. Even in Oslo, there was no room for a peacebuilding image of partnership. Trickster's moment had expired.[57]

War culture prevailed. The president affirmed that the Nobel Peace Prize was a symbol of "our highest aspirations" to "bend history in the direction of justice." Toward this end, he assumed the title "Commander in Chief" of a nation "at war" and made "just war" the measure of his actions. In defending his nation against the evil of terrorism, he would remain true to the rules of just war by prohibiting torture and affirming the Geneva Conventions. Peace was to be pursued through purified "instruments of war." From this heroic standpoint, the source of injustice was fully externalized. The American Proviso to the just-war doctrine—the presumption, in Stephen Carter's words, that "it is not possible to wage just war against the United States"—rendered the war on terror and its methods ostensibly ethical.[58] There was no mirror in which to glimpse the reflection of projected evil, let alone a democratic wish to reconcile the nation's dark side with its idealized self-image. The myth of exceptionalism, of America's unique virtue, justified and even demanded an imperial attitude of domination so that good might triumph over evil.[59]

Obama's presidential mantra, from West Point onward, was "to disrupt, dismantle, and ultimately defeat al-Qa'ida." His call to arms named the enemy precisely but in a way that widened rather than narrowed the sphere of war. In endorsing this counterterrorism strategy, the president observed that: "Despite our successes, we continue to face a significant terrorist threat from al-Qa'ida, its affiliates, and its adherents. Our terrorist adversaries have shown themselves to be agile and adaptive; defeating them requires that we develop and pursue a strategy that is even more agile and adaptive. To defeat al-Qa'ida, we must define with precision and clarity who we are fighting, setting concrete and realistic goals tailored to the specific challenges we face in different regions of the world." This was his policy, he insisted, since the day he took office. No lingering memory of Cairo qualified his "unrelenting focus on the task at hand."[60]

Partnership, now an instrument in the president's counterterrorism strategy, reduced to a term for forging new alliances in an ever-expanding war on terrorism. The "core" of al-Qaeda was located in Afghanistan and Pakistan, but the threat was shifting toward the "periphery," that is, wherever al-Qaeda "affiliates" and "adherents" might be found. The term "adherents," in particular, globalized the sphere of war. It meant nothing less than "individuals who have formed collaborative relationships with, act on behalf of, or are otherwise inspired to take action in furtherance of the goals of al-Qa'ida—the organization and the ideology—including by engaging in violence regardless of whether such violence is targeted at the United States, its citizens, or its interests." Affiliated movements had "taken root" in "the Middle East, East Africa, the Maghreb and Sahel regions of northwest Africa, Central Asia, and Southeast Asia." This was an "evolving threat" from groups and individuals inspired by the ideology, even without giving allegiance to the organization, of al-Qaeda. Its reach was global, from narcotics traffickers to Hizballah, Hamas, and FARC (the Revolutionary Armed Forces of Colombia) to individuals engaged in domestic terrorism against the US Homeland. It was a global threat that would "persist."[61]

Thus, the discourse of the Obama presidency did not break out of the "war on terror" mindset.[62] As Corinna Mullin has observed, the legacy of the George W. Bush presidency was affirmed in a discourse that, while somewhat more nuanced and less overtly Manichean, continued to oppose US identity to an evil Islamist Other. America remained a beacon of democracy, reason, and progress. Islamist movements were still viewed within a counterterrorism and national security framework that conflated all forms of terrorism in various parts of the world. Just as the basic paradigm of the war-on-terror discourse was sustained, "very few concrete changes" took place in the Obama administration "at the policy level." No incentive existed to reflect upon how past actions of the United States or the West in general had contributed to current motivations for terrorist activities. The enemy was reduced still to an image of irrational, backward, and violent religious fanatics. A barbarian foe confronted a noble, rational, humane, and civilized America. The deliberate cruelty of "their" violence was contrasted with the restrained and unfortunate necessity of "our" violence. All of this, Mullin concludes, distorted and exaggerated the nature and severity of the threat posed by Islamist "extremists" to the security and interests of a self-proclaimed enlightened United States.[63]

This rhetorical stance of American exceptionalism, uninhibited by a strong democratic imaginary, persisted in Obama's reelection campaign. The presidential debates, when they touched on matters of foreign policy, rehearsed the theme of national innocence and virtue. The first debate was devoted to domestic policy. In the second debate, the president marked as a major achievement that he had "gone after Al Qaeda's leadership like never before": "Osama bin Laden is dead." In reference to the recent attack on the US embassy in Libya, he drew upon the language of his predecessor to insist that "we are going to find out who did this and we're going to hunt them down, because one of the things I've said throughout my presidency is when folks mess with Americans, we go after them." Mitt Romney's only challenge was to accuse the president of failing to label the assault on the US embassy a terrorist attack, which Romney took as a sign of a Middle East policy that was "unraveling" for lack of a sufficiently supportive stance on Israel or adequate determination to defeat terrorism. Obama had begun his administration with an "apology tour" of the Middle East, according to Romney, and had been "leading from behind" ever since.[64]

These themes carried over to the third and final debate, which was supposed to feature foreign policy. The "enormous threat" of "radical violent extremism" was on the rise, Romney insisted. Terrorism certainly was not "on the run" or "hiding." Al Qaeda's core leadership had been "decimated," Obama replied. Romney insisted that his strategy, too, was to "go after the bad guys . . . to kill them, to take them out of the picture." Rebuking Romney for campaign inconsistencies on foreign policy issues, Obama said he had learned as commander in chief that you have to be clear to allies and enemies where you stand in order to advance an effective counterterrorism strategy. Romney seemed content to adopt, without acknowledgment, Obama's foreign policy as his own, and Obama was quick to point out that Romney did not have any "different ideas." Romney would spend more on the military to insure that America could fulfill its responsibility to defend freedom and promote the principles of peace around the world. "America remains the one indispensible nation," Obama replied. "As Commander in Chief," the president concluded, "I will maintain the strongest military in the world, keep faith with our troops and go after those who would do us harm."[65]

A discourse of continuity prevailed over change. War culture, once again, was sustained. The "blood pact with the devil," in Jung's words, is never lost.[66] We can only hope to manage it through the integrative function of a developed consciousness.

The Trickster Myth

Disruption, irony, ambivalence, shape shifting, perspective taking, reflecting: these are the ways of trickster to destabilize cultural orthodoxies. Tricksters exploit cracks in the foundational myths of a people. They are unwelcome but necessary agents of change in times of trial and tribulation—an unappreciated resource for revising the national imaginary. As they twist and turn the truisms of national identity to make the familiar appear strange, they hold up a mirror in which to see the reflection of the unwanted Other.

The trickster myth is counterpoint to the devil myth of US war culture.

It exploits the tension subsumed under the sign of democracy, exposing the projection of evil to the possibility of critical reflection and expanded consciousness. The virtue of an exceptional people is invested in a democratic prospect that is desired but distrusted, coveted but postponed. Democracy is both sacred and profane in a fallen world, vulnerable to domestic corruption and foreign threat, and thus subject to protective containment. Tricksters maneuver on this unsettled cultural terrain.

The nation's ambivalence toward democracy is the trickster's opportunity, short of transforming war culture, to expose the devil within. The contradiction between democratic values and the mindset of war can be accentuated, but irony in and of itself does not integrate a fractured identity into a democratic ethos. Reflecting critically on US war culture is akin to Prometheus stealing fire from Zeus for humans to use. Taking a democratic perspective to critique US war culture disturbs the sanctity of the political order. It is an impious act that violates the conventional wisdom of the republic.

A powerful force is released when demonized images of foreign enemies are recognized as projections of democratic anxieties. It is a disconcerting force that must be reconciled. If the unveiled image of the devil cannot be integrated into a transformed national identity, the shock of recognition will expend its force in hostile projections. The special calling of an exceptional people is an untenable national identity that struggles to sustain its pristine self-image by displacing blame. Differences are rendered deviant and criticisms are rejected in a collective ritual of nervous denial. The residual voice of democracy is faint, hollow, and contained. When tricksters call America to account for its democratic pretenses, they challenge the nation to confront a deep-seated contradiction. Their challenge is an invitation not readily accepted.

The trickster myth, as a corrective to the devil myth, is a precursor to reclaiming the nation's suppressed democratic ethos. The American trickster dons the threadbare garment of democracy to lure the nation into self-contradiction and self-recognition. The trickster's modus operandi is an exercise in democratic shape shifting. In broad outline, as we have seen, it is a rhetorical figure for attributing subjectivity to outsiders and articulating relations of interdependency with them. It functions like a stereoscopic gaze—deepening, broadening, and complicating a demonizing perspective that is narrow, shallow, and simplistic. In moments of agonistic crisis, the democratic trickster opens a space for self-examination. The trickster moment is a fleeting expression, a spark, of the nation's stifled democratic spirit. It is an invitation to transcend war culture by embracing democracy.

Conclusion

I speak the pass-word primeval, I give the sign of democracy,
By God! I will accept nothing which all cannot have their
counterpart of on the same terms.

Walt Whitman, *Leaves of Grass*

Ode to Democracy

Democracy is a tricky word. It can evoke an alarming image of political chaos, bestow a legitimizing gesture on wars of empire, or express a genuine aspiration to collective self-governance. It refers to a system of government and to a political culture. As a mode of self-rule, it might be more or less participatory, but it is typically a system of representative rather than direct governance. In the United States, democracy operates under the ideological dominion of liberalism and the economic rule of capitalism. Whereas democracy values community and equality foremost and strives to operate in the public sphere and through civil society, liberalism is a philosophy of individualism and freedom, and capitalism is an economic system of private ownership and commercial pursuits, both of which resist regulation by or for the people of the state. Liberalism's individualism and capitalism's consumerism typically trump democracy's aspirations for rich relationships of citizenship in a collected polity, but the underlying spirit of democracy survives.

America's democracy is a myth. It is a necessary fiction, a foundational story of a people's origins and purpose. It gives meaning to the national experience and infuses the story of American exceptionalism with promise. It is a vision of the mission of a chosen people, the dream of their salvation in a fallen world, and the emblem of their special virtue. Their wish is to make the world safe for democracy by democratizing the world. Democracy expresses the sacred relationship of collective being.[1] It is the political soul of the people.

Democracy is a true story. It is true to the sentiment, the beliefs, and the character of the nation. It is the ethos of the country fraught with anxiety.

Americans are apprehensive about their identity as a democratic people. There is something awesome and foreboding about the compelling prospect of democracy. The shadow of demagoguery darkens the democratic imaginary. A wish for reassuring unity and uniformity in the midst of discomfiting dissent and diversity distorts the democratic soul and tests the national resolve. At any given moment, America is more or less true to the story of a democratic people but never divests itself of the title of democracy. The quest defines the nation. How the story is told matters.

Democracy runs shallow and deep. The nation navigates the shoals of democracy but dreams of fathoming its depths. Today's weak democracy might become tomorrow's strong democracy. Beneath the thin façade lie deep aspirations for a more meaningful democratic experience. The democratic imagination in America has historical roots, and because it "has become the ultimate standard by which we evaluate and judge our political institutions and practices," in Russell Hanson's estimation, "the meaning of democracy is not, nor can it be, a matter of political indifference."[2]

Democracy is a recurring wish. Its potent political fiction of restoring power to the people and its enduring myth of collective participation resist the ideology of radical individualism and the rule of private interests in the liberal state. Its impulse, as James Morone observes, is to "reform and change . . . counter to the liberal status quo."[3] While democracy has never found its full expression in the nation's political institutions, the urge persists.

Democracy is a cultural legacy. The very possibility of a democratic sensibility depends on its expression in the nation's literature, visual and performing arts, and political oratory. The contours of democracy are imagined in poetry. Despite "the dispiriting truths of everyday life in America," Cornell West professes his ardent belief, shared by so many others, in a tradition of "democratic ideals." This very dissonance between hope and disappointment, West maintains, provoked the democratic voices of Ralph Waldo Emerson, Walt Whitman, Herman Melville, Mark Twain, Eugene O'Neill, James Baldwin, John Coltrane, Toni Morrison, and other "primary agents" of America's "deep democratic tradition."[4]

Democracy exists in political ritual. Just as an inspired but nebulous vision of democracy is given particular narrative form, the story of democracy is enacted and remembered in ritual. Ritual performances can connect a people to the spirit of democracy. Exercising the vote, listening to a president's State of the Union Address, debating issues of public policy, attending city council meetings, joining peaceful protests, publishing editorials, working for political campaigns, participating in social movements, monitoring the news, petitioning elected representatives, and other civic rites are the tangible practices that can instantiate democracy.

The democratic aesthetic is transformative. An enriched discourse of democracy is not superficial, irrational, tumultuous, or vulgar. It does not whip the mob into frenzy or aestheticize political life in the way Walter Benjamin warned of style substituting for substance in a fascist politics that subverts critical reason and culminates in war.[5] As Jon Simons observes, aestheticizations of politics are not necessarily fascist or totalitarian if they articulate democratic values of pluralism, diversity, and dissent.[6]

Randolph Bourne sustained his dissent from World War I against all odds "by engaging in irony and forming radical communities of aesthetic judgment," according to Christopher Kamrath. Bourne vigorously asserted values "that exceeded the war imperative."[7] He advocated a cultural practice that opened political space for critical debate, making it more plastic and less rigid. His turn to aesthetics was an attempt to salvage democratic ag- onistics and defy a domestication of war that delimited the possibilities of public speech. With the collapse of the public sphere and imposition of a re- gime of war propaganda, Bourne resisted a police state that suppressed free- dom of speech. He crafted a speaking position of ironic perspective-taking to build a more creative, flexible, and inclusive democratic community. A poetic vision was required, he insisted, to cultivate a national culture pre- disposed against war. Rather than a retreat from democratic engagement, Bourne's dissent operated in the cultural sphere outside the mainstream of wartime politics. His was a democratic aesthetic that would transform the political culture.

Democracy is a "cultural way of being," West writes.[8] At the level of culture, the "intimate link between aesthetics and democracy," in Thomas Docherty's view, opens the people to an understanding of alterity.[9] The possibility of transformation occurs when citizens become aware of their humanizing differences and recognize that "becoming human" is a "condi- tion of being-with-otherness." Dialogue and debate are ongoing exercises of collective judgment attentive to otherness in political contexts of contin- gency, competing perspectives, and un-decidability. They open the citizenry to being "conditioned by alterity." The beauty of democracy exists in self- altering moments of perceiving "uniformity amidst variety."[10]

Emerson grasped this transformative relationship of the one to the many, identity to identification, difference to similarity. To converge and diverge simultaneously is a democratic experience that changes the individual in so- ciety and places the citizen in polity. Emerson's emphasis was on the indi- vidual transformed, whether everyday citizen or public scholar, on noncon- formist democratic individuality creating a genuine democratic community that questioned dogma, welcomed fresh ideas, cultivated flexibility, loathed envy and imitation, eschewed prejudice, materialism, and empire, and cul- tivated a multiplicity of perspectives. He imagined a cosmopolitan citizenry that transcended narrow nationalism and imperial rule, which required a speaking, listening, and critical-thinking public engaged in mutual persuasion to overcome ignorance of others and narrow self-indulgence.[11]

Emerson wrote and spoke as democracy's prose poet. He was a student of history and rhetoric, an enemy of slavery and advocate of emancipation, an ordained minister banned thirty years from Harvard Divinity School for the heresy of affirming Jesus's humanity, and a creative spirit who believed in the transcendence of the individual, "the passage of the soul into higher forms."[12] He crafted a consummate image of the democratic individual. He understood the social world to be always in flux and considered the creation of the democratic nation to be an ongoing process. He preached the value of change and reform. He was receptive to new influences and opposed to foolish consistency. His individualism was cosmopolitan laced with a sense of interconnectedness. Human beings lived "in division, in parts, in particles," but "the soul of the whole" existed in each person as "the universal beauty, to which every part and particle is equally related." The oversoul "abolishes time and space" and "circumscribes all things." This was for Emerson a democratic spirit, "a certain wisdom of humanity which is common to the greatest men with the lowest, and which our ordinary education often labors to silence and obstruct. . . . The learned and the studious of thought have no monopoly of wisdom."[13]

The transforming experience of democracy was the genius of the self-reliant citizen expressed publicly in conversation and confrontation with self-reliant others. Emerson reconciled the one to the many in the agora of democratic agonistics. There was no democratic mass or herd in his representation of the demos. The limitation of the "private will" was ultimately "overpowered" in spite of itself through the "intercourse of society," where "your genius will speak from you, and mine from me." This was "the wisdom of humanity" common to all great democratic poets.[14]

The national poet of democracy, Walt Whitman, inspired by Emerson, expressed in free verse a fusion of the commonplace and vernacular with the transcendent and sublime. He spoke to the diversity and unity of the country in a voice that merged journalistic, oratorical, and biblical styles. He celebrated the commoner, the working class, and the immigrant nation, lamented the loss of American Indian cultures, and rejected black slavery. He glorified nature and loved the American landscape. He commended all parts of the whole, whether of the physical body or the body politic. He loved diversity and embraced equality, even as he remained nervous about universal suffrage. Just as he tried to nurse the broken bodies of Civil War soldiers—north and south—back to health, his poetry imagined a national wholeness containing a great diversity. His unified diversity would absorb division without stifling competition and contestation. Democratic affection was Whitman's enduring theme, fusing body and soul into the vision of a new covenant of true democracy.[15]

Whitman's vision of the third phase of national political development, following the firm constitutional foundation and ample material wealth achieved in the nation's first and second developmental phases, respectively, was to democratize society. His vision was a spiritual quest after "the idea of ensemble and of equal brotherhood." In this third vista, a "triumphant future" would speak of "America and democracy as convertible terms." The fundament of visionary work fell to poetry: "[I]n the region of imaginative, spinal and essential attributes, something equivalent to creation is, for our age and lands, imperatively demanded. For not only is it not enough that the new blood, new frame of democracy shall be vivified and held together merely by political means, superficial suffrage, legislation, &c., but it is clear to me that, unless it goes deeper, gets at least as firm and as warm a hold in men's hearts, emotions and belief, as, in their days, feudalism or ecclesiasticism, and inaugurates its own perennial sources, welling from the centre forever, its strength will be defective, its growth doubtful, and its main charm wanting." The reliable democratic identity was "the moral and artistic one." A true identity could exist only in the enactment of the vision articulated in the greatest democratic art and poetry. A nation bereft of such poetry suffered a hollowness of heart—an appalling spectacle "in an atmosphere of hypocrisy throughout." Nothing less than an "aesthetic conscience" could fulfill the "social aspects" of democracy in a country that otherwise marched vainly to empire.[16]

Whitman would reconcile individualistic freedom to a positive principle of society with a fulsome idea of "the People—of their measureless wealth of latent power and capacity." The People were God's "divine aggregate," not the aggregate of "the veritable horn'd and sharp-tail'd Devil." The present democracy exists only in "embryo" form; its fruition "resides altogether in the future." The real gist of the word "democracy" "still sleeps, quite unawaken'd" by "a programme of culture, drawn out, not for a single class alone, or for the parlors or lecture-rooms, but with an eye to practical life." For too long "have the People been listening to poems in which common humanity, deferential, bends low, humiliated, acknowledging superiors." A great democratic literature of the future will fully express a "loving comradeship" as the "offset of our materialistic and vulgar American democracy" of the present. Toward this end, "the test of a great literatus" of democracy "shall be the absence in him of the idea of the covert, the lurid, the maleficent, the devil, the grim estimates inherited from the Puritans, hell, natural depravity, and the like."[17]

Social connectedness, in Whitman's understanding, emanated from democratic individuality. His magnum opus, *Leaves of Grass*, he explained, was "the song of a great democratic individual . . . the chants . . . of an aggregated, inseparable, unprecedented, vast, composite, electric *democratic nationality*."[18] George Kateb sees in Whitman's vision not a tribal or strictly national identity but a philosophy of the culture of democracy. Whitman's greatness, in Kateb's view, was his effort to sing a democratic soul of receptivity. In "Song of Myself," Kateb's Whitman teaches a political theory of democratic connectedness as self-recognition and mutual acceptance: "Rejection of any other human being, for one reason or another, for apparently good reasons as well as for bad ones, is self-rejection." We are connected to one another in all of our differences by an "inner multiplicity." In Whitman's own words, "I am large, I contain multitudes." As Kateb remarks, this makes us individually and collectively "composite, not even composed."[19] Democracy is the discovery of the diversity of the self.

Emerson and Whitman start with the assumption of the individual and work toward a sense of community. In this tradition, the individual self experimentally embraces its multiplicity. Transformation occurs through a partial transcendence. Democratic community is experienced when individuals temporarily intersect and identities minimally converge into transitory relations of mutually empowering interdependence, where parts form a whole in complementary association with one another. It is a poetic vision that posits a common humanity with which the self-reliant individual becomes conversant. Democratic community is a moving ensemble of individuals, a process of harmonious heterogeneity, simultaneously divergent and convergent, forever dissonant but momentarily and at least minimally reconcilable.

Other democratic poets working in this tradition of the transcendent individual have challenged the hypocrisy of racism and the tyranny of empire. Both the individual and the nation can be trapped by an untruth about the racist past and "immobilized in the prison of [an] undiscovered self," as James Baldwin understood from the standpoint of an excluded black and gay man who, in West's estimation, "never lost sight of the democratic potential of America" because "he took for granted the humanity of black people—no matter how dehumanized by whites—and always affirmed the humanity of white people—no matter how devilish their treatment of blacks."[20] Baldwin's great insight was as follows: "A vast amount of the energy that goes into what we call the Negro problem is produced by the white man's profound desire not to be judged by those who are not white, not to be seen as he is, and at the same time a vast amount of the white anguish is rooted in the white man's equally profound need to be seen as he is, to be released from the tyranny of his mirror. . . . Love takes off the masks that we fear we cannot live without and know we cannot live within."[21] And as Toni Morrison, inspired by Herman Melville's critique of white progress and racial superiority, puts the matter succinctly, "The trauma of racism is, for the racist and the victim, the severe fragmentation of the self."[22]

The beauty of democracy is realized when the self is transformed into a collectivity without sacrificing the diversity of the whole. Uniformity is not a democratic ideal, nor is fragmentation of the commons. Democracy, as a politics of contestation, is enriched by the interdependence of differences. Competing perspectives differentiate and exercise the body politic. They hold one another accountable in the realm of political opinion. They maintain the process of deliberating and the cycle of decision making so that fallible judgments do not calcify into self-righteous dogmas. Democracy sustains diversity by transcending alienation. The developed democratic self recognizes the humanity of its many faces. It does not make enemies readily or attribute evil to otherness effortlessly. It is inclined against demonizing. It is a collective whole that privileges dissent as a vital transaction with otherness. Democracy's openness to exchange builds toward an attitude of positive peace to overturn one day the present presumption of war.[23]

Democratic culture is constituted, and its aesthetic of transcending alienation is realized, in the art of communication. Democracy is an art of political communication and persuasion—a rhetorical art. The ancient Athenian Greeks conceived of rhetoric as the discourse of democratic politics.[24] They invented rhetoric and democracy together. For the Greeks, "public rhetoric not only *revealed* social tension," as Josiah Ober observes, but also served as "a primary vehicle for *resolving* tension," which was an ongoing process.[25] John Dewey grasped this vital linkage between rhetoric and democracy when he argued that publics skilled in self-governance are articulate publics engaged in free social inquiry.[26] A great democratic community promotes dissent to resist the oppression of orthodoxy, to "break through the crust of conventionalized and routine consciousness."[27] The exchange necessary to bringing democracy into its own, in Dewey's view, is "a subtle, delicate, vivid and responsive art of communication" that breathes life into the transmission and circulation of information, ideas, and attitudes.[28] Only by developing "the methods and conditions of debate, discussion and persuasion" in the "give and take" of "thought and emotion" on matters of common concern might publics exercise good judgment.[29]

The democratic aesthetic and the art of political rhetoric converge on dissent, which is the quintessentially democratic practice. Rhetoric, understood in Dewey's philosophy as an art of becoming, performs its democratic function by advancing, in Nathan Crick's words, "minority viewpoints in exigent circumstances such that they have an opportunity to transform public opinion."[30] Rhetorical democracy is genuine democracy in the sense that it enables a minority view to become a majority opinion. It works to broaden and enrich experience, to motivate change, to imagine a richer version of a diverse humanity politically engaging one another. A rhetorical art of democratic dissent, as distinguished from a debased rhetoric that demonizes otherness, articulates the interconnectedness of strangers. As dissent opens the democratic self to otherness, it opens the nation to the world.

To envision a democratic future, drawn from the wellspring of America's political imaginary without the encumbrance of war and empire, is to imagine a culture of constructive dissent that no longer chases the devil. Under the sign of democratic dissent, differences would be addressed in a process of regeneration that recognizes the complexity and interdependency of a common yet diverse humanity. Such a culture would engage otherness rather than subdue it. It would transform enemies into political adversaries.

Here we encounter the riddle of trickster meeting the devil. When the projected image of evil, reflected in trickster's mirror, is momentarily retrieved for self-examination, its dissonance with the pristine myth of American exceptionalism proves too intense to contain. This American trickster deploys the discourse of democracy to trap the nation in self-contradiction. America's residual faith in the democratic principle is strong enough to retrieve but too weak to retain the projected image of evil savagery. Thus, the deadly cycle of hostile projections continues. The limits of trickster's deed reveal the need to strengthen the nation's democratic culture. Yet, the democratic aesthetic of transcending alienation presumes an art of political rhetoric that promotes otherness through dissent. The conundrum is how a political culture that tenuously retrieves its dark projections only to indulge them another time might develop the capacity to engage diversity—to accommodate a multiplicity of perspectives in a more developed democratic self. Recovering and diffusing the projected image of the devil requires integrating the enemy with the hero, the shadow of otherness with the conceit of the avenging angel, not to prevent future projections but to foil blind belief in devil images when inevitably we project again.

If the trick, in fleeting moments of crisis, is to attribute enough subjectivity to demonized enemies to glimpse one's own flaws indirectly through another's eyes, then how might a people acquire an enduring commitment to self-critique by dissent? Is it not the case that the rhetorical art of democratic dissent is the work of the trickster, and that a democratic attitude is necessary for trickster's work to succeed? If each presumes the other, then by what means, if not by the rhetorical turns of tricksters, does democracy become strong enough to transform the demonology of US war culture?

The riddle itself is a mythic formulation. Its solution requires a shift of perspective. A poetic vision of democracy is an amorphous sensibility that takes shape in the stories inspired by the dream. The stories come to life in the performance of rituals. Rituals are cyclical, not linear, progressions. Thus, the story of democracy spirals forward around a central vision. The strength of its trajectory corresponds to the quality of the rituals through which it is exercised and the frequency of their performance in resisting the temptation to demonize otherness. The mythic dream grasps the possibility of bridging the human divide. The dream is timeless. The possibility it senses is always available for development into an actuality. The simultaneity of myth and ritual, their fusion, is what produces true democracy.

The strength of what emerges from this union develops according to the manner in which it is exercised. The rhetorical art of dissent makes democracy hearty, increasing over time the nation's collective capacity for constructive engagement and critical self-reflection. The more deftly the nation adopts the ways of trickster, the more robust its commitment to dissent becomes. The art of democratic dissent does not simply reverse the poles of positive and negative valence. It transforms the simplistic dualism between absolute good and evil by exposing pristine self-images to the ordinary dirt of human affairs. It affirms a common humanity even as it criticizes a particular social convention, challenges an accepted belief, a prevailing attitude, or an established policy, questions a privileged identity, or disputes an injustice. It is a lively and sharp critique without the attribution of demons.

Democracy by dissent is a corrective art, a discourse of ongoing political reform. Its role in the present instance is to resist a warmongering myth of American exceptionalism. Divested of political import, democracy is reduced to an empty sign that rationalizes the imperial wars of a chosen people against ubiquitous forces of evil savagery. Caricatured as a degenerative disease of illiberal rule, it conjures nightmares of a docile herd and mindless, destructive mob. An impulse to neutralize or contain democracy suggests that the problem is the potential rule of democracy—the threat of too much democracy. Understood as a curative practice for adding perspective, maintaining flexibility, and restoring balance, the problem is too little democracy. Recognized as a discourse of dissent that emanates from the political margins, democracy's transformative work can be appreciated as a productive rather than destructive exercise.

The art of democratic dissent is a diverse people's discourse of accountability to one another. Even though discordant, it transcends alienation by bridging and coordinating differences, not by denying, denigrating, eliminating, dissolving, or suppressing them. It bridges social, political, and cultural divisions by attributing subjectivity to adversaries. It coordinates differences by articulating the ways in which they might complement each other.

This is democracy's well-played role within its political realm. At its best, it promotes tolerance and cautions against violence. The development of the democratic self, connecting it to its inner multiplicity, is the proper role of the rhetorical art of dissent. A democratic rhetoric is not a slave to any ideology. Developing democracy's potential for engaging differences is the nation's greatest prospect for acknowledging and eventually integrating into its collective identity the complexities of the human condition. When and if that potential is realized, the devil's deadly grip on the nation's defining sense of mission will surely loosen.

Notes

Introduction

1. W. Scott Poole, *Satan in America: The Devil We Know* (Lanham, MD: Rowman and Littlefield, 2009), xi.

2. Sheldon S. Wolin, *Democracy Incorporated: Managed Democracy and the Specter of Inverted Totalitarianism* (Princeton, NJ: Princeton University Press, 2008), 17–20.

3. One outbreak of this recurring attitude of divine mission, this time under conditions of economic decline, is reported by Lisa Miller, "Priority Check," *Newsweek*, December 20, 2010, 10.

4. Thomas Shepard, "A Defense of the Answer," in *The American Puritans: Their Prose and Poetry*, ed. Perry Miller (New York: Anchor Books, 1956), 24.

5. See Richard Slotkin, *The Fatal Environment: The Myth of the Frontier in the Age of Industrialization, 1800–1890* (New York: Atheneum, 1985), 10–12. In this book and *Gunfighter Nation: The Myth of the Frontier in Twentieth Century America* (New York: Atheneum, 1992), Slotkin has identified the concept of "Regeneration through Violence" and the narrative of the "Last Stand" as essential components of the Frontier myth behind the American territorial expansion of the nineteenth century and the nascent US imperialism of the early twentieth century.

6. John Wise, "Vindication of the Government of New England Churches," in Miller, *American Puritans*, 135.

7. Arthur Miller, *Timebends: A Life* (New York: Grove Press, 1987), 337.

8. Herman Melville, *Moby Dick; or, The Whale* (1851; repr., New York: Barnes and Noble, 1994), 162.

9. See Bernard Shaw's passage "On Diabolonian Ethics" in his Preface to *Three Plays for Puritans* (1901; repr., New York: Penguin Books, 1946), 22–29.

10. Melville, *Moby Dick*, 365.

11. Ira Chernus, *Monsters to Destroy: The Neoconservative War on Terror and Sin* (Boulder, CO: Paradigm, 2006), 4.

12. Melville, *Moby Dick*, 162.

13. Reza Aslan, *Zealot: The Life and Times of Jesus of Nazareth* (New York: Random House, 2013), 54 (emphasis in the original).

14. Christopher G. Flood, *Political Myth* (New York: Routledge, 2002), 41, 44; Nicholas Jackson O'Shaughnessy, *Politics and Propaganda: Weapons of Mass Seduction* (Ann Arbor: University of Michigan, 2004), 87–89, 94–97; David Campbell, *Writing Security: United States Foreign Policy and the Politics of Identity* (Minneapolis: University of Minnesota Press, 1998), 3; Richard T. Hughes, *Myths America Lives By* (Urbana: University of Illinois Press, 2003), 2–3, 5–8, 19.

15. Joseph Mali, *The Rehabilitation of Myth* (Cambridge, UK: Cambridge University Press, 1992), 5, 13, 129, 151; Giambattista Vico, *New Science*, trans. David Marsh (1744; repr., London: Penguin Books, 1999), 159, paragraph 404.

16. Umberto Eco, ed., *On Ugliness*, trans. Alastair McEwen (New York: Rizzoli, 2007), 90–104.

17. Béatrice Han, *Foucault's Critical Project: Between the Transcendental and the Historical* (Stanford, CA: Stanford University Press, 2002), 107; Hubert L. Dreyfus and Paul Rabinow, *Michel Foucault: Beyond Structuralism and Hermeneutics*, 2nd ed. (Chicago: University of Chicago Press, 1983), 105–6.

18. Michel Foucault, "Nietzsche, Genealogy, History," in *The Foucault Reader*, ed. Paul Rabinow (New York: Pantheon Books, 1984), 82.

19. Ronald F. Wendt, "Answers to the Gaze: A Genealogical Poaching of Resistances," *Quarterly Journal of Speech* 82.3 (1996): 257.

20. Jennifer A. Ziegler, "The Story behind an Organizational List: A Genealogy of Wildland Firefighters' 10 Standard Fire Orders," *Communication Monographs* 74.4 (2007): 422; David Berry, "Radical Mass Media Criticism: An Introduction," in *Radical Mass Media Criticism: A Cultural Genealogy*, ed. David Berry and John Theobald (Montreal: Black Rose Books, 2006), 13–14; see also Rudi Visker, *Michel Foucault: Genealogy as Critique*, trans. Chris Turner (London: Verso, 1995), 48–49; Michael Clifford, *Political Genealogy after Foucault: Savage Identities* (New York: Routledge, 2001), 20; and Sara Mills, *Michel Foucault* (London: Routledge, 2003), 64, 76–77.

21. Dreyfus and Rabinow, *Michel Foucault*, 118–25.

22. Foucault, "Nietzsche, Genealogy, History," 79–83, 93.

23. William G. Doty, *Mythography: The Study of Myths and Rituals*, 2nd ed. (Tuscaloosa: University of Alabama Press, 2000), xiii, 25–26, 280–81, 458.

24. Doty, 47.

25. Susan Faludi, *The Terror Dream: Fear and Fantasy in Post-9/11 America* (New York: Metropolitan Books, 2007), 4–7.

26. Mary Beth Norton has argued convincingly that Salem can be fully understood only in the context of the threat posed to English settlers in New England by the French and Indian wars of the seventeenth century. See Mary Beth Norton, *In the Devil's Snare: The Salem Witchcraft Crisis of 1692* (New York: Vintage Books, 2003).

27. Ray Bradbury, "The Tramp and the Dictator" (2001), Disc 2, in *Charles*

Chaplin's The Great Dictator, DVD, directed by Charles Chaplin (1940; repr., The Criterion Collection, 2011).

28. The doors of the temple of Janus in Rome were always open during times of war, and closed in times of peace. During Rome's first seven hundred years the doors of the temple were only closed during three brief periods: (1) in the reign of Numa; (2) after the first defeat of Carthage; (3) in the reign of Augustus Caesar. Edith Hamilton, *Mythology* (Boston: Little, Brown, 1942), 51.

29. Lewis Hyde, *Trickster Makes This World: Mischief, Myth and Art* (New York: North Point Press, 1998), 14, 268.

30. John S. Wilson, "O'Neill on the World and *The Iceman*," in *Conversations with Eugene O'Neill*, ed. Mark W. Estrin (Jackson: University Press of Mississippi, 1990), 164–65. For a reconstruction of O'Neill's "lost" cycle, see Donald Gallup, *Eugene O'Neill and his Eleven-Play Cycle: "A Tale of Possessors Self-Dispossessed"* (New Haven: Yale University Press, 1998).

31. Robert Louis Stevenson, *Dr. Jekyll and Mr. Hyde* (1886; repr., New York, Bantam Books, 1985), 80.

32. Mark Twain, *Roughing It* (New York: Harper, 1913), chapter 5.

33. Kenneth Burke, *A Rhetoric of Motives* (1950; repr., Berkeley: University of California Press, 1969), xv.

34. Kenneth Burke, *Permanence and Change*, 3rd ed. (Berkeley: University of California Press, 1984), 272.

35. Michel Sherry, *In the Shadow of War* (New Haven: Yale University Press, 1997).

36. Fred Anderson and Andrew Cayton, *The Dominion of War: Empire and Liberty in North America, 1500–2000* (New York: Viking, 2005).

37. Andrew Bacevich, *The New American Militarism: How Americans are Seduced by War* (Oxford: Oxford University Press, 2005); Andrew Bacevich, *Washington Rules: America's Path to Permanent War* (New York: Holt, Henry, 2011).

38. Kelly Denton-Barhaug, *U.S. War Culture, Sacrifice, and Salvation* (Sheffield: Equinox, 2011).

39. David Holloway, *Cultures of War on Terror: Empire, Ideology, and the Remaking of 9/11* (Montreal, Quebec: McGill-Queens University Press, 2008).

Chapter 1

1. Thomas Merton, *New Seeds of Contemplation* (1961; repr., Boston: Shambhala Publications, 2003), 116.

2. John D. Roth, *Choosing Against War: A Christian View* (Intercourse, PA: Good Books, 1989), 54–60, 64, 18, 117; Walter Wink, *The Powers That Be: Theology for a New Millennium* (New York: Doubleday, 1998), 42–62.

3. Elisabeth Anker, "Villains, Victims and Heroes: Melodrama, Media, and September 11," *Journal of Communication* 55 (2005): 23; see also Samuel P. Winch, "Constructing an 'Evil Genius': New Uses of Mythic Archetypes to Make Sense of bin Laden," *Journalism Studies* 6 (2005): 285–99.

4. Michael Rogin, *Ronald Reagan, the Movie: And Other Episodes in Political Demonology* (Berkeley: University of California Press, 1987), 2–3, 23.

5. Seymour Martin Lipset, *American Exceptionalism: A Double-Edged Sword* (New York: W. W. Norton, 1996), 19–20.

6. Michael Hirsh, *At War with Ourselves: Why America Is Squandering Its Chance to Build a Better World* (Oxford, UK: Oxford University Press, 2003), 70–73.

7. Denise M. Bostdorff, "George W. Bush's Post-September 11 Rhetoric of Covenant Renewal: Upholding the Faith of the Greatest Generation," *Quarterly Journal of Speech* 89 (2003): 303.

8. John M. Murphy, "'Our Mission and Our Moment': George W. Bush and September 11th," *Rhetoric & Public Affairs* 6 (2003): 626–27.

9. David Hoogland Noon, "Operation Enduring Analogy: World War II, the War on Terror, and the Uses of Historical Memory," *Rhetoric & Public Affairs* 7 (2004): 357–58.

10. Stephen B. Chapman, "Imperial Exegesis: When Caesar Interprets Scripture," in *Anxious about Empire: Theological Essays on the New Global Realities*, ed. Wes Avram (Grand Rapids, MI: Brazos Press, 2004), 95–96 (emphasis in the original); see also Debra Merskin, "The Construction of Arabs as Enemies: Post-September 11 Discourse of George W. Bush," *Mass Communication and Society* 7 (2004): 157–75.

11. George W. Bush, "President Bush Delivers Commencement Address at Ohio State University," The White House, Office of the Press Secretary, June 14, 2002, http://georgewbush-whitehouse.archives.gov/news/releases/2002/06/20020614–1 .html; see also George W. Bush, "President Delivers Commencement Address at Concordia University," The White House, Office of the Press Secretary, May 14, 2004, http://georgewbush-whitehouse.archives.gov/news/releases/2004/05 /20040514–4.html.

12. Peter Baker, "Bush Tells Group He Sees a 'Third Awakening,'" *Washington Post*, September 13, 2006, A05.

13. Christian Spielvogel, "'You Know Where I Stand': Moral Framing of the War on Terrorism and the Iraq War in the 2004 Presidential Campaign," *Rhetoric & Public Affairs* 8 (2005): 552; George W. Bush, "State of the Union Address," The White House, Office of the Press Secretary, January 31, 2006, http://georgewbush -whitehouse.archives.gov/stateoftheunion/2006/.

14. James Arnt Aune, "The Argument from Evil in the Rhetoric of Reaction," *Rhetoric & Public Affairs* 6 (2003): 518. On the trope of evil, see John Angus Campbell, "Evil as the Allure of Perfection," *Rhetoric & Public Affairs* 6 (2003): 525.

15. Terry Eagleton, *Holy Terror* (New York: Oxford University Press, 2005), 131, 134.

16. Kenneth Burke, *The Rhetoric of Religion: Studies in Logology* (1961; repr., Berkeley: University of California Press, 1970), 1–5, 174–81, 190–200.

17. James Hillman, *A Terrible Love of War* (New York: Penguin, 2004), 25.

18. Robert L. Ivie, *Democracy and America's War on Terror* (Tuscaloosa: University of Alabama Press, 2005), 14, 34, 43–44, 90–91.

19. Arthur Miller, *Timebends* (New York: Grove Press, 1987), 337.

20. Simon Schama, *Citizens: A Chronicle of the French Revolution* (New York: Alfred A. Knopf, 1989), 858–59.

21. Stephen H. Daniel, *Myth and Modern Philosophy* (Philadelphia: Temple University Press, 1990), 10.

22. Benjamin Barber, *Strong Democracy: Participatory Politics for a New Age* (Berkeley: University of California Press, 1984), 20–21.

23. David Held, *Models of Democracy*, 2nd ed. (Stanford, CA: Stanford University Press, 1996), 94; Robert A. Dahl, *How Democratic Is the American Constitution?* (New Haven: Yale University Press, 2001), 24–25.

24. James Madison, "Number X: The Subject Continued," in *The Federalist Papers*, ed. Isaac Kramnick (1787; repr., New York: Penguin Books, 1987), 122–28.

25. James Madison, "Number LV: The Same Subject Continued in Relation to the Total Number of the Body," in Kramnick, *Federalist Papers*, 336.

26. Ivie, *Democracy and America's War on Terror*, 63–70; Gordon S. Wood, *The Creation of the American Republic, 1776–1787* (New York: W. W. Norton, 1969), 513–17, 562, 595–614; Edmund S. Morgan, *Inventing the People: The Rise of Popular Sovereignty in England and America* (New York: W. W. Norton, 1988), 267, 282–86.

27. Robert V. Remini, *Andrew Jackson: The Course of American Democracy, 1833–1845* (Baltimore: Johns Hopkins University Press, 1984), 270.

28. Kenneth Cmiel, *Democratic Eloquence: The Fight over Popular Speech in Nineteenth-Century America* (New York: William Morrow, 1990), 66–67, 71–73.

29. Michael J. Sproul, *Propaganda and Democracy: The American Experience of Media and Mass Persuasion* (New York: Cambridge University Press, 1997), 94.

30. Jeffrey K. Tulis, *The Rhetorical Presidency* (Princeton, NJ: Princeton University Press, 1987); Robert L. Ivie, "Tragic Fear and the Rhetorical Presidency: Combating Evil in the Persian Gulf," in *Beyond the Rhetorical Presidency*, ed. Martin J. Medhurst (College Station: Texas A&M University Press, 1996), 157–60.

31. Michael W. Doyle, "Kant, Liberal Legacies, and Foreign Affairs," in *Debating the Democratic Peace: An International Security Reader*, ed. Michael E. Brown, Sean M. Lynn-Jones, and Steven E. Miller (Cambridge, MA: Massachusetts Institute of Technology Press, 1996); Bruce Russett, *Grasping the Democratic Peace: Principles for a Post-Cold War World* (Princeton, NJ: Princeton University Press, 1993); Spencer R. Weart, *Never at War: Why Democracies Will Not Fight One Another* (New Haven: Yale University Press, 1998); Alan Gilbert, *Must Global Politics Constrain Democracy? Great-Power Realism, Democratic Peace, and Democratic Internationalism* (Princeton, NJ: Princeton University Press, 1999).

32. Ivie, *Democracy and America's War on Terror*, 92–116.

33. Quoted in Tony Smith, *The United States and the Worldwide Struggle for Democracy in the Twentieth Century* (Princeton, NJ: Princeton University Press, 1995), 313; Amos Perlmutter, *Making the World Safe for Democracy: A Century of Wilsonianism and Its Totalitarian Challengers* (Chapel Hill: University of North Carolina Press, 1997), 9, 161.

34. Quoted in Smith, *Worldwide Struggle*, 320.

35. Quoted in Ivie, *Democracy and America's War on Terror*, 113–14; see 111–16.

36. Robert Kagan, *Dangerous Nation* (New York: Alfred A. Knopf, 2006), 3–5.

37. Robert L. Ivie, "Savagery in Democracy's Empire," *Third World Quarterly* 26.1 (2005): 56.

38. Janice Hocker Rushing and Thomas S. Frentz, *Projecting the Shadow: The Cyborg Hero in American Film* (Chicago: University of Chicago Press, 1995), 220.

39. Sheldon S Wolin, *Politics and Vision: Continuity and Innovation in Western Political Thought*, 2nd ed. (Princeton, NJ: Princeton University Press, 2004), 601.

40. Aldous Huxley, *The Devils of Loudun* (1952; repr., New York: Barnes and Noble Books, 1996), 175 (emphasis in the original).

41. George W. Bush, "President Holds Prime Time News Conference," The White House, Office of the Press Secretary, October 11, 2001, http://georgewbush-whitehouse.archives.gov/news/releases/2001/10/20011011–7.html.

42. Joshua Gunn, "The Rhetoric of Exorcism: George W. Bush and the Return of Political Demonology," *Western Journal of Communication* 68.1 (2004): 1–23.

43. George W. Bush, "President Unveils Back to Work Plan." The White House, Office of the Press Secretary, October 4, 2001, http://georgewbush-whitehouse.archives.gov/news/releases/2001/10/20011004–8.html.

44. George W. Bush, "National Character Counts Week Proclamation," The White House, Office of the Press Secretary, October 23, 2001, http://georgewbush-whitehouse.archives.gov/news/releases/2001/10/20011023–23.html; George W. Bush, "International Campaign against Terror Grows," The White House, Office of the Press Secretary, September 25, 2001, http://georgewbush-whitehouse.archives.gov/news/releases/2001/09/20010925–1.html; George W. Bush, "President Directs Humanitarian Aid to Afghanistan," The White House, Office of the Press Secretary, October 4, 2001, http://georgewbush-whitehouse.archives.gov/news/releases/2001/10/20011004.html.

45. Bush, "International Campaign against Terror Grows."

46. Bush, "President Holds Prime Time News Conference"; Bush, "President Holds Prime Time News Conference."

47. George W. Bush, "President Pays Tribute at Pentagon Memorial." The White House, Office of the Press Secretary, October 11, 2001, http://georgewbush-whitehouse.archives.gov/news/releases/2001/10/20011011–1.html; Bush, "International Campaign against Terror Grows"; George W. Bush, "President's Remarks at Iowa Republican Dinner," The White House, Office of the Press Secretary, March 1, 2002, http://georgewbush-whitehouse.archives.gov/news/releases/2002/03/20020301–6.html; George W. Bush, "President: FBI Needs Tools to Track Down Terrorists," The White House, Office of the Press Secretary, September 25, 2001, http://georgewbush-whitehouse.archives.gov/news/releases/2001/09/20010925-5.html (emphasis added).

48. Marie-Louise von Franz, *Dreams* (Boston and London: Shambhala, 1991), 14 (emphasis in the original).

49. Von Franz, 14. Von Franz's reference can be found in Luke 6:41–42 (King James Version): "And why beholdest thou the mote that is in thy brother's eye, but perceivest not the beam that is in thine own eye?"

50. Carl Jung, "Aion: Phenomenology of the Self," in *The Portable Jung*, ed. Joseph Campbell (1951; repr., New York: Penguin Books, 1988), 146 (emphasis added).

51. George W. Bush, "President Unveils 'Most Wanted' Terrorists," The White House, Office of the Press Secretary, October 10, 2001, http://georgewbush -whitehouse.archives.gov/news/releases/2001/10/20011010–3.html; Bush, "President: FBI Needs Tools to Track Down Terrorists"; Bush, "President Holds Prime Time News Conference"; George W. Bush, "President Outlines War Effort," The White House, Office of the Press Secretary, October 17, 2001, http://georgewbush -whitehouse.archives.gov/news/releases/2001/10/20011017–15.html; George W. Bush, "America's Youth Respond to Afghan Children's Fund," The White House, Office of the Press Secretary, October 16, 2001, http://georgewbush-whitehouse .archives.gov/news/releases/2001/10/20011016–4.html; George W. Bush, "At O'Hare, President Says 'Get on Board,'" The White House, Office of the Press Secretary, September 27, 2001, http://georgewbush-whitehouse.archives.gov/news /releases/2001/09/20010927–1.html; Bush, "President: FBI Needs Tools to Track Down Terrorists."

52. Jung, "Aion," 146.

53. Bush, "President Unveils Back to Work Plan"; George W. Bush, "President Speaks on War Effort to Citadel Cadets," The White House, Office of the Press Secretary, December 11, 2001, http://georgewbush-whitehouse.archives.gov /news/releases/2001/12/20011211–6.html; George W. Bush, "President Outlines War Effort," The White House, Office of the Press Secretary, April 17, 2002, http:// georgewbush-whitehouse.archives.gov/news/releases/2002/04/20020417–1. html; George W. Bush, "President's Remarks in Lancaster, Pennsylvania," The White House, Office of the Press Secretary, July 9, 2004, http://georgewbush -whitehouse.archives.gov/news/releases/2004/07/20040709–10.html; George W. Bush, "President Speaks to the United Nations General Assembly," The White House, Office of the Press Secretary, September 21, 2004, http://www.unwatch .com/gwb92105.php; George W. Bush, "President's Remarks in 'Focus on Education with President Bush' Event," The White House, Office of the Press Secretary, September 22, 2004, http://georgewbush-whitehouse.archives.gov/news /releases/2004/09/20040922–10.html; George W. Bush, "President Discusses War on Terror," The White House, Office of the Press Secretary, October 28, 2005, http://georgewbush-whitehouse.archives.gov/news/releases/2005/10/20051028–1 .html; George W. Bush, "President Discusses War on Terror and Operation Iraqi Freedom," The White House, Office of the Press Secretary, March 20, 2006, http://georgewbush-whitehouse.archives.gov/news/releases/2006/03/20060320–7 .html; George W. Bush, "President Commemorates Veterans Day, Discusses War on Terror," The White House, Office of the Press Secretary, November 11, 2005, http://2001–2009.state.gov/s/ct/rls/rm/56852.htm; George W. Bush, "State of the Union Address," The White House, Office of the Press Secretary, February 2, 2005, http://georgewbush-whitehouse.archives.gov/news/releases/2005/02/20050202–11 .html; George W. Bush, "President's Address to the Nation," The White House, Office of the Press Secretary, September 11, 2006, http://georgewbush-whitehouse .archives.gov/news/releases/2006/09/20060911–3.html.

54. Hillman, *Terrible Love*, 190, 196.

55. Bush, "President Discusses War on Terror."

56. Bill Keller, "The Radical Presidency of George W. Bush; Reagan's Son," *New York Times*, January 26, 2003, online at http://www.nytimes.com/2003/01/06 /magazine/the-radical-presidency-of-george-w-bush-reagan-s-son.html?pagewanted =print&src=pm; see also Lou Cannon and Carl M. Cannon, *Reagan's Disciple: George W. Bush's Troubled Quest for a Presidential Legacy* (New York: Public Affairs, 2008).

57. Huxley, *Devils of Loudun*, 175.

58. Bush, "President Speaks of War Effort to Citadel Cadets."

59. Quoted in Evan S. Connell, *Son of the Morning Star* (New York: Harper Collins, 1991), 8, 21.

60. Robert Johnson, *The Complete Recordings*. 2 CDs, Columbia/Legacy, C2K 64916, Sony Music Entertainment, 1990, 46.

61. Gunn, "Rhetoric of Exorcism," 2.

62. George W. Bush, "Bush the Decider," YouTube, April 19, 2006, http:// www.youtube.com/watch?v=irMeHmlxE9s; Bob Woodward, *Bush at War* (New York: Simon and Schuster, 2002), 145–46; George Lakoff, *Whose Freedom: The Battle over America's Most Important Idea* (New York: Farrar, Straus and Giroux, 2006), 73–74, 96–97; Gene Healy and Timothy Lynch, "Power Surge: The Constitutional Record of George W. Bush," Cato Institute, May 1, 2006, http://www .cato.org/publications/white-paper/power-surge-constitutional-record-george-w -bush.

63. George W. Bush, "President Bush Addresses American Legion National Convention," The White House, Office of the Press Secretary, August 31, 2006, http://georgewbush-whitehouse.archives.gov/news/releases/2006/08/20060831–1 .html.

64. Bush, "President Speaks on War Effort to Citadel Cadets."

65. George W. Bush, "President Delivers 'State of the Union,'" The White House, Office of the Press Secretary, January 28, 2003, http://georgewbush-whitehouse .archives.gov/news/releases/2003/01/20030128–19.html; Bush, "President Delivers 'State of the Union'"; George W. Bush, "President Discusses Economic Stimulus with National Association of Manufacturers," The White House, Office of the Press Secretary, October 31, 2001, http://georgewbush-whitehouse.archives.gov /news/releases/2001/10/20011031–1.html; George W. Bush, "President Urges Support for America's Charities," The White House, Office of the Press Secretary, November 20, 2001, http://georgewbush-whitehouse.archives.gov/news/releases /2001/11/20011120–5.html; Bush, "President Outlines War Effort."

66. Bush, "President Outlines War Effort"; George W. Bush, "President Rallies Troops at Travis Air Force Base," The White House, Office of the Press Secretary, October 17, 2001, http://georgewbush-whitehouse.archives.gov/news/releases /2001/10/20011017–20.html; Bush, "President Discusses Economic Stimulus."

67. Bush, "President Outlines War Effort"; Bush, "President Directs Humanitarian Aid to Afghanistan"; Bush, "America's Youth Respond"; Bush, "National Character Counts Week"; George W. Bush, "President Asks American Chil-

dren to Help Afghan Children," The White House, Office of the Press Secretary, October 12, 2001, http://georgewbush-whitehouse.archives.gov/news/releases/2001/10/20011012–4.html.

68. George W. Bush, "President's Remarks During Hispanic Heritage Month Event," The White House, Office of the Press Secretary, October 12, 2001, http://georgewbush-whitehouse.archives.gov/news/releases/2001/10/20011012–6.html; Bush, "National Character Counts Week."

69. Bush, "President's Remarks at Iowa Republican Dinner"; Bush, "President's Remarks in 'Focus on Education'"; Bush, "President's Remarks in Lancaster, Pennsylvania."

70. John 1:5.

71. Elaine Pagels, *The Origin of Satan* (New York: Random House, 1995), 100.

72. Pagels, *Origin of Satan*, 100.

73. Huxley, *Devils of Loudun*, 237 (emphasis in the original).

74. Huxley, *Devils of Loudun*, 237; Pagels, *Origin of Satan*, 182.

75. Bush, "President's Address to the Nation"; George W. Bush, "President's Remarks at Columbus, Ohio Rally," The White House, Office of the Press Secretary, September 1, 2004, http://georgewbush-whitehouse.archives.gov/news/releases/2004/09/20040901–6.html; Bush, "President's Remarks in 'Focus on Education'"; Bush, "State of the Union," 2005; Bush, "President Discusses War on Terror."

76. Bush, "President Discusses War on Terror"; Bush, "President's Remarks at Columbus, Ohio"; Bush, "President's Remarks in Lancaster, Pennsylvania"; Bush, "President Speaks to the United Nation's General Assembly"; Bush, "State of the Union Address," 2005; Bush, "President's Address to the Nation," 2006; Bush, "President Discusses War on Terror."

77. Luke 4:13.

78. Bush, "President Discusses War on Terror."

79. Bush, "State of the Union Address," 2005; George W. Bush, "President Outlines Strategy for Victory in Iraq," The White House, Office of the Press Secretary, November 30, 2005, http://www.au.af.mil/au/awc/awcgate/whitehouse/20051130–2.htm; George W. Bush, "President Discusses War on Terror at FBI Academy," The White House, Office of the Press Secretary, July 11, 2005, http://georgewbush-whitehouse.archives.gov/news/releases/2005/07/20050711–1.html; Bush, "President's Remarks at Columbus, Ohio."

80. George W. Bush, "President Discusses Global War on Terror," The White House, Office of the Press Secretary, September 5, 2006, http://georgewbush-whitehouse.archives.gov/news/releases/2006/01/20060123–4.html; George W. Bush, "President Bush Discusses Progress in the Global War on Terror," The White House, Office of the Press Secretary, September 7, 2006, http://georgewbush-whitehouse.archives.gov/news/releases/2006/09/20060907–2.html; Mark 9:24.

81. Bush, "President Discusses Global War on Terror"; Bush, "President's Address to the Nation," 2006; Bush, "President Bush Discusses Progress in the Global War on Terror."

82. Robert L. Ivie, "The Rhetoric of Bush's 'War' on Evil," *KB Journal* 1 (Fall 2004), available online at http://www.kbjournal.org; Robert L. Ivie, "Fighting Terror

by Rite of Redemption and Reconciliation," *Rhetoric & Public Affairs* 10.2 (2007): 221–48; Burke, *Rhetoric of Religion*, 281–82. Burke's twentieth-century verbal image of a young, agile, and mercurial Satan wearing a fool's cap is quite unlike Jean-Jacques Feuchère's nineteenth-century bronze sculpture of a brooding, bat-winged, and taloned Satan postured like Rodin's *Thinker.*

83. Jung, 146.

84. George Bernard Shaw, "Preface to Major Barbara," in *Bernard Shaw's St. Joan, Major Barbara and Androcles and the Lion* (New York: Modern Library, 1952), 214.

85. Johnson, *Complete Recordings*, 46.

86. Susan Faludi, *The Terror Dream: Fear and Fantasy in Post-9/11 America* (New York: Metropolitan Books, 2007), 4–5, 7, 13, 15.

Chapter 2

1. Arthur Miller, *Timebends* (New York: Grove Press, 1987), 329–30.

2. Miller, *Timebends*, 330. See Marion Starkey, *The Devil in Massachusetts* (New York: Anchor Books, 1989).

3. Elia Kazan, *A Life* (New York: Alfred A. Knopf, 1988), 449; Miller, *Timebends*, 333. In Kazan's retelling, this conversation took place before his decision to cooperate with HUAC; in Miller's version, Kazan had already testified. See Kazan, *A Life*, 460–61, and Miller, *Timebends*, 332–35.

4. Miller, *Timebends*, 335, 336.

5. Elaine G. Breslaw, chapter 1, "Tituba's Roots," in *Tituba, Reluctant Witch of Salem* (New York: New York University Press, 1996), 3–20.

6. Paul Boyer and Stephen Nissenbaum, eds., *The Salem Witchcraft Papers* (New York: Da Capo Press, 1977), vol. 3, "Tituba," 745 and 756.

7. Starkey, *Devil in Massachusetts*, 29; Arthur Miller, *The Crucible* (New York: Penguin Books, 1976), 8; Marisa Conde, *I, Tituba, Black Witch of Salem* (Charlottesville: University Press of Virginia, 1992); Charles W. Upham, *Salem Witchcraft* (Williamstown, MA: Corner House, 1971), vol. 2, 2.

8. Boyer and Nissenbaum, "Sarah Osborne," *Salem Witchcraft Papers*, vol. 2, 611.

9. Boyer and Nissenbaum, "Examination of Tituba—A Second Version," *Salem Witchcraft Papers*, vol. 3, 750–55.

10. Boyer and Nissenbaum, "Sarah Bibber v. George Burroughs," *Salem Witchcraft Papers*, vol. 1, 167; "Elizabeth Hubbard v. George Burroughs," vol. 1, 170; "Elizar Keyser v. George Burroughs," vol. 1, 176–77.

11. Boyer and Nissenbaum, "Ann Putnam Jr. v. George Burroughs," *Salem Witchcraft Papers*, vol. 1, 164; "Mercy Lewis v. George Burroughs," vol. 1, 168; "Elizabeth Hubbard v. George Burroughs," vol. 1, 170.

12. Boyer and Nissenbaum, "Mary Walcott v. George Burroughs," *Salem Witchcraft Papers*, vol. 1, 174; "Abigail Hobbs and Mary Warren v. George Burroughs," vol. 1, 172; "Mary Warren v. George Burroughs, John Alden, Martha Corey, and Ann Pudeator," vol. 1, 173; "Examination of Deliverance Hobbs in Prison," vol. 2, 423.

13. See Irving Rouse, *The Taínos: Rise and Decline of the People Who Greeted Columbus* (New Haven: Yale University Press, 1992), 39–42, and Julian Granberry and Gary S. Vescelius, *Languages of the Pre-Columbian Antilles* (Tuscaloosa: University of Alabama Press, 2004), 14–15.

14. Fray Ramón Pané, *Relación de las antiguedades de los indios*, ed. José Juan Arrom (México: Siglo XXI, 1998), 3. Arrom's important edition of Pané has been translated into English: Fray Ramón Pané, *An Account of the Antiquities of the Indians*, ed. José Juan Arrom, trans. Susan Griswold (Durham, NC: Duke University Press Books, 2000).

15. Breslaw, *Tituba, Reluctant Witch*, 24–25 and 30; Pané, *Relación de las antiguedades*, 16–17; Upham, "The Confession of Ann Putnam," *Salem Witchcraft*, vol. 2, 510.

16. Pané, *Relación de las antiguedades*, 22–23; 21–22; 23–24. All translations from Pané, as edited by Arrom, are by Giner.

17. Boyer and Nissenbaum, "Ann Putnam, Sr., v. Rebecca Nurse, Sarah Cloyce, Bridget Bishop, and Elizabeth Cary," *Salem Witchcraft Papers*, vol. 2, 601.

18. Boyer and Nissenbaum, "Robert Downer v. Susannah Martin," *Salem Witchcraft Papers*, vol. 2, 572.

19. Boyer and Nissenbaum, "Examination of Tituba—A Second Version," *Salem Witchcraft Papers*, vol. 3, 753.

20. Boyer and Nissenbaum, *Salem Witchcraft Papers*, vol. 3, 752.

21. Sebastián Robiou Lamarche, *Taínos y Caribes* (San Juan, Puerto Rico: Editorial Punto y Coma, 2005), 95.

22. Boyer and Nissenbaum, "Examination of Tituba—A Second Version," *Salem Witchcraft Papers*, vol. 3, 752. See the story of the Taíno bird *inriri* in Lamarche, 91.

23. John Hale, *A Modest Enquiry into the Nature of Witchcraft, 1702* (Bainbridge, NY: York-Mail Print, 1973), 31; Boyer and Nissenbaum, "Benjamin Hutchinson v. George Burroughs," *Salem Witchcraft Papers*, vol. 1, 172.

24. "Commentary by Director Nicholas Hytner and writer Arthur Miller," *The Crucible*, DVD (1996; Twentieth Century Fox Entertainment, 2004).

25. At the behest of Mary Sibley, a witch-cake was fed to a village dog in order to discover the culprit witch who was disturbing the children. See Hale, *Modest Enquiry*, 23–24.

26. Upham, *Salem Witchcraft*, vol. 2, 95.

27. Boyer and Nissenbaum, "John Proctor," *Salem Witchcraft Papers*, vol. 2, 677.

28. Robert Calef, "More Wonders of the Invisible World," in *The Witchcraft Delusion in New England*, ed. Samuel G. Drake (New York: Burt Franklin, 1970), vol. 3, 23–24.

29. Pané, *Relación de las antiguedades*, 27–28.

30. Pané, *Relación de las antiguedades*, 26 and 33.

31. Bartolomé de las Casas, *Apologética Historia de las Indias*, quoted in Appendix C, "Fray Bartolomé de las Casas," in Pané, *Relación de las antiguedades*, 78.

32. Quoted in Miguel Rivera, "Introducción," in Diego de Landa, *Relación de las cosas de Yucatán* (Madrid: Historia 16, 1985), 23.

33. Cotton Mather, *Magnalia Christi Americana: or, the Ecclesiastical History of New England* (London, 1702), quoted in Alden T. Vaughan and Edward W. Clark, eds., *Puritans among the Indians: Accounts of Captivity and Redemption, 1676–1724* (Cambridge, MA: Harvard University Press, 1981), 135.

34. Mary Rowlandson, "The Soveraignty and Goodness of God, Being a Narrative of the Captivity, Sufferings and Removes of Mrs. Mary Rowlandson," in *Puritans among the Indians*, ed. Vaughan and Clark, 35.

35. Upham, *Salem Witchcraft*, vol. 2, 2.

36. Cotton Mather, "Wonders of the Invisible World" in *Witchcraft Delusion*, ed. Drake, vol. 1, 159 (italics in the original).

37. Mary Beth Norton, *In the Devil's Snare: The Salem Witchcraft Crisis of 1692* (New York: Vintage Books, 2003), 5 and 59.

38. Patricia Roberts-Miller, *Voices in the Wilderness: Public Discourse and the Paradox of Puritan Rhetoric* (Tuscaloosa: University of Alabama, 1999), 19, 132, 136–37, 140. Roberts-Miller defines monologic discourse as "a form of public argumentation that purports to get audiences to adopt the right course of action through clearly stating and logically demonstrating true propositions." Roberts-Miller, *Voices in the Wilderness*, 123.

39. S. Russell, "Witchcraft, Genealogy, Foucault," *British Journal of Sociology* 52, no. 1 (2001): 121–37.

40. Upham, *Salem Witchcraft*, vol. 1, 8.

41. Laurie Winn Carlson has advanced the intriguing notion that the ailments in Salem were caused by an epidemic of *Encephalitis lethargica* or sleeping sickness—a disease for which there is no cure even today. See Laurie Winn Carlson, *A Fever in Salem* (Chicago: Ivan R. Dee, 1999).

42. Upham, *Salem Witchcraft*, vol. 2, 85.

43. Marie-Louis von Franz, "The Process of Individuation," in *Man and His Symbols*, Carl Jung (New York: Laurel Editions, 1968), 175.

44. "Thereupon [Tezcatlipoca] presented the mirror to Quetzalcoatl saying . . . 'It is here in the mirror you shall appear.'" John Bierhorst, ed., "Quetzalcoatl," *Four Masterworks of American Indian Literature* (Tucson: University of Arizona Press, 1974), 30.

45. Marie-Louis von Franz, *Dreams* (Boston: Shambhala, 1991), 15.

46. Boyer and Nissenbaum, "Martha Corey," *Salem Witchcraft Papers*, vol. 1, 248; Boyer and Nissenbaum, "Rebecca Nurse," vol. 2, 585; Boyer and Nissenbaum, "Elizabeth Proctor," *Salem Witchcraft Papers*, vol. 2, 660; Boyer and Nissenbaum, "Mary Esty," *Salem Witchcraft Papers*, vol. 1, 304.

47. Boyer and Nissenbaum, "John Proctor," *Salem Witchcraft Papers*, vol. 2, 682.

48. Boyer and Nissenbaum, "Margaret Jacobs," *Salem Witchcraft Papers*, vol. 2, 491–92.

49. Boyer and Nissenbaum, "John Proctor," *Salem Witchcraft Papers*, vol. 2, 690.

50. Starkey, *Devil in Massachusetts*, 191. The Salem witch-hunters believed that the devil could only appear in the likeness of those under his rule.

51. Starkey, *Devil in Massachusetts*, 214. The accused were asked to "touch" the

persons with fits at the hearings. If their fits disappeared at that moment, the evil was thought to have returned to the witch.

52. Thomas Brattle, "letter (1692)," in Frances Hill, *The Salem Witch Trials Reader* (n.p.: Da Capo Press, 2000), 94.

53. Starkey, *Devil in Massachusetts*, 214.

54. Von Franz, in Jung, *Man and His Symbols*, 182.

55. Calef in Drake, *Witchcraft Delusion*, 48.

56. Brattle in Hill, *Salem Witch Trials*, 92.

57. Starkey, *Devil in Massachusetts*, 168.

58. Starkey, *Devil in Massachusetts*, 210.

59. Calef in Drake, *Witchcraft Delusion*, vol. 3, 132–33.

60. Quoted in Richard Francis, *Judge Sewall's Apology: The Salem Witch Trials and the Forming of an American Conscience* (New York: Harper Collins, 2005), 181.

61. Calef in Drake, *Witchcraft Delusion*, vol. 3, 134–35.

62. Hale, *Modest Enquiry*, 9.

63. Marilynne K. Roach, *The Salem Witch Trials* (New York: Cooper Square Press, 2002), 568.

64. "The Confession of Ann Putnam, (1706)," in Hill, *Salem Witch Trials*, 108.

65. Starkey, *Devil in Massachusetts*, 258–60.

66. Von Franz, *Dreams*, 14, 17.

67. "The Confession of Ann Putnam (1706)," in Hill, *Salem Witch Trials*, 108.

68. Calef in Drake, *Witchcraft Delusion*, 132–33.

69. Calef in Drake, *Witchcraft Delusion*, 134.

70. Samuel Parris, "Salem Village Church Book of Record," in Hill, *Salem Witch Trials*, 156.

71. Carl Jung, "Psychology of the Transference," in *The Basic Writings of C. G. Jung*, ed. Violet S. de Laszlo (New York: Modern Library, 1959), 401.

72. Carl Jung, "Psychology of the Transference," 338.

73. Jim Wallis, *God's Politics* (New York: Harper San Francisco, 2005), 7; Robert L. Ivie, *Dissent from War* (Bloomfield, CT: Kumarian Press, 2007), 62–67; Walter Wink, *The Powers that Be: Theology for a New Millennium* (New York: Galilee Doubleday, 1998), 42–62.

74. Arthur Miller, quoted in E. Miller Budick, "History and Other Spectres in Arthur Miller's *The Crucible*," in Harold Bloom, ed. *Arthur Miller's The Crucible* (Philadelphia: Chelsea House Publishers, 1999), 96.

Chapter 3

1. Elizabeth Custer, *Boots and Saddles* (Norman: University of Oklahoma Press, 1961), 218–20.

2. O. G. Libby, ed., "The Arikara Narrative of the Campaign Against the Hostile Dakotas, June, 1876," *North Dakota Historical Collections 6* (Bismarck, ND: Historical Society of North Dakota, 1920), 78; James Donovan, *A Terrible Glory: Custer and the Little Bighorn, the Last Great Battle of the American West* (New York:

Little, Brown, 2008); Donovan, *Terrible Glory*, 201–3; Robert M. Utley, *The Lance and the Shield* (New York: Henry Holt, 1993), 144.

3. Joseph Medicine Crow, "Custer and His Crow Scouts," in *Little Bighorn Remembered: The Untold Story of Custer's Last Stand*, ed. Herman J. Viola (New York: Times Books, 1999), 114; Donovan, *Terrible Glory*, 214; Evan S. Connell, *Son of the Morning Star* (New York: Harper Perennial, 1991), 2–3.

4. William Arrowsmith, "Introduction," Euripides, *Alcestis* (Oxford: University of Oxford Press, 1974), 23–26; Carl Jung, "The Personal and the Collective Unconscious," in *The Basic Writings of C. G. Jung*, ed. Violet S. de Laszlo (New York: Modern Library, 1959), 107–18.

5. Edgar I. Stewart, "Introduction," George Armstrong Custer, *My Life on the Plains* (1874; repr., Norman: University of Oklahoma Press, 1988), ix; George Armstrong Custer, *My Life*, 123; Dee Brown, *Bury My Heart at Wounded Knee* (New York: Holt, Rinehart and Winston, 1971), 168 and 170; Stewart, "Introduction," George Armstrong Custer, xviii-xxvi; John G. Neihardt, "The Song of the Indian Wars," in *The Twilight of the Sioux* (Lincoln: University of Nebraska, 1971), 107.

6. Richard Slotkin, *The Fatal Environment: The Myth of the Frontier in an Age of Industrialization, 1800–1890* (New York: Atheneum, 1985), 455–56, 462; quoted in Connell, *Son of the Morning Star*, 331; *New York Herald*, August 2, 1876, quoted in Donovan, *Terrible Glory*, 322; *New York Times*, July 17, 1876, quoted in Donovan, *Terrible Glory*, 324; Robert M. Utley, *Custer and the Great Controversy: The Origin and Development of a Legend* (Pasadena, CA: Westernlore Press, 1980), 41.

7. Henry Wadsworth Longfellow, *The Complete Poetical Works of Henry Wadsworth Longfellow* (Cutchogue, NY: Buccaneer Books, 1993); Homer, *The Iliad*, trans. Robert Fitzgerald (New York: Penguin Books, 1991), Book 1, lines 244, 717; Book 4, line 212; Book 10, line 281; Frederick Whittaker, *A Complete Life of General George A. Custer* (1876; repr., Lincoln: University of Nebraska Press, 1993), 2:614.

8. Joseph Campbell, *The Hero with a Thousand Faces* (Princeton: Princeton University Press, 1973), 3; Joseph Campbell, *Primitive Mythology* (New York: Penguin Books, 1987), 42; Robert Taft, "The Pictorial Record of the Old West: Custer's Last Stand—John Mulvany, Cassily Adams, and Otto Becker," in *The Custer Reader*, ed. Paul Andrew Hutton (Lincoln: University of Nebraska Press, 1992), 435.

9. Taft, "The Pictorial Record of the Old West: Custer's Last Stand—John Mulvany, Cassily Adams, and Otto Becker," in *Custer Reader*, ed. Hutton (Lincoln: University of Nebraska Press, 1992), 435–36; 439–41; note 48, 457; and 424.

10. Hemingway, *For Whom the Bell Tolls* (New York: Charles Scribner's Sons, 1940), 366; Whittaker, *Complete Life*, 2:602 and 2:614; Nathaniel Philbrick, *The Last Stand: Custer, Sitting Bull and the Battle of the Little Bighorn* (New York: Viking, 2010), 83; Utley, *Custer and the Great Controversy*, 133–34.

11. For pictograms by Amos Bad Heart Buffalo, White Bird, Kills Two, Lame Deer, and Kicking Bear, see Leslie Tillett, ed., *Wind on the Buffalo Grass: The In-*

dians' Own Account of the Battle at the Little Bighorn River (New York: Thomas Y. Crowell, 1976), 49–140, 143; for Wooden Leg, No Two Horns, White Swan, and One Bull, see Viola, *Untold Story*, 37, 65, 117, 122; for Standing Bear, see John G. Neihardt, *Black Elk Speaks* (Lincoln: University of Nebraska Press, 2004), foll. 126.

12. Jorge Luis Borges, *Collected Fictions* (New York: Penguin Books, 1998), 293; W. B. Yeats, *The Celtic Twilight* (1893; repr., Dorset, Great Britain: Prism Press, 1990), 4; Richard Slotkin, *Gunfighter Nation: The Myth of the Frontier in Twentieth Century America* (New York: Atheneum, 1992), 318.

13. Phillip Thomas Tucker, *Exodus from the Alamo: The Anatomy of the Last Stand Myth* (Philadelphia: Casemate, 2010), xi, 322, 329, 323. Walter Lord, *A Time to Stand: The Epic of the Alamo* (Lincoln: University of Nebraska Press, 1961), 191.

14. Robert M. Utley, *Cavalier in Buckskin: George Armstrong Custer and the Western Military Frontier* (Norman: University of Oklahoma Press, 1988), 116, 120.

15. William G. Doty, *Mythography* (Tuscaloosa: University of Alabama, 2000), 463; Henry Blackman Sell and Victor Weybright, *Buffalo Bill and the Wild West* (New York: Oxford University Press, 1955), 147.

16. We part from Campbell's definition of ritual: "A ritual is the enactment of a myth. By participating in a ritual you are participating in a myth." Joseph Campbell, "The First Storytellers," *Joseph Campbell and the Power of Myth*, DVD, Disc 1 (1988; repr., Del Mar, CA: Mystic Fire Video/Wellspring, 2005); Neihardt, *Black Elk Speaks*, 145.

17. Aristotle, *Poetics*, trans. Gerald F. Else (Ann Arbor: University of Michigan, 1973), 26–27.

18. William F. Cody, *The Life of Hon. William F. Cody, Known as Buffalo Bill: An Autobiography* (1879; repr., Alexandria, VA: Time-Life Books, 1982), 344 and 298; Slotkin, *Fatal Environment*, 408; Brian W. Dippie, *Custer's Last Stand* (Missoula: University of Montana Press, 1976), 77–78.

19. Dippie, 87; Martí (1853–1895), Apostle of Cuban Independence, was also "one of the leading prose writers of the Spanish language and a recognized poet in a new literary movement called *Modernismo*." See Roberto González Echevarría, "An Introduction," in José Martí, *Selected Writings* (New York: Penguin Books, 2002), xvi; José Martí, "¡Magnífico espectáculo!," José Martí, *Obras Completas* (La Habana: Editorial Nacional de Cuba, 1963), 11: 31–43; Louis S. Warren, *Buffalo Bill's America: William Cody and the Wild West Show* (New York: Alfred A. Knopf, 2005), 256 and 272–73. In later years, the role of Custer would be assigned to Buck Taylor, "King of the Cowboys."

20. Charles Herner, *The Arizona Rough Riders* (Tucson: University of Arizona Press, 1970), 38; Michael A. Elliot, *Custerology: The Enduring Legacy of the Indian Wars and George Armstrong Custer* (Chicago: University of Chicago Press, 2007), 141; Michelle Delaney, *Buffalo Bill's Wild West Warriors: A Photographic History by Gertrude Kasebier* (New York: Harper Collins, 2007), 145; Slotkin, *Gunfighter Nation*, 83 and 85.

21. Utley, *The Lance and the Shield*, between 270–71, 265–66.

22. Martí, "¡Magnífico espectáculo!," 43.

23. John Neihardt, "Song of the Indian Wars," in *The Twilight of the Sioux* (Lincoln: University of Nebraska, 1971), 176.

24. Bartolomé de Las Casas, *Brevísima Relación de la Destruición de las Indias* (Madrid: Ediciones Cátedra, 2001), 78, 159. All translations from Las Casas' *Relación* by Oscar Giner. For a complete, workmanlike translation in English of Las Casas' text, see *A Short Account of the Destruction of the Indies*, ed. and trans. Nigel Griffin (New York: Penguin Books, 1992).

25. Las Casas, *Brevísima Relación*, 107–8; Bartolomé de Las Casas, *Historia de las Indias* (México: Fondo de Cultura Económica, 1965), vol. 2, lib. III, cap. XXV, 522.

26. Hugh Thomas, *Rivers of Gold* (New York: Random House Trade Paperback, 2005), 137; Las Casas, *Brevísima Relación*, 160 (castellanos were golden coins from the Middle Ages); Francisco López de Xerez, *Verdadera Relación de la Conquista del Perú*, quoted in Kim MacQuarrie, *The Last Days of the Incas* (New York: Simon and Schuster, 2007), 96; MacQuarrie, *Last Days*, 133.

27. Peter Shaffer, *The Royal Hunt of the Sun* (New York: Stein and Day, 1965), 14. Shaffer's play is an incisive contemporary dramatization of the story of Pizarro and Atahualpa.

28. Edward Lazarus, *Black Hills White Justice* (New York: Harper Collins, 1991), 90, 92.

29. Robert M. Utley, *Last Days of the Sioux Nation* (New Haven: Yale University Press, 1965), 22–23. See also Clyde A. Milner II, Carol O'Connor, and Martha A. Sandweiss, eds., *The Oxford History of the American West* (Oxford: Oxford University Press, 1994), 247–49; Utley, *The Lance and the Shield*, 200, 232.

30. Lazarus, *Black Hills White Justice*, 108–9; Vine Deloria Jr., *Custer Died for Your Sins* (Norman: University of Oklahoma Press, 1988), 46.

31. Utley, *The Last Days of the Sioux Nation*, 50; Lazarus, 90–92, 109–12.

32. Utley, *Last Days of the Sioux Nation*, 54–59, and James Mooney, *The Ghost Dance* (North Dighton, MA: JG Press, 1996), 186–90, and 133–36.

33. Mooney, *Ghost Dance*, 182–83.

34. Mooney, *Ghost Dance*, 66, 139, 127.

35. The following account of Ghost Dance beliefs, unless noted in the text, is based on a letter written by James McLaughlin, October 17, 1890 (Mooney, *Ghost Dance*, 149); a sermon preached by Ghost Dance priest Short Bull, October 31, 1890 (Mooney, *Ghost Dance*, 150–51); and both a summary by George Sword, an Oglala who was captain of Indian police at Pine Ridge, and the testimony of Kuwapi as interviewed by William Selwyn, a Yankton Sioux (Mooney, appendix to ch. 10, 158–163).

36. Written account by Mrs. Z. A. Parker of a dance observed June 20, 1890, quoted in Mooney, *Ghost Dance*, 278–79, 150.

37. Utley, *Last Days of the Sioux Nation*, 92–94, and *The Lance and the Shield*, 285–286.

38. Utley, *Last Days of the Sioux Nation*, 111, and Mooney, *Ghost Dance*, 211–12.

39. The following account of Sitting Bull's death follows the versions found in

Utley, *Last Days*, 155–64, and *The Lance and the Shield*, ch. 24, 293–305; Mooney, *Ghost Dance*, 217–23; and James McLaughlin, "An Account of Sitting Bull's Death, 1891," www.pbs.org/weta/thewest/resources/archives/eight/sbarrest.htm (accessed May 3, 2013).

40. Mooney, *Ghost Dance*, 217.

41. Mark Owen with Kevin Maurer, *No Easy Day: The Autobiography of a Navy Seal* (New York: Dutton, Penguin Group, 2012), 247.

42. Utley, *Last Days of the Sioux Nation*, 166; McLaughlin, "An Account of Sitting Bull's Death, 1891."

43. Mooney, *Ghost Dance*, 290; Mary Collins, a Congregational missionary at Standing Rock, and Catherine Weldon Johnson, a friend and supporter of Sitting Bull, quoted in Utley, *The Lance and the Shield*, 286 and 291–92; McLaughlin, "An Account of Sitting Bull's Death"; Utley, *Lance and the Shield*, 286.

44. Mooney, *Ghost Dance*, 148–62.

45. Mooney, *Ghost Dance*, 83; Karl Marx and Friedrich Engels, *The Communist Manifesto*, trans. Samuel Norse, (London: Penguin Classics, 1985), 79.

46. Carl Jung quoted in Gerhard Wehr, *An Illustrated Biography of C. G. Jung* (Boston: Shambhala, 1989), 64.

47. Stephen W. Silliman, "The 'Old West' in the Middle East: U.S. Military Metaphors in Real and Imagined Indian Country," *American Anthropologist* 110.2 (2008): 237, 239.

48. Silliman, 241–42; Robert D. Kaplan, *Imperial Grunts: The American Military on the Ground* (New York: Random House, 2005), 367; John A. Wickham, "September 11 and America's War on Terrorism: A New Manifest Destiny," *American Indian Quarterly* 26.1 (2002): 116–44; John Brown, "'Our Indian Wars Are Not Over Yet'—Ten ways to Interpret the War on Terror as a Frontier Conflict," January 20, 2006, *TomDispatch.com*, http://www.commondreams.org/cgi-bin/print.cgi?file=/views06/0120-20.htm (accessed August 5, 2013).

Chapter 4

1. Ian Kershaw, *Hitler, 1936–1945: Nemesis* (New York: W. W. Norton, 2000), 841.

2. Amy Kaplan, "'Left Alone with America': The Absence of Empire in the Study of American Culture," in *Cultures of United States Imperialism*, ed. Amy Kaplan and Donald E. Pease (Durham, NC: Duke University Press, 1993), 12–13; Amy Kaplan, *The Anarchy of Empire in the Making of U.S. Culture* (Cambridge, MA: Harvard University Press, 2002), 6, 11–12; Barbara A. Biesecker, "Remembering World War II: The Rhetoric and Politics of National Commemoration at the Turn of the 21st Century," *Quarterly Journal of Speech* 88.4 (2002): 394; Vanessa B. Beasley sees a similar pattern in the operation of presidential inaugurals, "The Rhetoric of Ideological Consensus in the United States: American Principles and American Pose in Presidential Inaugurals," *Communication Monographs* 68.2 (2001): 181–82.

3. Kenneth Burke, "The Rhetoric of Hitler's 'Battle,'" reprinted in *The Phi-*

losophy of Literary Form: Studies in Symbolic Action, 3rd ed. (Berkeley: University of California Press, 1973), 191–92, 218–19.

4. Burke, "Hitler's 'Battle,'" 219–20, 193, 196, 202–4 (emphasis in the original).

5. Bernard Shaw, "Don Juan in Hell," from *Man and Superman* in *Nine Plays by Bernard Shaw* (1903; repr., New York: Dodd, Mead, 1935), 619.

6. Harry Truman, "Statement by the President of the United States," The White House, Washington, DC, August 6, 1945, Harry S. Truman Library, Papers of Eban A. Ayers, http://www.trumanlibrary.org/whistlestop/study_collections /bomb/small/mb10.htm (accessed January 8, 2009). Also online at http://www .pbs.org/wgbh/americanexperience/features/primary-resources/truman-hiroshima/ (accessed February 1, 2013). James W. Hikins, "The Rhetoric of 'Unconditional Surrender' and the Decision to Drop the Atomic Bomb," *Quarterly Journal of Speech* 69 (November 1983): 379–80, 399–400.

7. Robert L. Ivie, "William McKinley: Advocate of Imperialism," *Western Speech* 36.1 (1972): 15–17, 23; Vincente L. Farael, "White Love: Surveillance and Nationalist Resistance in the U.S. Colonization of the Philippines," in *Cultures of Unites States Imperialism*, 185–87; Myles Beaupre, "'What Are the Philippines Going to Do to Us?': E. L. Godkin on Democracy, Empire, and Anti-imperialism," *Journal of American Studies* 46.3 (2012): 712–13.

8. Susan A. Brewer, *Why America Fights: Patriotism and War Propaganda from the Philippines to Iraq* (New York: Oxford University Press, 2009), 14–15, 36–37, 40, 42.

9. Brewer, *Why America Fights*, 42–43.

10. Pricilla Murolo, "Wars of Civilization: The US Army Contemplates Wounded Knee, the Pullman Strike, and the Philippine Insurrection," *International Labor and Working-Class History* 80 (Fall 2011): 83, 85–88, 91.

11. Paul A. Kramer, "Race-Making and Colonial Violence in the U.S. Empire: The Philippine-American War as Race War," *Diplomatic History* 30.2 (2006): 171–72, 185, 201, 203, 190–94; Phillip Ablett, "Colonialism in Denial: US Propaganda in the Philippine-American War," *Social Alternatives* 23.3 (2004): 25.

12. Robert L. Ivie, "Savagery in Democracy's Empire," *Third World Quarterly* 26.1 (2005): 56–59.

13. Erin Steuter and Deborah Wills, *At War with Metaphor: Media, Propaganda, and Racism in the War on Terror* (Lanham, MD: Lexington Books, 2008), xv–xvi.

14. Committee on Public Information, *German War Practices*, ed. Dana C. Munro, George C. Sellery, and August C. Krey (1917).

15. Winston Churchill, "Prime Minister Winston Churchill's Broadcast 'Report on the War,'" April 27, 1942, http://www.ibiblio.org/pha/timeline/410427awp .html (accessed February 8, 2013); Winston Churchill, "Prime Minister Winston Churchill's Broadcast on the Soviet-German War," June 22, 1941, http://www .ibiblio.org/pha/timeline/410622dwp.html (accessed February 8, 2013).

16. Brewer, *Why America Fights*, 59.

17. These posters are readily found at various sites on the Internet, including a power-point presentation entitled "World War I Propaganda Posters," http://

sprague2.net/. . ./World%20War%20I%20Propaganda%20Posters.ppt (accessed February 9, 2013).

18. Accessed online at http://www.artstor.org.ezproxy.lib.indiana.edu /artstor/ViewImages?id=8D1EczUtPCgoOSY0Y1N7R3spXXMhf1x8&userId= gDBAdA %3D%3D (accessed March 2, 2013).

19. Celia Malone Kingsbury, *For Home and Country: World War I Propaganda on the Home Front* (Norman: University of Nebraska Press, 2010), 92.

20. Erik Van Schaack, "The Coming of the Hun! American Fears of a German Invasion, 1918," *The Journal of American Culture* 28.3 (2005): 284–86, 291.

21. *The Kaiser, the Beast of Berlin*, directed by Rupert Julian, released on March 9, 1918, Rupert Julian Productions, silent black and white film, 70 minutes. In the interwar years, an anti-isolationist film was released to portray Hitler as the beast of Berlin. See Cynthia J. Miller, "The B Movie Goes to War in Hitler, *Beast of Berlin*," in *Why We Fought: America's Wars in Film and History*, ed. Peter C. Rollins and John E. O'Connor (Lexington: University Press of Kentucky, 2008), 226–41.

22. An image of the poster is available online at http://www.flickr.com/photos /nostri-imago/2868678553/ (accessed February 8, 2013).

23. Edward W. Said, *Orientalism* (1978; repr., New York: Vintage Books, 1979), 4, 71–73, 205–7; Marja Vuorinen, "Introduction: Enemy Images as Inversions of the Self," in *Enemy Images in War Propaganda*, ed. Marja Vuorinen (Newcastle upon Tyne: Cambridge Scholars Publishing, 2012), 1–4; Harold D. Lasswell, *Propaganda Technique in World War I* (1927; repr., Cambridge, MA: MIT Press, 1971), 69, 77, 96, 102, 195.

24. On the Pullman strike, see Murolo, "Wars of Civilization," 77. Although Debs is remembered as a political visionary whose ideas were rejected in his own day but largely adopted after his time, this reconstruction of his image undermines the significance of his dissent from the system. As Lee and Andrews suggest, "The American story of liberal progress shapes individual characters to its purpose. The disdainful becomes the celebrated; the failed becomes the visionary; and the tragic is transformed into a narrative of reconciliation." Ronald Lee and James R. Andrews, "A Story of Rhetorical-Ideological Transformation: Eugene V. Debs as Liberal Hero," *Quarterly Journal of Speech* 77.1 (1991): 32. The jailhouse conversion to Socialism narrative may be more legendary than historical in its clarity and timing, as indicated by James Darsey, "The Legend of Eugene Debs: Prophetic *Ethos* as Radical Argument," *Quarterly Journal of Speech* 74.4 (1988): 440. On the Canton, Ohio, speech and its aftermath, see Ernest Freeberg, *Democracy's Prisoner: Eugene V. Debs, The Great War, and the Right to Dissent* (Cambridge, MA: Harvard University Press, 2008), 46, 52–53, 72, 96–101.

25. Eugene V. Debs, "Anti-War Speech at Canton, Ohio," June 16, 1918, E. V. Debs Internet Archive, http://www.marxists.org/archive/debs/works/1918/canton .htm (accessed February 11, 2013).

26. Debs, "Anti-War Speech at Canton, Ohio."

27. Randolph Bourne, "War Is the Health of the State" (1918), http://www .antiwar.com/bourne.php (accessed February 11, 2013).

28. Brewer, *Why America Fights*, 88; Franklin Roosevelt, "State of the Union" Address, January 6, 1942, http://www.let.rug.nl/usa/presidents/franklin-delano -roosevelt/state-of-the-union-1942.php (accessed February 9, 2013).

29. Charles Chaplin, *My Autobiography* (1964; repr., New York: Penguin Classics, 2003), 387–88.

30. Charles Chaplin, *The Great Dictator* (Charles Chaplin Film Corporation, 1940).

31. Adrian Daub, "'Hannah, Can You Hear Me?'—Chaplin's *Great Dictator*, 'Schtonk,' and the Vicissitudes of Voice," *Criticism* 51.3 (2009): 469, 473–74, 478– 79; Robert Cole, "Anglo-American Anti-fascist Film Propaganda in a Time of Neutrality: *The Great Dictator*, 1940," *Historical Journal of Film, Radio and Television* 21.2 (2001): 140, 142–43, 145, 149; Jodi Sherman, "Humor, Resistance, and the Abject: Roberto Benigni's *Life Is Beautiful* and Charlie Chaplin's *The Great Dictator*," *Film & History* 32.2 (2002): 75.

32. Chaplin, *My Autobiography*, 458.

33. Walt Disney, *Spirit of '43* (1943), http://www.youtube.com/watch?v= fHj0p7DCAfU (accessed February 15, 2013).

34. Brewer, *Why America Fights*, 108.

35. These films, produced by Major Frank Capra for the War Department, Special Services Division, Office of War Information, Bureau of Motion Pictures in cooperation with the US Army Signal Corps, included *Prelude to War* (1942), *The Nazis Strike* (1943), *Divide and Conquer* (1943), *The Battle of Britain* (1943), *The Battle of Russia* (1943), *The Battle of China* (1944), and *War Comes to America* (1945).

36. Peter C. Rollins, "Frank Capra's *Why We Fight* Film Series and Our American Dream," *Journal of American Culture* 19.4 (1996): 81, 84; see also Jordi Xifra and Ramon Girona, "Frank Capra's *Why We Fight* and Film Documentary Discourse in Public Relations," *Public Relations Review* 38.1 (2012): 45.

37. Chaplin, *My Autobiography*, 387; Frank Capra, *The Name above the Title: An Autobiography* (New York: Macmillan, 1971), 325–43. On Capra's intent to refute, see Ian S. Scott, "*Why We Fight* and *Projections of America*: Frank Capra, Robert Riskin, and the Making of World War II Propaganda," in *Why We Fought*, ed. Rollins and O'Connor, 244.

38. For a general discussion of racism and other propaganda themes in Hollywood films aimed at demonizing the enemy during World War II, see Andrew J. Falk, *Upstaging the Cold War: American Dissent and Cultural Diplomacy, 1940–1960* (Amherst: University of Massachussets Press, 2010), 1–38.

39. Kathleen M. German, "Frank Capra's *Why We Fight* Series and the American Audience," *Western Journal of Speech Communication* 54 (Spring 1990): 241, 244.

40. Rollins, "Frank Capra's *Why We Fight* Film Series," 85.

41. Franklin Roosevelt, "Declaration of War," delivered on December 8, 1945, to a joint session of Congress and broadcast over radio to the American public; History Matters, http://historymatters.gmu.edu/d/5166/ (accessed March 8, 2013).

42. *News Parade: Bombing of Pearl Harbor* (Castle Films, 1942).

43. Franklin Roosevelt, "Declaration of War."

44. The film was released on August 9, 1945, the same day the atomic bomb was dropped on Nagasaki and three days after the atomic bomb was dropped on Hiroshima.

45. Claudia Springer, "Military Propaganda: Defense Department Films from World War II and Vietnam," *Cultural Critique* 3 (Spring 1986): 152.

46. John W. Dower, *War Without Mercy: Race and Power in the Pacific War* (New York: Pantheon Books, 1986), 9–10, 20.

47. Steuter and Wills, *At War with Metaphor*, 38.

48. Another strategy considered for diminishing the perceived threat from this internal racial enemy was to disperse and assimilate people of Japanese ancestry. See Allan W. Austin, "East Pioneers: Japanese American Resettlement during World War II and the Contested Meaning of Exile and Incarceration," *Journal of American Ethnic History* (Winter 2007): 58, 66, 68–70.

49. *Japanese Relocation*, Office of War Information, Bureau of Motion Pictures, 1943.

50. John Howard, *Concentration on the Home Front: Japanese Americans in the House of Jim Crow* (Chicago: University of Chicago Press, 2008).

51. Samuel T. Caruso, "After Pearl Harbor: Arizona's Response to the Gila River Relocation Center," *Journal of Arizona History* 14.4 (1973): 335.

52. David Davis, "A Field in the Desert that Felt Like Home," *Sports Illustrated* November 16, 1998, 3. For a discussion of the internal tensions in the camp associated with these cultural sites and functions, see Arthur A. Hansen, "Cultural Politics in the Gila River Relocation Center 1942–1943," *Arizona and the West* 27.4 (1985): 327–62. Michi Weglyn, *Years of Infamy: The Untold Story of America's Concentration Camps* (New York: Morrow, 1976).

53. Austin, "East Pioneers," 58.

54. Takeya Mizuno, "Censorship in a Different Name: Press 'Supervision' in Wartime Japanese American Camps 1942–1943," *Journalism and Mass Communication Quarterly* 88.1 (2011): 121–41.

55. "U.S. Initial Post-Surrender Policy for Japan," SWNCC 150/4, State-War-Navy Coordinating Committee, September 21, 1945, http://www.ndl.go.jp /constitution/e/shiryo/01/022_2/022_2tx.html (accessed February 28, 2013).

56. Henry R. Luce, "The American Century," *Life Magazine* (February 17, 1941): 61–65.

57. Brewer, *Why America Fights*, 90.

58. Neil MacFarquhar, "Saddam Hussein, Defiant Dictator Who Ruled Iraq with Violence and Fear, Dies," *New York Times*, December 30, 2006, http://www .nytimes.com/2006/12/30/world/middleeast/30saddam.html?pagewanted=all& _r=0 (accessed January 17, 2014).

59. Edward T. Linenthal, "The Boundaries of Memory: The United States Holocaust Memorial Museum," *American Quarterly* 46.3 (1994): 410.

60. Marouf Hasian Jr., "Remembering and Forgetting the 'Final Solution': A Rhetorical Pilgrimage through the U.S. Holocaust Memorial Museum," *Critical Studies in Media Communication* 21.1 (2004): 79–81.

61. Tim Cole, "Nativization and Nationalization: A Comparative Landscape Study of Holocaust Museums in Israel, the US and the UK," *Journal of Israeli History: Politics, Society, Culture* 23.1 (2004): 138, 134. On this point, see also Lilenthal, "The Boundaries of Memory," 428–29.

62. Fath Davis Ruffins, "Culture Wars Won and Lost: Ethnic Museums on the Mall, Part I: The National Holocaust Museum and the National Museum of the American Indian," *Radical History Review* 68 (1997): 90, 83.

63. Amanda J. Cobb, "The National Museum of the American Indian: Sharing the Gift," *American Indian Quarterly* 29.3-4 (2005): 364–65, 379, 381 (emphasis in the original). See also Ruffins, "Culture Wars Won and Lost," 97.

64. Joanne Barker and Clayton Dumont, "Contested Conversations: Presentations, Expectations, and Responsibility at the National Museum of the American Indian," *American Indian Culture and Research Journal* 30.2 (2006): 136, 124.

Chapter 5

1. Paul D. Voelker, "Politics, But Literature: The Example of Eugene O'Neill's Apprenticeship," *The Eugene O'Neill Newsletter*, http://www.eoneill.com/library/newsletter/viii_2/viii-2b.htm (accessed May 21, 2013); Eugene O'Neill, *The Plays of Eugene O'Neill* (New York: Random House, 1954), 3:248; José Martí, "Class War in Chicago: A Terrible Drama," in Martí, *Selected Writings* (New York: Penguin Books, 2002), 203.

2. José Martí, "El proceso de los siete anarquistas de Chicago," in Martí, *Obras Completas* (La Habana: Editorial Nacional de Cuba, 1963), 11:55; *Chicago Tribune*, May 5, 1886; *New York Times*, May 6, 1886, in "The Haymarket Riot and Trial: Selected Newspaper Articles," *The Haymarket Riot Trial, 1886*, in Douglas O. Linder, *Famous Trials*, http://law2.umkc.edu/faculty/projects/ftrials/haymarket/haymarketnews.html (accessed May 31, 2013).

3. José Martí, "Grandes motines obreros," *Obras Completas*, 10:452; and José Martí, "El proceso de los siete anarquistas" *Obras Completas*, 11:56.

4. Martí, "Un drama terrible," *Obras Completas*, 11:343; Martí, "Grandes motines obreros," *Obras Completas*, 10:454; and Martí, *Selected Writings*, 209.

5. A. M. Nagler, ed., *A Sourcebook in Theatrical History* (New York: Dover Publications, 1952), 47; James Mooney, *The Ghost Dance* (North Dighton, MA: JG Press, 1996), 148.

6. Martí, *Selected Writings*, 201.

7. John P. Altgeld, "The Pardon of the Haymarket Prisoners," *The Haymarket Riot Trial 1886*, in Douglas O. Linder, *Famous Trials*, http://law2.umkc.edu/faculty/projects/ftrials/haymarket/pardon.html (accessed June 3, 2013).

8. Karl Marx and Friedrich Engels, *The Communist Manifesto*, trans. Samuel Moore (1848; repr., New York: Penguin Books, 1985), 78, 93, 80, 85, and 94.

9. Marx and Engels, *Communist Manifesto*, 84; Mooney, *Ghost Dance*, 34 and 45; Rev. 21:1 and 22:14.

10. US Senate, Subcommittee of the Committee on the Judiciary, *Bolshevik Propaganda Hearings*, 65th. Cong., 3rd sess., Washington, DC: GPO, 1919.

11. John Steinbeck, *The Grapes of Wrath* (1939; repr., New York: Bantam Books, 1970), 35 and 54.

12. Steinbeck, 24, 189, 139, 328–29.

13. Steinbeck, 260–61, 95. Ward Howe's poem was first printed in the *Atlantic Monthly*, February 1862.

14. Yunte Huang, *Charlie Chan: The Untold Story of the Honorable Detective and His Rendezvous with History* (New York: W. W. Norton, 2010), 269.

15. Titles and publication dates of Hammett's novels are: *Red Harvest* (1927), *The Dain Curse* (1928), *The Maltese Falcon* (1929), *The Glass Key* (1930), and *The Thin Man* (1933); Richard Layman, *Shadow Man: The Life of Dashiell Hammett* (New York: Harcourt, Brace, Jovanovich, 1981), 181.

16. Layman, *Shadow Man*, 203; Lillian Hellman, *Scoundrel Time* (Boston: Little, Brown, 1976), 50; Hellman, "Introduction," in Dashiell Hammett, *The Big Knockover: Selected Stories and Short Novels* (New York: Vintage Books, 1989), xii.

17. Layman, *Shadow Man*, 219; "Hammett's full testimony before United States Second District Court Judge Sylvester Ryan, July 9, 1951, in New York City," appendix, in Layman, *Shadow Man*, 259.

18. Hellman, "Introduction," in Hammett, *Big Knockover*, x; Layman, *Shadow Man*, 260.

19. Bertolt Brecht, "We Nineteen," in *Thirty Years of Treason: Excerpts from Hearings before the House Committee on Un-American Activities, 1938–1968*, ed. Eric Bentley (New York: The Viking Press, 1971), 224; Garry Wills, "Introduction," in Hellman, *Scoundrel Time*, 31–32.

20. O'Neill, 3:172.

21. Hugh Thomas, *Cuba: The Pursuit of Freedom* (New York: Harper and Row, 1971), 410 and 445; Robin Andersen, *A Century of Media, A Century of War* (New York: Peter Lang, 2006), 109.

22. Ché Guevara, *Guerrilla Warfare* (Lincoln: University of Nebraska Press, 1998), 5.

23. David Halberstam, *The Fifties* (New York: Villard Books, 1993), 378 and 386–87; Richard Gott, *Cuba: A New History* (New Haven: Yale University Press, 2005), 153; Mark Twain, *Collected Tales, Sketches, Speeches, & Essays* (New York: The Library of America, 1992), 475.

24. Guevara, *Guerrilla Warfare*, 11.

25. Thomas, *Cuba*, 1490, 1056, and 1051.

26. Thomas, *Cuba*, 1302; Howard Jones, *The Bay of Pigs* (Oxford: Oxford University Press, 2008), 172.

27. Jones, *Bay of Pigs*, 82; Thomas, *Cuba*, 1358.

28. Thomas, *Cuba*, 1369.

29. Peter Wyden, *Bay of Pigs: The Untold Story* (New York: Simon and Schuster, 1979), 291.

30. Smedley D. Butler, *War Is a Racket* (Port Townsend, WA: Feral House, 2003), 55; Jones, 133 and 168.

31. Fidel Castro Speaks Before Havana Rally, "Castro Speech Data Base," *Latin American Network Information Center*, http://lanic.utexas.edu/project/castro

/db/1959/19590121.html (accessed November 11, 2013); Trisha Ziff, *Che Guevara: Revolutionary and Icon* (New York: Abrams Image, 2006), 15.

32. Guevara, "Message to the Tricontinental," *Guerrilla Warfare*, 171.

33. Ziff, *Che Guevara*, 17; Gott, *Cuba*, 3.

34. Ernesto Ché Guevara, *El diario del Che en Bolivia* (New York: Ocean Press, 2006), 190.

35. John Berger, "Image of Imperialism," in *Selected Essays* (New York: Vintage Books, 2003), 114; Derek Walcott, "Che," in *Collected Poems, 1948–1984* (New York: Farrar, Straus and Giroux, 2001), 123; Ziff, *Che Guevara*, 20. See the Frémez poster in Ziff, 43.

36. Steinbeck, 463; Ziff, *Che Guevara*, 22.

37. Unless noted, quotes from the film are from John Milius and Francis Ford Coppola, *Apocalypse Now Redux: The Screenplay* (New York: Hyperion, 2000).

38. Conversation with Lee Benjamin, April 25 and 26, 2013.

39. George S. Patton, "Speech to the Third Army Troops, England, Spring 1944" in *American Speeches: Political Oratory from Abraham Lincoln to Bill Clinton*, ed. Ted Widmer (New York: The Library of America, 2006), 449. James William Gibson, *The Perfect War: Technowar in Vietnam* (New York: Atlantic Monthly Press, 2000), 26.

40. Peter Cowie, *The Apocalypse Now Book* (New York: Da Capo Press, 2001), 96; Arthur Kopit, *Indians* (New York: Bantam Books, 1971). Published versions of the text juxtapose Mooney's photographs of Wounded Knee with photos of the Vietnam War.

41. Joseph Campbell, *The Hero with a Thousand Faces* (Princeton, NJ: Princeton University Press, 1973), 81.

42. Anthony Storr, ed., *The Essential Jung* (New York: MJF Books, 1983), 109–10.

43. "Quetzalcoatl," in *Four Masterworks of American Indian Literature*, ed. John Bierhorst (Tucson: University of Arizona Press, 1984), 30; William Golding, *Lord of the Flies* (New York: Capricorn Books, 1959), 133.

44. Marlon Brando with Robert Lindsey, *Songs My Mother Never Taught Me* (New York: Random House, 1994), 431.

Chapter 6

1. War propaganda is "a fantasy of enmity where we seek self-definition through constructing our antithesis," according to Nicholas Jackson O'Shaughnessy, *Politics and Propaganda: Weapons of Mass Seduction* (Ann Arbor: University of Michigan Press, 2005), vii.

2. On the notion of a comic corrective, see Kenneth Burke, *Attitudes Toward History*, 3rd ed. (Berkeley: University of California Press, 1984), 39–44.

3. Lewis Hyde, *Trickster Makes This World: Mischief, Myth and Art* (New York: North Point Press, 1998), 14, 268.

4. C. G. Jung, *Four Archetypes: Mother/Rebirth/Sprit/Trickster*, trans. R. F. C. Hull (Princeton, NJ: Princeton University Press, 1969), 142, 140, 144.

5. Most commonly, according to William Hynes, tricksters are figures of (1) ambiguity, anomaly, polyvalence, (2) disruption, impropriety, alchemy, (3) disguise, transmorphism, shape-shifting, (4) inversion, profanity, toppling, (5) cultural transformation through mediation and imitation of the Gods, and (6) bricolage. See William H. Hynes, "Mapping the Characteristic of Mythic Tricksters: A Heuristic Guide," in *Mythical Trickster Figures: Contours, Contexts, and Criticisms*, ed. William J. Hynes and William G. Doty (Tuscaloosa: University of Alabama Press, 1993), 33–45.

6. William J. Hynes, "Inconclusive Conclusions: Tricksters; Metaplayers and Revealers," in *Mythical Trickster Figures*, 212. Romand Coles, "Of Tensions and Tricksters: Grassroots Democracy Between Theory and Practice," *Perspectives on Politics* 4.3 (2006): 547.

7. Burke, *Attitudes*, 308–10, 312–14. See 309 for Burke's quotation of Shakespeare's *Romeo and Juliet* regarding virtue turning to vice.

8. Burke, *Attitudes*, 27; Kenneth Burke, *Permanence and Change: An Anatomy of Purpose*, 2nd rev. ed. (1954; repr., Indianapolis, IN: Bobbs-Merrill, 1965), 69–70; Burke, *Permanence and Change*, 90, 133; Burke, *Permanence and Change*, 133, 163.

9. Burke, *Permanence and Change*, 108 (emphasis in the original).

10. Trickster "can find the lewd in the sacred and the sacred in the lewd," Hynes notes, so that "no prohibition is safe from trickster." Hynes, "Mapping Mythic Tricksters," 42.

11. Demonizing enemies involves denying them a complex subjectivity, "a subjectivity that includes the cultural and historical backgrounds, the political motivations, and the unconscious drives of the actors," according to Joseba Zulaika, *Terrorism: The Self-Fulfilling Prophecy* (Chicago: University of Chicago Press, 2009), 19, 50–51.

12. Jung, *Four Archetypes*, 151.

13. Thomas H. Etzold and John Lewis Gaddis, eds., *Containment: Documents on American Policy and Strategy, 1945–1950* (New York: Columbia University Press, 1978), 385–442.

14. Ernest R. May and Philip D. Zelikow, eds. *The Kennedy Tapes: Inside the White House During the Cuban Missile Crisis* (Cambridge, MA: Belknap, 1997), 107; John F. Kennedy, "Televised Address on Cuban Missile Crisis," October 22, 1962, in Theodore C. Sorensen, ed., *"Let the Word Go Forth": The Speeches, Statements, and Writings of John F. Kennedy, 1947 to 1963* (New York: Delacorte Press, 1988), 272–78.

15. Steven R. Goldzwig and George N. Dionosopoulos, *In a Perilous Hour: The Public Address of John F. Kennedy* (Westport, CT: Greenwood Press, 1995), 112, 116.

16. For a more detailed account of how Kennedy and his advisors worked through the crisis with Khrushchev, as a function of the stereoscopic gaze, see Robert L. Ivie, "Finessing the Demonology of War: Toward a Practical Aesthetic of Humanising Dissent," *Javnost—The Public* 14.4 (2007): 37–54.

17. May and Zelikow, eds., *The Kennedy Tapes*, 59, 61–62, 88, 99–100, 105, 107, 127, 129, 134, 142, 144, 176–79, 186, 256, 281–82, 480 (emphasis in the original).

See also Graham Allison and Philip Zelikow, *Essence of Decision: Explaining the Cuban Missile Crisis* (New York: Longman, 1999), 355–57.

18. Martin Luther King Jr., "Beyond Vietnam: A Time to Break the Silence," April 4, 1967, delivered at Riverside Church in New York City. *American Rhetoric Online Speech Bank*, http://www.americanrhetoric.com/speeches/mlkatimetobreaksilence .htm (accessed April 12, 2013).

19. Jim Wallis is a prolific author, speaker, and preacher, media commentator, evangelical theologian, and founder of the *Sojourners* magazine and network of progressive Christians working for peace and justice. He has served on the advisory board of President Barack Obama's Office of Faith-Based and Neighborhood Partnerships.

20. Jim Wallis, "A Peaceful Response to September 11, 2001," in *The Antiwar Movement*, ed. Randy Scherer (San Diego, CA: Greenhaven Press, 2004), 134–35, 138–39. This essay was originally published in 2001 in *Sojourners* magazine following 9/11 but before the US invasion of Afghanistan.

21. Jim Wallis, *God's Politics: A New Vision for Faith and Politics in America* (New York: Harper San Francisco, 2005), xxi, 3–4, 67–68, 94.

22. Wallis, *God's Politics*, 5, 13, 16, 101, 105.

23. Wallis, *God's Politics*, 22–23, 30, 97, 105, 109, 119, 141, 144–45, 149, 151–52, 154 (emphasis in the original).

24. Wallis, *God's Politics*, 45–47, 144, 154, 190.

25. Wallis, *God's Politics*, 138–46, 149, 163, 171, 191, 201.

26. Dan Glaister, "Clinton and Obama Swap Fireworks for Détente," *Guardian*, February 1, 2008, http://www.guardian.co.uk/world/2008/feb/01/uselections2008 .barackobama.

27. Robert L. Ivie and Oscar Giner, "More Good, Less Evil: Contesting the Mythos of National Insecurity in the 2008 Presidential Primaries," *Rhetoric & Public Affairs* 12.2 (2009): 279–301; Robert L. Ivie and Oscar Giner, "American Exceptionalism in a Democratic Idiom: Transacting the Mythos of Change in the 2008 Presidential Campaign," *Communication Studies* 60.4 (2009): 359–75.

28. Barack Obama, "Remarks of Senator Barack Obama to the Chicago Council on Global Affairs," April 23, 2007, Council on Foreign Relations, Essential Documents, http://www.cfr.org/us-election-2008/remarks-senator-barack-obama -chicago-council-global-affairs/p13172 (accessed November 31, 2012).

29. Barack Obama, *The Audacity of Hope: Thoughts on Reclaiming the American Dream* (New York: Three Rivers Press, 2006), 310.

30. As Felicia Stewart observes, Obama's "intent to seek interdependence and interconnectivity" is manifest throughout his rhetoric; "his words celebrate diverse cultures." Felicia R. Stewart, "Exploring Afrocentricity: An Analysis of the Discourse of Barack Obama," *Journal of African American Studies* 15 (2011): 273, 276. Obama's civic rhetoric is at once cosmopolitan and local in its sensitivity to diversity, according to Ronald C. Arnett, "Civic Rhetoric: Meeting the Communal Interplay of the Provincial and the Cosmopolitan; Barack Obama's Notre Dame Speech, May 17, 2009," *Rhetoric & Public Affairs* 14.4 (2011): 632. The narrative of

his campaign rhetoric was marked by an attempt to envision "an America united as a nation based on commonly held political principles referred to as 'the American Creed,'" argues Stefanie Hammer, "The Role of Narrative in Political Campaigning: An Analysis of Speeches by Barack Obama," *National Identities* 12.3 (2010): 270. His vision is of a people in a continuing process of constituting themselves, according to Derek Sweet and Margret McCue-Enser, "Constituting 'the People' as Rhetorical Interruption: Barack Obama and the Unfinished Hopes of an Imperfect People," *Communication Studies* 61.5 (2010): 602–22.

31. Obama expressed these views in an interview with Robin Toner on March 15, 2008, as reported in Robin Toner, "Obama's Test: Can a Liberal be a Unifier?" *New York Times*, March 25, 2008, http://www.nytimes.com/2008/03/25/us /politics/25obama.html?pagewanted=all (accessed November 1, 2012).

32. Democratic Debate Transcript, Texas, February 21, 2008, *CNNPolitics. com*, http://www.cnn.com/2008/POLITICS/02/21/debate.transcript/ (accessed November 1, 2012).

33. Transcript, "The Democratic Debate in South Carolina," *New York Times*, January 21, 2008, http://www.nytimes.com/2008/01/21/us/politics/21demdebate -transcript.html?pagewanted=all (accessed November 1, 2012).

34. Obama's speech on race pursued a theme of consilience over othering, argues David A. Frank, "The Prophetic Voice and the Face of the Other in Barack Obama's 'A More Perfect Union' Address, March 18, 2008," *Rhetoric & Public Affairs* 12.2 (2009): 167–94.

35. Transcript, "Barack Obama's Speech on Race," *New York Times*, March 18, 2008, http://www.nytimes.com/2008/03/18/us/politics/18text-obama.html ?pagewanted=all (accessed November 2, 2012). Obama would transcend the issues of race by "achieving the American Dream for all citizens," observe Robert C. Rowland and John M. Jones, "One Dream: Barack Obama, Race, and the American Dream," *Rhetoric & Public Affairs* 14.1 (2011): 127.

36. Obama, "Remarks to Chicago Council"; Obama, *Audacity of Hope*, 316–17, 321; Democratic Debate, Nevada, January 15, 2008, *Los Vegas Sun*, http://www .lasvegassun.com/news/2008/jan/15/debate-transcript/ (accessed November 1, 2012).

37. Transcript, "The Second Presidential Debate," *New York Times*, October 7, 2008, http://elections.nytimes.com/2008/president/debates/transcripts/second -presidential-debate.html (retrieved November 2, 2012).

38. "There is not a black Obama and a white Obama," Susanna Dilliplane observes; "as a single person, he confounds such binary thinking." Susanna Dilliplane, "Race, Rhetoric, and Running for President: Unpacking the Significance of Barack Obama's 'A More Perfect Union' Speech," *Rhetoric & Public Affairs* 15.1 (2012): 142.

39. Obama, "Remarks to Chicago Council"; Barack Obama, "Renewing American Leadership," *Foreign Affairs* (July/August 2007), http://www.foreignaffairs.com /articles/62636/barack-obama/renewing-american-leadership (accessed November 2, 2012); Obama, "Renewing American Leadership."

40. Cornel West, *Democracy Matters: Winning the Fight Against Imperialism* (New York: Penguin Press, 2004), 15, 214.

41. Obama, *Audacity of Hope*, 316, 321.

42. Robert L. Ivie, "Depolarizing the Discourse of American Security: Constitutive Properties of Positive Peace in Barack Obama's Rhetoric of Change," in *Philosophy after Hiroshima*, ed. Edward Demenchonok (Newcastle Upon Tyne, UK: Cambridge Scholars Publishing, 2009), 242.

43. On the notion of egocide, see David H. Rosen, *Transforming Depression: Egocide, Symbolic Death, and New Life* (New York: G. P. Putnam's Sons, 1993).

44. Robert L. Ivie, *Democracy and America's War on Terror* (Tuscaloosa: University of Alabama Press, 2005), 14–15, 43–44, 90–91.

45. Robert A. Dahl, *How Democratic Is the American Constitution?* (New Haven: Yale University Press, 2001), 24–25.

46. Barack Obama, "Remarks of the President on a New Beginning," The White House, Office of the Press Secretary (Cairo, Egypt), June 4, 2009, http://www.whitehouse.gov/the_press_office/remarks-by-the-president-at-cairo-university-6-04-09/ (accessed November 11, 2012).

47. Obama, "A New Beginning."

48. Robert L. Ivie, "Obama at West Point: A Study in Ambiguity of Purpose," *Rhetoric & Public Affairs* 14.4 (2011): 727–28, 744–45.

49. Barack Obama, "President Obama on Afghanistan, General McChrystal & General Petraeus," The White House Blog, June 23, 2010, http://www.whitehouse.gov/blog/2010/06/23/president-obama-afghanistan-general-mcchrystal-general-petraeus (accessed November 19, 2012); Foon Rhee, "Cheney Hits Obama on Afghanistan," *Boston Globe*, December 1, 2009, http://www.boston.com/news/politics/politicalintelligence/2009/12/cheney_hits_oba.html (accessed November 19, 2012).

50. Tom Englehardt, *The American Way of War: How Bush's Wars Became Obama's* (Chicago: Haymarket Books, 2010), 5, 177–84, 191–92. See also Ruth Conniff, "Obama's Ominous Speech on Afghanistan," *The Progressive*, December 1, 2009, http://www.progressive.org/rc120109.html (accessed November 20, 2012). In her words, "It must give Obama a queasy feeling to be laying out essentially the same arguments the Bush administration made, with all their evident pitfalls, when it launched us on the endless 'war on terror.'"

51. Ewen MacAskill, "Barack Obama's War: The Final Push in Afghanistan," *Guardian*, December 1, 2009, http://www.guardian.co.uk/world/2009/dec/01/barack-obama-speech-afghanistan-war/print (accessed November 20, 2012); Phyllis Bennis, "Annotate This! President Obama's Afghanistan Escalation Speech," Foreign Policy in Focus, Washington, DC, December 2, 2009, http://www.fpif.org/articles/annotate_this_president_obamas_afghanistan_escalation_speech (accessed November 20, 2012).

52. Barack Obama, text, "Obama's Address on the War in Afghanistan," *New York Times*, December 1, 2009, http://www.nytimes.com/2009/12/02/world/asia/02prexy.text.html?pagewanted=all (accessed November 20, 2012).

53. "Obama's Address on the War in Afghanistan."

54. Barack Obama, "Remarks of the President at the Acceptance of the Nobel Peace Prize," The White House, Office of the Press Secretary (Oslo, Norway), December 10, 2009, http://www.whitehouse.gov/the-press-office/remarks-president -acceptance-nobel-peace-prize/ (accessed November 21, 2012).

55. Obama, "Nobel Peace Prize"; Robert E. Terrill, "An Uneasy Peace: Barack Obama's Nobel Peace Prize Lecture," *Rhetoric & Public Affairs* 14.4 (2011): 765.

56. Obama, "Nobel Peace Prize."

57. Indeed, it would have been historic, even for a president of Obama's exceptional rhetorical skill, argues Rob Kroes, if he had managed not to be "co-opted" into a "militarized view of the world and American foreign policy." Rob Kroes, "The Power of Rhetoric and the Rhetoric of Power: Exploring a Tension within the Obama Presidency," *European Journal of American Studies*, Special Issue (December 2012): 9

58. Obama, "Nobel Peace Prize"; Stephen L. Carter, *The Violence of Peace: America's Wars in the Age of Obama* (New York: Beast Books, 2011), xi; see also 69–73.

59. Godfrey Hodgson, *The Myth of American Exceptionalism* (New Haven: Yale University Press, 2009), xvii.

60. Barack Obama, Letter of Endorsement, "National Strategy for Counterterrorism," The White House, Washington, DC, June 28, 2011, http://www .whitehouse.gov/sites/default/files/counterterrorism_strategy.pdf (accessed November 23, 2012).

61. "National Strategy for Counterterrorism," The White House, Washington, DC, June 28, 2011, 1–4, 11, 13, 18, http://www.whitehouse.gov/sites/default/files /counterterrorism_strategy.pdf (accessed November 23, 2012).

62. On this point, see Trevor McCrisken, "Ten Years On: Obama's War on Terrorism in Rhetoric and Practice," *International Affairs* 87.4 (2011): 781–801. See also Joseph G. Peschek, "The Obama Presidency and the Politics of 'Change' in Foreign Policy," *New Political Science* 32.2 (2010): 272–78; and Samer Nassif Abboud, "Image, Rhetoric, and Reality: The Obama Administration and the Middle East," *New Political Science* 32.2 (2010): 278–84.

63. Corinna Mullin, "The US Discourse on Political Islam: Is Obama's a Truly Post-'War on Terror' Administration?" *Critical Studies on Terrorism* 4.2 (2011): 263, 266–68, 271–74. For a critique of Obama's nonprogressive war policy, see Nicolas J. S. Davies, "Obama at War," in *Grading the 44th President: A Report Card on Barack Obama's First Term as a Progressive Leader*, ed. Luigi Esposito and Laura L. Finley (Santa Barbara, CA: Praeger, 2012), 143–61.

64. "Second Presidential Debate Full Transcript," *ABC News*, October 17, 2012, 6, 8, http://abcnews.go.com/Politics/OTUS/2012-presidential-debate-full -transcript-oct-16/story?id=17493848#.ULDPs47A7ao (accessed November 24, 2012).

65. "Transcript: Presidential Debate, October 22, 2012," *Politico*, October 22, 2012, http://www.politico.com/news/stories/1012/82712.html (accessed November 24, 2012).

66. Jung, *Four Archetypes*, 148.

Conclusion

1. Ralph Ketcham, *The Idea of Democracy in the Modern Era* (Lawrence: University Press of Kansas, 2004), 12–17.

2. Russell L. Hanson, *The Democratic Imagination in America: Conversations with Our Past* (Princeton, NJ: Princeton University Press, 1985), 5.

3. James A. Morone, *The Democratic Wish: Popular Participation and the Limits of American Government*, rev. ed. (New Haven: Yale University Press, 1998), 4, 7–9, 18–19.

4. Cornel West, *Democracy Matters: Winning the Fight Against Imperialism* (New York: Penguin Press, 2004), 66–67.

5. Walter Benjamin, "The Work of Art in the Age of its Technical Reproducibility: Third Version," trans. Harry Zohn and Edmund Jephcott. In *Walter Benjamin: Selected Writings; Volume 4, 1938–1940*, ed. Howard Eiland and Michael W. Jennings (1939; repr., Cambridge, MA: Belknap, 2003), 269–70.

6. Jon Simons, "Introduction: Democratic Aesthetics," *Culture, Theory & Critique* 50.1 (2009): 1–5; see also Jon Simons, "Aestheticisation of Politics: From Fascism to Radical Democracy," *Journal of Cultural Research* 12.3 (2008): 207–29.

7. Christopher Kamrath, "Randolph Bourne's Malcontents: Cultural Politics, Democratic Practice, and the Domestication of War, 1917–1918," *Culture, Theory & Critique* 50.1 (2009): 59–60.

8. West, *Democracy Matters*, 68.

9. Thomas Docherty, *Aesthetic Democracy* (Stanford, CA: Stanford University Press, 2006), ix.

10. Docherty, *Aesthetic Democracy*, xiii, xix, 158.

11. For a discussion of these Emersonian themes, see West, *Democracy Matters*, 68–76.

12. Ralph Waldo Emerson, *The Collected Works of Ralph Waldo Emerson*, vol. 3, ed. Robert Spiller (Cambridge, MA: Harvard University Press, 1971), 14.

13. Ralph Waldo Emerson, "The Over-Soul," *Essays: First Series*, ed. Joseph Slater (1841 and 1843; Cambridge, MA: Belknap, 1979); the text of this essay is available online at http://www.emersoncentral.com/oversoul.htm (accessed December 22, 2012).

14. Emerson, "The Over-Soul."

15. See Ed Folsom and Kenneth M. Price, "Walt Whitman," *The Walt Whitman Archive*, online at http://www.whitmanarchive.org/biography/walt_whitman/index.html (accessed December 23, 2012).

16. Walt Whitman, "Democratic Vistas," (1871) American Studies at the University of Virginia, online at http://xroads.virginia.edu/%7EHyper/Whitman/vistas/vistas.html (accessed December 24, 2012).

17. Whitman, "Democratic Vistas."

18. Walt Whitman, "Preface, 1872, To 'As a Strong Bird on Pinions Free,'" Bartleby.com, online at http://www.bartleby.com/229/2005.html (accessed December 24, 2012). Emphasis in the original.

19. George Kateb, "Walt Whitman and the Culture of Democracy," *Political Theory* 18.4 (1990): 552–53.

20. West, *Democracy Matters*, 81. Baldwin's essay on "The Creative Process" about the prison of the undiscovered self is quoted in West, *Democracy Matters*, 80.

21. James Baldwin, *The Fire Next Time* (1963; repr., New York: Vintage Books, 1992), 95.

22. Toni Morrison, *Playing in the Dark: Whiteness and the Literary Imagination* (1992), quoted in West, *Democracy Matters*, 96.

23. Positive peace means the democratic exercise of power in nonviolent pursuit of economic, social, and political justice. Negative peace refers to an absence of war only, whereas positive peace is an absence of all kinds of violence, including the structural violence of human exploitation. Positive peace is the continuing, nonviolent struggle for human fulfillment. See Robert L. Ivie, "Hierarchies of Equality: Positive Peace in a Democratic Idiom," *The Handbook of Communication Ethics*, ed. George Cheney, Steve May, and Debashish Munshi (New York: Routledge, 2011), 374–86.

24. Mogens Herman Hansen, *The Athenian Democracy in the Age of Demosthenes: Structure, Principles, and Ideology*, trans. J. A. Crook (1991; repr., Norman: University of Oklahoma Press, 1999), 12. See also Harvey Yunis, *Taming Democracy: Models of Political Rhetoric in Classical Athens* (Ithaca, NY: Cornell University Press, 1996).

25. Josiah Ober, *Mass and Elite in Democratic Athens: Rhetoric, Ideology and the Power of the People* (Princeton, NJ: Princeton University Press, 1989), 308 (emphasis in the original).

26. Dewey did not use the term "rhetoric," but as Robert Danisch observes, it captures the essence of Dewey's effort to craft a philosophy of democratic action as a practical art of communication. Robert Danisch, *Pragmatism, Democracy, and the Necessity of Rhetoric* (Columbia: University of South Carolina Press, 2007), 42.

27. John Dewey, *The Public and Its Problems* (1927; repr., Athens: Swallow Press/Ohio University Press, 1991), 183.

28. Dewey, *The Public*, 184.

29. Dewey, *The Public*, 208–9, 218.

30. Nathan Crick, *Democracy and Rhetoric: John Dewey on the Arts of Becoming* (Columbia: University of South Carolina Press, 2010), 12.

Selected Bibliography

Allison, Graham, and Philip Zelikow. *Essence of Decision: Explaining the Cuba Missile Crisis*, 2nd ed. New York: Longman, 1999.

Anderegg, Michael. *Inventing Vietnam: The War in Film and Television*. Philadelphia, PA: Temple University Press, 1991.

Bacevich, Andrew J. *The New American Militarism: How Americans Are Seduced by War*. New York: Oxford University Press, 2005.

———. *Washington Rules: America's Path to Permanent War*. New York: Henry Holt, 2010.

Balmer, Randall Herbert. *God in the Whitehouse, A History: How Faith Shaped the Presidency from John F. Kennedy to George W. Bush*. New York: Harper, 2008.

Barber, Benjamin. *Fear's Empire: War, Terrorism, and Democracy*. New York: W. W. Norton, 2004.

Beatty, Keith. *The Scar That Binds: American Culture and the Vietnam War*. New York: New York University Press, 2000.

Bentley, Eric, ed. *Thirty Years of Treason: Excerpts from Hearings before the House Committee on Un-American Activities, 1938–1968*. New York: Viking Press, 1971.

Bercovitch, Sacvan. *The American Jeremiad*. Madison: University of Wisconsin Press, 1978.

———. *The Puritan Origins of the American Self*. New Haven: Yale University Press, 1975.

———. *The Rites of Assent: Transformations in the Symbolic Construction of America*. New York: Routledge, 1993.

Berger, John. *Selected Essays*. New York: Vintage Books, 2003.

Bernstein, Richard J. *The Abuse of Evil: The Corruption of Politics and Religion since 9/11*. Cambridge, UK: Polity Press, 2005.

Bierhorst, John, ed. *Four Masterworks of American Indian Literature*. Tucson: University of Arizona Press, 1984.

Boyer, Paul, and Stephen Nissenbaum, eds. *The Salem Witchcraft Papers*. Volumes 1–3. New York: Da Capo Press, 1977.

Boggs, Carl, and Tom Pollard. *The Hollywood War Machine: U.S. Militarism and Popular Culture*. Boulder, CO: Paradigm, 2006.

Bonn, Scott A. *Mass Deception: Moral Panic and the U.S. War on Iraq*. New Brunswick, NJ: Rutgers University Press, 2010.

Borges, Jorge Luis. *Collected Fictions*. New York: Penguin Books, 1998.

Bouton, Terry. *Taming Democracy: 'The People,' the Founders, and the Troubled Ending of the American Revolution*. New York: Oxford University Press, 2009.

Brando, Marlon, with Robert Lindsey. *Songs My Mother Taught Me*. New York: Random House, 1994.

Brands, H. W. *The Devil We Knew: Americans and the Cold War*. New York: Oxford University Press, 1994.

Breslaw, Elaine G. *Tituba, Reluctant Witch of Salem*. New York: New York University Press, 1996.

Brewer, Susan A. *Why America Fights: Patriotism and War Propaganda from the Philippines to Iraq*. New York: Oxford University Press, 2009.

Brown, Dee. *Bury My Heart at Wounded Knee*. New York: Holt, Rinehart and Winston, 1971.

Burke, Anthony. *Beyond Security, Ethics and Violence: War against the Other*. New York: Routledge, 2007.

Burke, Edmund, III, and David Prochaska, eds. *Genealogies of Orientalism: History, Theory, Politics*. Lincoln: University of Nebraska Press, 2008.

Burke, Kenneth. *Attitudes Toward History*. 3rd ed. Berkeley: University of California Press, 1984.

———. *Permanence and Change*. 3rd ed. Berkeley: University of California Press, 1984.

———. *The Philosophy of Literary Form: Studies in Symbolic Action*. 3rd ed. Berkeley: University of California Press, 1973.

———. *A Rhetoric of Motives*. 1950; repr. Berkeley: University of California Press, 1969.

Bush, George W. Presidential News and Speeches. The White House, http://georgewbush- whitehouse.archives.gov/news/ (accessed August 4, 2013).

———. *Public Papers of the Presidents of the United States: George W. Bush*. National Archives and Records Administration. GPO Access. http://www.gpoaccess.gov/pubpapers/gwbush.html (accessed August 4, 2013).

Calloway, Colin G. *New Worlds for All: Indians, Europeans, and the Remaking of Early America*. Baltimore: Johns Hopkins University Press, 1998.

Campbell, Craig, and Fredrik Lodevall. *America's Cold War: The Politics of Insecurity*. Cambridge, MA: Belknap, 2009.

Campbell, David. *Writing Security: United States Foreign Policy and the Politics of Identity*. Rev. ed. Minneapolis: University of Minnesota Press, 1998.

Campbell, Joseph. *The Hero with a Thousand Faces*. Princeton, NJ: Princeton University Press, 1973.

———. *Historical Atlas of World Mythology*. 2 vols. New York: Harper and Row, 1968.

———, ed. *The Portable Jung*. New York: Viking Press, 1988.

———. *Primitive Mythology*. New York: Penguin Books, 1987.

Canizares-Esguerra, Jorge. *Puritan Conquistadors: Iberianizing the Atlantic, 1550–1770*. Palo Alto, CA: Stanford University Press, 2006.

Capra, Frank. *Why We Fight*, the War Department, Special Services Division, Office of War Information, Bureau of Motion Pictures in cooperation with the US Army Signal Corps, 1942–1945.

Castro, Fidel. "Castro Speech Data Base." *Latin American Network Information Center*, http://lanic.utexas.edu/project/castro/db/1959/19590121.html

Chaplin, Charles. *The Great Dictator*. Charles Chaplin Film Corporation, 1940.

———. *My Autobiography*. 1964; repr. New York: Penguin Classics, 2003.

Chernus, Ira. *Monsters to Destroy: The Neoconservative War on Terror and Sin*. Boulder, CO: Paradigm, 2006.

Chomsky, Noam. *Rethinking Camelot: JFK, the Vietnam War, and U.S. Political Culture*. Cambridge, MA: South End Press, 1999.

Clifford, Michael. *Political Genealogy after Foucault: Savage Identities*. New York: Routledge, 2001.

Cody, William F. *The Life of Hon. William F. Cody, Known as Buffalo Bill: An Autobiography*. 1879; repr. Alexandria, VA: Time-Life Books, 1982.

Cole, Philip A. *The Myth of Evil: Demonizing the Enemy*. New York: Greenwood, 2006.

Connell, Evan S. *Son of the Morning Star: Custer and the Little Bighorn*. New York: Harper Perennial, 1991.

Conrad, Joseph. *Heart of Darkness*. New York: W. W. Norton, 1971.

Coppola, Francis Ford. *Apocalypse Now: The Complete Dossier*. 2 DVDs. Zoetrope Corporation, 2000.

Cowie, Peter. *The Apocalypse Now Book*. New York: Da Capo Press, 2001.

Crick, Nathan. *Democracy and Rhetoric: John Dewey on the Arts of Becoming*. Columbia: University of South Carolina Press, 2010.

Custer, Elizabeth. *Boots and Saddles*. Norman: University of Oklahoma Press, 1961.

Custer, George Armstrong. *My Life on the Plains*. 1874; repr. Norman: University of Oklahoma Press, 1988.

Daniel, Stephen H. *Myth and Modern Philosophy*. Philadelphia: Temple University Press, 1990.

Danisch, Robert. *Pragmatism, Democracy, and the Necessity of Rhetoric*. Columbia: University of South Carolina Press, 2007.

Dawson, Ashley. *Exceptional State: Contemporary U. S. Culture and the New Imperialism*. Durham, NC: Duke University Press, 2007.

Delaney, Michelle. *Buffalo Bill's Wild West Warriors: A Photographic History by Gertrude Kasebier*. New York: Harper Collins, 2007.

Deloria, Vine, Jr. *Custer Died for Your Sins: An Indian Manifesto*. Norman: University of Oklahoma Press, 1988.

De Mallie, Raymond J., ed. *The Sixth Grandfather: Black Elk's Teachings Given to John G. Neihardt*. Lincoln: University of Nebraska Press, 1984.

Demos, John Putnam. *Entertaining Satan: Witchcraft and the Culture of Early New England.* 2nd ed. New York: Oxford University Press, 2004.

Denton-Barhaug, Kelly. *U.S. War Culture, Sacrifice, and Salvation.* Sheffield: Equinox, 2011.

Derber, Charles, and Yale R. Magrass. *Morality Wars: How Empires, the Born Again, and the Politically Correct Do Evil in the Name of Good.* Boulder, CO: Paradigm, 2010.

Domke, David. *God Willing: Political Fundamentalism in the White House, the "War on Terror," and the Echoing Press.* London: Pluto Press, 2004.

Donovan, James. *A Terrible Glory: Custer and the Little Bighorn—the Last Great Battle of the American West.* New York: Little, Brown, 2008.

Doty, William G. *Mythography: The Study of Myths and Rituals.* 2nd ed. Tuscaloosa: University of Alabama Press, 2000.

Dower, John W. *War Without Mercy: Race and Power in the Pacific War.* New York: Pantheon Books, 1986.

Drake, Samuel G., ed. *The Witchcraft Delusion in New England.* 3 vols. 1866; repr. New York: Burt Franklin, 1970.

Dreyfus, Hubert L., and Paul Rabinow. *Michel Foucault: Beyond Structuralism and Hermeneutics.* 2nd ed. Chicago: University of Chicago Press, 1983.

Ehrenreich, Barbara. *Blood Rites: Origins and History of the Passions of War.* New York: Henry Holt, 1997.

Elliott, Michael A. *Custerology: The Enduring Legacy of the Indian Wars and George Armstrong Custer.* Chicago: University of Chicago Press, 2007.

Emerson, Ralph Waldo. *The Collected Works of Ralph Waldo Emerson.* Edited by Robert Spiller. Cambridge, MA: Harvard University Press, 1971.

———. *Essays: First Series.* Edited by Joseph Slater. 1841 and 1843; repr. Cambridge, MA: Belknap, 1979.

Englehardt, Tom. *The American Way of War: How Bush's Wars Became Obama's.* Chicago: Haymarket Books, 2010.

Espinosa, Gastón. *Religion and the American Presidency: George Washington and George W. Bush, with Commentary and Primary Sources.* New York: Columbia University Press, 2009.

Estrin, Mark, ed. *Conversations with Eugene O'Neill.* Jackson: University Press of Mississippi, 1990.

Etzold, Thomas H., and John Lewis Gaddis, eds. *Containment: Documents on American Policy and Strategy, 1945–1950.* New York: Columbia University Press, 1978.

Euripides. *Alcestis.* Translated by William Arrowsmith. Oxford: Oxford University Press, 1974.

Faludi, Susan. *The Terror Dream: Fear and Fantasy in Post-9/11 America.* New York: Henry Holt, 2007.

Flanagan, Jason C. *Imagining the Enemy: American Presidential War Rhetoric from Woodrow Wilson to George W. Bush.* Claremont, CA: Regina Books, 2009.

Flood, Christopher G. *Political Myth.* New York: Routledge, 2002.

Fogelsong, David S. *The American Mission and the "Evil Empire": The Crusade for a "Free Russia" since 1881.* New York: Cambridge University Press, 2007.

Foucault, Michel. *Discipline and Punish: The Birth of the Prison.* Translated by Alan Sheridan. New York: Pantheon, 1977.

———. "Nietzsche, Genealogy, History." In *The Foucault Reader,* edited by Paul Rabinow, 76–100, New York: Pantheon Books, 1984.

Francis, Richard. *Judge Sewall's Apology: The Salem Witch Trials and the Forming of an American Conscience.* New York: Harper Collins, 2005.

Franklin, H. Bruce. *Vietnam and Other American Fantasies.* Amherst: University of Massachusetts Press, 2000.

Freeberg, Ernest. *Democracy's Prisoner: Eugene V. Debs, The Great War, and the Right to Dissent.* Cambridge, MA: Harvard University Press, 2008.

Freedman, Lawrence. *Kennedy's Wars: Berlin, Cuba, Laos, and Vietnam.* New York: Oxford University Press, 2002.

Fuller, Robert C. *Naming the Antichrist: The History of an American Obsession.* New York: Oxford University Press, 1996.

Fursenko, Aleksandr, and Timothy Naftali. *"One Hell of a Gamble": Khrushchev, Castro, and Kennedy, 1968–1964.* New York: W. W. Norton, 1997.

Gaddis, John Lewis. *Surprise, Security, and the American Experience.* Cambridge, MA: Harvard University Press, 2004.

Gallup, Donald C. *Eugene O'Neill and His Eleven-Play Cycle: "A Tale of Possessors Self-Dispossessed."* New Haven: Yale University Press, 1998.

Geertz, Clifford. *The Interpretation of Cultures.* New York: Basic Books, 1973.

Gibson, James William. *The Perfect War: Technowar in Vietnam.* New York: Atlantic Monthly Press, 2000.

Gilman, Richard. *Common and Uncommon Masks: Writings on Theatre, 1961–1970.* New York: Vintage Books, 1972.

Giner, Oscar. "Zoot Suit," *Theater* 10, no. 2 (Spring 1979): 123–28.

———. "The Death of Marlon Brando." *Communication and Critical/Cultural Studies* 2, no. 2, (June 2005): 83–106.

———. "Portraits of Rebellion: Geronimo's Portrait of 1884." In *Rhetoric, Materiality and Politics,* edited by Barbara Biesecker and John Lucaites, 277–92. New York: Peter Lang Publishing Inc., 2009.

Girard, René. *I See Satan Fall Like Lightening.* Translated by James G. Williams. Maryknoll, NY: Orbis Books, 2001.

———. *The Scapegoat.* Translated by Yvonne Freccero. Baltimore, MD: Johns Hopkins University Press, 1986.

———. *Violence and the Sacred.* Translated by Parick Gregory. 1988. New York: Continuum, 2005.

Godbeer, Richard. *The Devil's Dominion.* Cambridge: Cambridge University Press, 1994.

Goldzwig, Steven R., and George N. Dionosopoulos. *In a Perilous Hour: The Public Address of John F. Kennedy.* Westport, CT: Greenwood Press, 1995.

Gott, Richard. *Cuba: A New History.* New Haven: Yale University Press, 2005.

Granberry, Julian, and Gary S. Vescelius. *Languages of the Pre-Columbian Antilles.* Tuscaloosa: University of Alabama Press, 2004.

Greene, Jack P. *The Intellectual Construction of America: Exceptionalism and Identity from 1492 to 1800.* Chapel Hill: University of North Carolina Press, 1993.

Greenwald, Glenn. *Tragic Legacy: How a Good vs. Evil Mentality Destroyed the Bush Administration.* New York: Crown Publishing Group, 2008.

Guevara, Ernesto Che. *El diario del Che en Bolivia.* New York: Ocean Press, 2006.

———. *Guerrilla Warfare.* Lincoln: University of Nebraska Press, 1998.

Hagopian, Patrick. *The Vietnam War in American Memory: Veterans, Memorials, and the Politics of Healing.* Amherst: University of Massachusetts Press, 2009.

Halberstam, David. *The Fifties.* New York: Villard Books, 1993.

Hale, John. *A Modest Enquiry into the Nature of Witchcraft, 1702.* Bainbridge, NY: York-Mail Print, 1973.

Hall, Mitchell K. *Vietnam War.* 2nd ed. New York: Longman, 2007.

Hallin, Daniel C. *The "Uncensored War": The Media and Vietnam.* Berkeley: University of California Press, 1989.

Halper, Stefan, and Jonathan Clarke. *America Alone: The New-Conservative and the Global Order.* New York: Cambridge University Press, 2004.

Hammett, Dashiell. *Crime Stories and Other Writings.* New York: Library of America, 2001.

Han, Béatrice. *Foucault's Critical Project: Between the Transcendental and the Historical.* Stanford, CA: Stanford University Press, 2002.

Hanson, Russell L. *The Democratic Imagination in America: Conversations with Our Past.* Princeton, NJ: Princeton University Press, 1985.

Hedges, Chris. *War Is the Force that Gives Us Meaning.* New York: Public Affairs, 2002.

Hellman, Lillian. *Scoundrel Time.* Boston: Little, Brown, 1976.

Hemingway, Ernest. *For Whom the Bell Tolls.* New York: Charles Scribner's Sons, 1940.

Hersey, John. *Hiroshima.* New York: Bantam Books, 1968.

Hersh, Seymour M. *My Lai 4: A Report on the Massacre and Its Aftermath.* New York: Random House, 1970.

Hess, Gary R. *Presidential Decisions for War: Korea, Vietnam, the Persian Gulf, and Iraq.* 2nd ed. Baltimore: Johns Hopkins University Press, 2009.

———. *Vietnam: Explaining America's Lost War.* Malden, MA: Blackwell, 2009.

Hodges, Adam. *The "War on Terror" Narrative: Discourse and Intertextuality in the Construction and Contestation of Sociopolitical Reality.* New York: Oxford University Press, 2011.

Hodgson, Godfrey. *The Myth of American Exceptionalism.* New Haven: Yale University Press, 2009.

Hoffer, Peter Charles. *The Devil's Disciples: Makers of the Salem Witchcraft Trials.* Baltimore, MD: Johns Hopkins University Press, 1996.

———. *The Salem Witchcraft Trials: A Legal History.* Lawrence: University of Press of Kansas, 1997.

Hofstadter, Richard. *The Paranoid Style in American Politics.* New York: Knopf, 1965.

Holloway, David. *Cultures of War on Terror: Empire, Ideology, and the Remaking of 9/11*. Montreal, Quebec: McGill-Queens University Press, 2008.

Howard, John. *Concentration on the Home Front: Japanese Americans in the House of Jim Crow*. Chicago: University of Chicago Press, 2008.

Hughes, Richard T. *Christian America and the Kingdom of God*. Urbana: University of Illinois Press, 2009.

———. *Myths America Lives By*. Urbana: University of Illinois Press, 2003.

Hutton, Paul Andrew, ed. *The Custer Reader*. Lincoln: University of Nebraska Press, 1992.

Huxley, Aldous. *The Devils of Loudun*. 1952; New York: Barnes and Noble Books, 1996.

Hyde, Lewis. *Trickster Makes His World: How Disruptive Imagination Creates Culture*. New York: Canongate Books, 2008.

Hynes, William J., and William G. Doty, eds. *Mythical Trickster Figures: Contours, Contexts, and Criticisms*. Tuscaloosa: University of Alabama Press, 1993.

Ingebretsen, Edward J. *At Stake: Monsters and the Rhetoric of Fear in Public Culture*. Chicago: University of Chicago Press, 2001.

Ivie, Robert L. *Democracy and America's War on Terror*. Tuscaloosa: University of Alabama Press, 2005.

———. *Dissent from War*. Bloomfield, CT: Kumarian Press, 2007.

Jackson, Helen. *A Century of Dishonor: A Sketch of the United States Government's Dealings with Some of the Indian Tribes*. 1882; New York: Barnes and Noble Books, 1994.

Jewett, Robert. *Captain America and the Crusade against Evil: The Dilemma of Zealous Nationalism*. Grand Rapids, MI: William B. Eerdmans, 2004.

———. *Mission and Menace: Four Centuries of American Religious Zeal*. Minneapolis, MN: Fortress Press, 2008.

Johnson, Robert. *The Complete Recordings*. 2 CDs, Columbia/Legacy, C2K 64916. Sony Music Entertainment, 1990.

Jones, Howard. *The Bay of Pigs*. Oxford: Oxford University Press, 2008.

Jung, Carl. *The Basic Writings of C. G. Jung*. Edited by Violet S. de Laszlo. New York: Modern Library, 1959.

———. *Four Archetypes: Mother/Rebirth/Sprit/Trickster*. Translated by R. F. C. Hull. Princeton, NJ: Princeton University Press, 1969.

Kalb, Marvin, and Deborah Kalb. *Haunting Legacy: Vietnam and the American Presidency from Ford to Obama*. Washington, DC: Brookings Institution Press, 2011.

Kane, John. *Between Virtue and Power: The Persistent Moral Dilemma of U.S. Foreign Policy*. New Haven: Yale University Press, 2008.

Kaplan, Amy. *The Anarchy of Empire in the Making of U.S. Culture*. Cambridge, MA: Harvard University Press, 2002.

Kaplan, Amy, and Donald E. Pease, eds. *Cultures of United States Imperialism*. Durham: Duke University Press, 1993.

Karnow, Stanley. *Vietnam: A History*. New York: Penguin Books, 1984.

Kazin, Michael, and Joseph A. McCartin, eds. *Americanism: New Perspectives on the History of an Ideal*. Chapel Hill: University of North Carolina Press, 2006.

Keen, David. *Endless War? Hidden Functions of the War on Terror*. London: Pluto Press, 2006.

Kellner, Douglas. *From 9/11 to Terror War: The Dangers of the Bush Legacy*. Lanham, MD: Rowman and Littlefield, 2003.

Kershaw, Ian. *Hitler, 1936–1945: Nemesis*. New York: W. W. Norton, 2000.

Ketcham, Ralph. *The Idea of Democracy in the Modern Era*. Lawrence: University Press of Kansas, 2004.

Kingsbury, Celia Malone. *For Home and Country: World War I Propaganda on the Home Front*. Norman: University of Nebraska Press, 2010.

Kinney, Katherine. *Friendly Fire: American Images of the Vietnam War*. New York: Oxford University Press, 2000.

Kloppenberg, James T. *Reading Obama: Dreams, Hope, and the American Political Tradition*. Princeton, NJ: Princeton University Press, 2011.

Kolko, Gabriel. *The Age of War: The United States Confronts the World*. Boulder, CO: Lynne Reinner, 2006.

Kopit, Arthur. *Indians*. New York: Bantam Books, 1971.

Lakoff, George. *Moral Politics: What Conservatives Know That Liberals Don't*. Chicago: University of Chicago Press, 1996.

Las Casas, Bartolomé de. *Brevísima Relación de la Destruición de las Indias*. Madrid: Ediciones Cátedra, 2001.

———. *Historia de las Indias*. México: Fondo de Cultura Económica, 1965.

Lasswell, Harold D. *Propaganda Technique in World War I*. 1927; repr. Cambridge, MA: Massachusetts Institute of Technology Press, 1971.

Lawrence, John Shelton, and Robert Jewett. *The Myth of the American Superhero*. Grand Rapids, MI: William B. Eerdmans, 2002.

Layman, Richard. *Shadow Man: The Life of Dashiell Hammett*. New York: Harcourt, Brace, Jovanovich, 1981.

Lazarus, Edward. *Black Hills White Justice: The Sioux Nation versus the United States, 1775 to the Present*. New York: HarperCollins, 1991.

Leeming, David, and Jake Page. *Myths, Legends, and Folktales of America: An Anthology*. New York: Oxford University Press, 2000.

Lifton, Robert Jay, and Greg Mitchell. *Hiroshima in America: A Half Century of Denial*. New York: Avon Books, 1995.

Lincoln, Bruce. *Holy Terror: Thinking about Religion after September 11*. Chicago: University of Chicago Press, 2003.

Lipset, Seymour Martin. *American Exceptionalism: A Double-Edged Sword*. New York: W. W. Norton, 1996.

Little, Douglas. *American Orientalism: The United States and the Middle East since 1945*. 3rd ed. Chapel Hill: University of North Carolina Press, 2008.

Lockhart, Charles. *The Roots of American Exceptionalism: History, Institutions, and Culture*. New York: Palgrave, 2003.

Longfellow, Henry Wadsworth. *The Complete Poetical Works of Henry Wadsworth Longfellow*. Cutchogue, NY: Buccaneer Books, 1993.

Lord, Walter. *A Time to Stand: The Epic of the Alamo*. Lincoln: University of Nebraska Press, 1961.

MacQuarrie, Kim. *The Last Days of the Incas*. New York: Simon and Schuster, 2007.

Madsen, Deborah L. *American Exceptionalism*. Jackson: University Press of Mississippi, 1998.

Maggi, Armando. *Satan's Rhetoric: A Study of Renaissance Demonology*. Chicago: University of Chicago Press, 2001.

Mali, Joseph. *Mythistory: The Making of a Modern Historiography*. Chicago: University of Chicago Press, 2003.

Marshall, Joseph M., III. *The Journey of Crazy Horse: A Lakota History*. New York: Viking, 2004.

Martí, José. *Obras Completas*. 23 vols. La Habana: Editorial Nacional de Cuba, 1963.

———. *Selected Writings*. New York: Penguin Books, 2002.

Martin, Geoff, and Erin Steuter. *Pop Culture Goes to War: Enlisting and Resisting Militarism in the War on Terror*. Lanham, MD: Lexington Books, 2010.

Marx, Karl, and Friedrich Engels. *The Communist Manifesto*. 1848; London: Penguin Classics, 1985.

May, Ernest R., and Philip D. Zelikow, eds. *The Kennedy Tapes: Inside the White House During the Cuban Missile Crisis*. Cambridge, MA: Belknap, 1997.

Mayer, Jane. *The Dark Side: The Inside Story on How the War on Terror Turned Into a War on American Ideals*. New York: Doubleday, 2008.

McAdams, Dan P. *George W. Bush and the Redemptive Dream: A Psychological Portrait*. New York: Oxford University Press, 2011.

McKrisken, Trevor B. *American Exceptionalism and the Legacy of Vietnam: U.S. Foreign Policy since 1974*. New York: Palgrave Macmillan, 2003.

Melville, Herman. *Moby Dick; or, The Whale*. 1851; New York: Barnes and Noble, 1988.

Messadie, Gerald. *A History of the Devil*. Translated by Marc Romano. New York: Kodansha International, 1997.

Milius, John, and Francis Ford Coppola. *Apocalypse Now Redux*. New York: Hyperion, 2000.

Miller, Arthur. *The Crucible*. New York: Penguin, 1953.

———. *Timebends: A Life*. New York: Grove Press, 1987.

Miller, Perry, ed. *The American Puritans: Their Prose and Poetry*. New York: Anchor Books, 1956.

———. *Errand into the Wilderness*. 1956; repr. Cambridge, MA: Belknap, 1984.

Mills, Sara. *Michel Foucault*. London: Routledge, 2003.

Mooney, James. *The Ghost Dance*. North Dighton, MA: JG Press, 1996.

Moore, Robin. *The Green Berets*. New York: Skyhorse Publishing, 2007.

Monroe, James. *Hellfire Nation: The Politics of Sin in American History*. New Haven: Yale University Press, 2003.

Morgan, Edmund S. *Inventing the People: The Rise of Popular Sovereignty in England and America*. New York: W. W. Norton. 1988.

———, ed. *Puritan Political Ideas, 1558–1794*. Indianapolis: Bobbs-Merrill, 1965.

Morone, James A. *The Democratic Wish: Popular Participation and the Limits of American Government.* Rev. ed. New Haven: Yale University Press, 1998.

Morris, Edmund. *Theodore Rex.* New York: Random House, 2001.

Muchembled, Robert. *A History of the Devil: From the Middle Ages to the Present.* Translated by Jean Birrell. Cambridge, UK: Polity Press, 2004.

Munk, Linda. *The Devil's Mousetrap: Redemption and Colonial American Literature.* New York: Oxford University Press, 1997.

Nadel, Alan. *Containment Culture: American Narratives, Postmodernism, and the Atomic Age.* Durham: Duke University Press, 1995.

Neihardt, John G. *Black Elk Speaks.* Lincoln: University of Nebraska Press, 2004.

———. *The Twilight of the Sioux.* Lincoln: University of Nebraska, 1971.

Noble, David W. *Death of a Nation: American Culture and the End of Exceptionalism.* Minneapolis: University of Minnesota Press, 2002.

Norton, Mary Beth. *In the Devil's Snare: The Salem Witchcraft Crisis of 1692.* New York: Vintage Books, 2003.

Obama, Barack. *The Audacity of Hope: Thoughts on Reclaiming the American Dream.* New York: Three Rivers Press, 2006.

———. Speeches and Remarks. The White House. http://www.whitehouse.gov/briefing-room/speeches-and-remarks (accessed August 4, 2013).

O'Leary, Stephen. *Reading the Signs of the Times.* New York: Oxford University Press, 1994.

O'Neill, Eugene. *The Plays of Eugene O'Neill.* 3 vols. New York: Random House, 1954.

O'Shaughnessy, Nicholas Jackson. *Politics and Propaganda: Weapons of Mass Seduction.* Ann Arbor: University of Michigan Press, 2004.

Pagels, Elaine. *The Origin of Satan.* New York: Random House, 1995.

———. *Revelations: Visions, Prophecy and Politics in the Book of Revelation.* New York: Viking, 2012.

Pané, Fray Ramón. *Relación de las antiguedades de los indios.* Edited by José Juan Arrom. México: Siglo XXI, 1998.

Pease, Donald E. *The New American Exceptionalism.* Minneapolis: University of Minnesota Press, 2009.

Pedersen, Carl G. *Barack Obama's America.* Edinburgh: Edinburgh University Press, 2009.

Pfaff, William. *The Irony of Manifest Destiny: The Tragedy of America's Foreign Policy.* New York: Walker, 2010.

Philbrick, Nathaniel. *The Last Stand: Custer, Sitting Bull and the Battle of the Little Bighorn.* New York: Viking, 2010.

Poole, W. Scott. *Satan in America: The Devil We Know.* Lanham, MD: Rowman and Littlefield, 2009.

Rapley, Robert. *Witch Hunts: Salem to Guantanamo Bay.* Montreal: McGill-Queen's University Press, 2005.

Roberts-Miller, Patricia. *Voices in the Wilderness: Public Discourse and the Paradox of Puritan Rhetoric.* Tuscaloosa: University of Alabama, 1999.

Rogin, Michael. *Ronald Reagan the Movie: And Other Episodes in Political Demonology*. Berkeley: University of California Press, 1987.

Rollins, Peter C., and John E. O'Connor. *Why We Fought: America's Wars in Film
and History*. Lexington: University Press of Kentucky, 2008.

Rosen, David H. *Transforming Depression: Egocide, Symbolic Death, and New Life*.
New York: G. P. Putnam's Sons, 1993.

Rosenthal, Bernard. *Records of the Salem Witch-Hunt*. New York: Cambridge University Press, 2009.

Rothenberg, Jerome, ed. *Shaking the Pumpkin: Traditional Poetry of the Indian North
Americas*. Albuquerque: University of New Mexico Press, 1991.

Rouse, Irving. *The Taínos: Rise and Decline of the People Who Greeted Columbus*. New
Haven: Yale University Press, 1992.

Rushing, Janice Hocker, and Thomas S. Frentz. *Projecting the Shadow: The Cyborg
Hero in American Film*. Chicago: University of Chicago Press, 1995.

Russell, Jeffrey Burton. *Mephistopheles: The Devil in the Modern World*. Ithaca, NY:
Cornell University Press, 1990.

Said, Edward W. *Culture and Imperialism*. New York: Vintage Books, 1993.

———. *Orientalism*. New York: Vintage Book, 1978.

Saito, Natsu. *Meeting the Enemy: American Exceptionalism and International Law*.
New York: New York University Press, 2010.

Schaeffer, John D. *Sensus Communis: Vico, Rhetoric, and the Limits of Relativism*.
Durham: Duke University Press, 1990.

Schmitz, David R. *The Tet Offensive: Politics, War, and Public Opinion*. Lanham:
Rowman and Littlefield, 2005.

Schoultz, Lars. *The Infernal Little Cuban Republic: The United States and the Cuban
Revolution*. Chapel Hill: University of North Carolina Press, 2009.

Schultzinger, Robert D. *A Time for Peace: The Legacy of the Vietnam War*. New York:
Oxford University Press, 2008.

Schwab, Orrin. *Redeemer Nation: America and the World in the Technocratic Age, 1914
to the Present*. Salt Lake City: American Universities and Colleges Press, 2004.

Semmerling, Tim Jon. *Evil Arabs in American Popular Film: Orientalist Fear*. Austin:
University of Texas Press, 2006.

Settje, David. *Faith and War: How Christians Debated the Cold and Vietnam Wars*.
New York: New York University Press, 2011.

Shaffer, Peter. *The Royal Hunt of the Sun*. New York: Stein and Day, 1965.

Shaw, Bernard. *Nine Plays*. 1903; New York: Dodd, Mead, 1935.

———. *Three Plays for Puritans*. 1901; New York: Penguin Books, 1946.

Sherry, Michael S. *In the Shadow of War: The United States since the 1930s*. New
Haven: Yale University Press, 1995.

Shulman, George M. *American Prophecy: Race and Redemption in American Political
Culture*. Minneapolis: University of Minnesota Press, 2008.

Slocum, J. Davi, ed. *Hollywood and War: Film Reader*. New York: Taylor and Francis,
2006.

Slotkin, Richard. *The Fatal Environment: The Myth of the Frontier in the Age of Industrialization, 1800–1890*. New York: Atheneum, 1985.

――. *Gunfighter Nation: The Myth of the Frontier in Twentieth Century America.* New York: Atheneum, 1992.

Smith, Henry Nash. *Virgin Land: The American West as Symbol and Myth.* Cambridge, MA: Harvard University Press, 1950.

Smith, Tony. *A Pact with the Devil: Washington's Bid for World Supremacy and the Betrayal of the American Promise.* Vol. 1. New York: Taylor and Francis, 2006.

Sorensen, Theodore C., ed. *The Speeches, Statements, and Writings of John F. Kennedy, 1947 to 1963.* New York: Random House, 1991.

Spanos, William V. *American Exceptionalism in the Age of Globalization: The Specter of Vietnam.* Albany: State University Press of New York, 2008.

――. *America's Shadow: An Anatomy of Empire.* Minneapolis: University of Minnesota Press, 2000.

Starkey, Marion Lena. *The Devil in Massachusetts: A Modern Enquiry into the Salem Witch Trials.* 1949; New York: Anchor Books, 1989.

Steinbeck, John. *The Grapes of Wrath.* 1939; New York, Bantam Books, 1970.

――. *Working Days: The Journals of the Grapes of Wrath, 1938–1941.* New York: Viking, 1989.

Stephanson, Anders. *Manifest Destiny: American Expansionism and the Empire of Right.* New York: Hill and Wang, 1995.

Storr, Anthony, ed. *The Essential Jung.* New York: MJF Books, 1983.

Summers, Montigue. *The History of Witchcraft and Demonology.* Mineola, NY: Dover Publications, 2007.

Taylor, Philip M. *Munitions of the Mind: A History of Propaganda from the Ancient World to the Present Day.* 3rd ed. Manchester: Manchester University Press, 2003.

Thomas, Hugh. *Cuba: The Pursuit of Freedom.* New York: Harper and Row, 1971.

――. *Rivers of Gold: The Rise of the Spanish Empire, from Columbus to Magellan.* New York: Random House Trade Paperback, 2005.

Tucker, Phillip Thomas. *Exodus from the Alamo: The Anatomy of the Last Stand Myth.* Philadelphia: Casemate, 2010.

Tillett, Leslie, ed. *Wind on the Buffalo Grass: The Indians' Own Account of the Battle at the Little Big Horn River, and the Death of Their Life on the Plains.* New York: Thomas Y. Crowell, 1976.

Turner, Frederick Jackson. *The Frontier in American History.* New York: Holt, Rinehart and Winston, 1962.

Tuveson, Earnest Lee. *Redeemer Nation: The Idea of America's Millennial Role.* Chicago: University of Chicago Press, 1980.

Twain, Mark. *Collected Tales, Sketches, Speeches, & Essays.* New York: Library of America, 1992.

――. *Roughing It.* New York: Harper, 1913.

Upham, Charles W. *Salem Witchcraft.* Vol. 2. 1867; Williamstown, MA: Corner House, 1971.

Utley, Robert M. *Custer and the Great Controversy: The Origin and Development of a Legend.* Pasadena, CA: Westernlore Press, 1980.

———. *The Lance and the Shield: The Life and Times of Sitting Bull*. New York: Henry Holt, 1993.

———. *The Last Days of the Sioux Nation*. New Haven: Yale University Press, 1965.

Vaughan, Alden T., and Edward W. Clark, eds. *Puritans among the Indians: Accounts of Captivity and Redemption, 1676–1724*. 1702; Cambridge, MA: Harvard University Press, 1981.

Vico, Giambattista. *New Science*. Translated by David Marsh. 1744; London: Penguin Books, 1999.

Viola, Herman J., ed. *Little Bighorn Remembered: The Untold Story of Custer's Last Stand*. New York: Times Books, 1999.

Visker, Rudi. *Michel Foucault: Genealogy as Critique*. Translated by Chris Turner. London: Verso, 1995.

Von Franz, Marie-Louise. *Dreams*. Boston: Shambhala, 1991.

Von Hendy, Andrew. *The Modern Construction of Myth*. Bloomington: Indiana University Press, 2002.

Vuorinen, Marja, ed. *Enemy Images in War Propaganda*. Newcastle upon Tyne: Cambridge Scholars Publishing, 2012.

Wallis, Jim. *God's Politics: A New Vision for Faith and Politics in America*. New York: Harper San Francisco, 2005.

Warren, Louis S. *Buffalo Bill's America: William Cody and the Wild West Show*. New York: Alfred A. Knopf, 2005.

Weart, Spencer R. *Nuclear Fear: A History of Images*. Cambridge, MA: Harvard University Press, 1988.

Wehr, Gerhard. *An Illustrated Biography of C. G. Jung*. Boston: Shambhala, 1989.

Weisberg, Jacob. *The Bush Tragedy*. New York: Random House, 2008.

West, Cornel. *Democracy Matters: Winning the Fight Against Imperialism*. New York: Penguin Press, 2004.

Whitfield, Stephen J. *The Culture of the Cold War*. Baltimore: Johns Hopkins University Press, 1991.

Whitman, Walt. *The Portable Walt Whitman*. Edited by Michael Warner. New York: Penguin Books, 2004.

Whittaker, Frederick. *A Complete Life of General George A. Custer*. 1876; repr. Lincoln: University of Nebraska Press, 1993.

Wiebe, Robert H. *Self-Rule: A Cultural History of American Democracy*. Chicago: University of Chicago Press, 1996.

Wilentz, Sean. *The Rise of American Democracy: Jefferson to Lincoln*. New York: W. W. Norton, 2005.

Winkler, Carol K. *In the Name of Terrorism: Presidents on Political Violence in the Post-World War II Era*. Albany: State University of New York Press, 2006.

Wolin, Sheldon S. *Democracy Incorporated: Managed Democracy and the Specter of Inverted Totalitarianism*. Princeton, NJ: Princeton University Press, 2008.

Woodward, Bob. *Obama's War: Avoiding a Quagmire in Afghanistan*. Washington, DC: Potomac Books, 2010.

Wyden, Peter. *Bay of Pigs: The Untold Story*. New York: Simon and Schuster, 1979.

Young, Marilyn B., and Robert Buzzanco, eds. *A Companion to the Vietnam War.* Malden, MA: Blackwell, 2002.

Young, Marilyn B., John J. Fitzgerald, and A. Tom Grunfeld. *The Vietnam War: A History in Documents.* New York: Oxford University Press, 2002.

Ziff, Trisha. *Che Guevara: Revolutionary and Icon.* New York: Abrams Image, 2006.

Zulaika, Joseba. *Terrorism: The Self-Fulfilling Prophecy.* Chicago: University of Chicago Press, 2009.

Index